Writing Matters
Developing Sentence Skills in Students of All Ages

Second Edition

William Van Cleave

Cover design by Steve Bowers.
Photos by Jennifer Carsten with additional photos by Chaidez Stevenson and Tess Jones.

Pictures are of students from my private practice in Greenville, SC and students at SeeWorth Academy (Oklahoma City, OK), a school where I've had the pleasure of serving as a consultant.

International Standard Book Number: 978-0-9798651-8-3.

To purchase additional copies, visit wvced.com.

Dedication

This text is dedicated to...
Glenn, Logan, and the Helmers;
Laurie, Wes, Martha, and the Quattlebaums;
Jennifer, Taylor, Topper, Victoria, and the Carstens;
Ginny, Jack, and the Goulds; Nina, Rob, and the Williams;
Georgette and Emerson Dickman; & Martha and Tracy Pellett,
for believing in me.

It is also dedicated to...
Will, Cindy, and the Wynkoops; Ethan, Caroline, and the Dovers;
Mac, Dana, and the McCalls; Charlie, Porter, and the Pruitts;
Robert and the Seiglers; Zach, Jackson, Ellie, and all the Cooters;
Andy and the Nelsons; Andrew Tallon, Merritt, and the Graces;
Nicolas and the Trocha/Correa family; Rita, Chuck, and the Stones;
Cody Hampton; Charles and the Einsteins; Will Vanvick;
Roger, Debbie, and the Stones; Ralph Bertelle; Christopher Carsten;
Will Spigner; and Luke, Katherine, and the Murdoch/Hall family,
for reminding me to believe in myself.

Thanks

Thanks to the Bauknights, the Blaszaks, The Briarwood School, the Brookers, Camperdown Academy, Jennifer Hasser, the Hills, the Hipps, the Johnsons, the Jones, The Kildonan School, the Luthis, the Schofields, SeeWorth Academy, the Stephensons, the Stewarts, the Julian and Megan Taylors, the Stefi and Shane Taylors, and Susie Wherry.

Thanks to the many teachers and students who have participated in my seminars, workshops, classes, and tutorials about writing. You have made me a better teacher of writing, and, in doing so, you have contributed to this book.

Thanks to the three teachers who taught me to write: Alyce Pollitt (middle school), Dean Robertson (high school), and Carolyn Durham (college). Thanks to Diana Hanbury King, who first showed me how to teach students to write. That said, I trust few people to edit my writing. Thanks to Susan McLeod, a true friend, a fine writer, and an excellent editor, who understands and appreciates the written word the way I do, for her helpful suggestions and insights.

William Van Cleave

Table of Contents

Making This Manual Matter

How to Use The Book:

Read "There Is Something The Matter," and mark portions that are relevant to your own teaching. This first chapter raises important questions teachers need to ask, addresses many of the skills peripherally associated with sentence writing, and establishes the book's mission.

"At The Heart of the Matter," the next chapter, explains the instructional approach, including components of a good writing lesson. To understand and implement the strategies in this text, instructors should read and understand this chapter.

Both sections of "The Matter at Hand" are broken into individual concept lessons for instruction. Make sure to read the Core Concept and Sample Activities in each section before beginning your teaching. As you plan to teach students a concept, read the Overview that precedes the Initial Lesson for that concept. It provides the instructor with broader knowledge than the lesson itself contains, arming her to address both questions and problems that may arise during instruction.

Along with good word lists and an excellent reference section, the appendices provide instructors with a sequence of skills that aligns with the Common Core State Standards.

Professional Development Opportunities:

The teaching strategies and concepts in this text stem from classroom and tutorial work with students, numerous opportunities to train teachers, and extensive reading in the field. Though the book is meant to arm instructors to teach writing effectively, professional development is both recommended and encouraged.

Teacher training in the *Writing Matters* approach is important for a number of reasons:

- Teachers need direct, explicit instruction in the teaching of writing. While this manual provides such instruction, the concepts are more likely to be implemented once a competent trainer has introduced and demonstrated the key concepts for instruction and allowed workshop participants to explore them actively.

- Instructors are often uncertain about how to approach writing in their teaching. Lack of comfort can lead to ineffective teaching or, worse, no teaching at all.

- Training in the *Writing Matters* style of teaching is both engaging and rewarding as teachers will significantly expand *what* they teach and, more importantly, *how* they teach. As a side benefit, many teachers will improve their own writing through professional development in *Writing Matters*.

Additionally, W.V.C.ED provides assistance to schools and districts in designing and implementing writing curricula. Alignment with the Common Core is also plausible.

There Is Something The Matter: An Introduction

In the past two decades, educators have done a better job of addressing struggling readers. Multisensory structured language methods have spread not just to specialized schools, where students are both diagnosed and classified, but also to mainstream public and private schools that have recognized the need for this kind of instruction for their students. Response to Intervention (R.T.I.) has further encouraged schools to step up and embrace instruction that is both immediate and effective. A better understanding and implementation of phonological awareness activities has been beneficial. Early screening has helped. Initiatives at both the state and national levels have improved reading skills as well. This is not to say that all our problems are solved, nor that the work is complete. Rather, it acknowledges that there is focus, that attention is being paid, that progress is definite and encouraging. Unfortunately, the same cannot be said for writing skills. Simply put, we have a long way to go. It has become my number one priority to share with as many instructors as possible effective strategies for teaching students to write.

In his novella, "The Body," on which the compelling coming-of-age film *Stand By Me* is based, Stephen King's narrator, Gordie LaChance, writes...

> The most important things are the hardest things to say. They are the things you get ashamed of, because words diminish them -- words shrink things that seemed limitless when they were in your head to no more than living size when they're brought out. But it's more than that, isn't it? The most important

things lie too close to wherever your secret heart is buried, like landmarks
to a treasure your enemies would love to steal away. And you may make
revelations that cost you dearly only to have people look at you in a funny
way, not understanding what you've said at all, or why you thought it was so
important that you almost cried while you were saying it. That's the worst, I
think. When the secret stays locked within not for want of a teller but for want
of an understanding ear.

Though LaChance writes of his inability to find an ear for the grief he feels over his brother's
death and his parents' subsequent distance, his words apply to many students as well.
For students who struggle with writing, most *everything* is hard to say. This is at once
frustrating and overwhelming. It must become our mission, then, to arm students with
the tools necessary to express themselves in writing. Many of our struggling students are
intellectually gifted. Some are wonderfully articulate with the spoken word. Still others
have incredible ideas, blocked by an inability to express them either verbally or in writing.
Regardless of the difficulty, however, these students must *learn* to *write*. Eventually, those
who plan to graduate from high school and attend college will also need to *write* in order to
learn.

The "writing matters" in this text are designed for teachers who wish to improve their
students' sentence writing skills. Standardized testing, required by most school districts
across the U.S., puts considerable pressure on administrators and teachers. Careers
sometimes depend upon students' scores on these high-stakes evaluative tools. Likewise,
parents and the larger community sometimes judge a school's worth based on these scores.
The writing prompt is the most common evaluative tool used on tests of student writing
ability. Too often, teachers skip sentence writing skills and move directly into paragraphs
and essays. Some begin the fall with sample writing prompts, asking students to put
all the pieces of a good response together simultaneously. Even without the pressure of
standardized testing, teachers often neglect grammar and sentence construction, either
concerned with research that suggests its lack of worth or uncomfortable teaching material
in which they have had little or no training.

Why is the development of writing skills so often neglected?

Testing Instruments: First, writing difficulties are far more challenging to measure than their reading counterparts. Who designs the testing instrument? Is it graded on a rubric, and if so, how are its criteria selected? Does spelling count? What about handwriting? Do we assess sentences by word count? Clause structure? Are we measuring at both the sentence and the paragraph levels? Is complexity of thought worth more than correct punctuation? Is the testing timed? Does it involve response to a provided text or current event or is it given on a topic of which students have prior knowledge?

What to teach: There is also great debate on what to teach. Recently, teachers who had attended one of my writing workshops returned home, filled with new ideas and puzzled by discrepancies between my thoughts and the curriculum in use at their learning center. Their director, who had not attended the workshop, e-mailed me a long and detailed series of discussion points. Her approach was exceptional -- non-confrontational and certainly not defensive. She wanted to make sure they were "doing it right," but she also wanted to see that what I taught matched the specific needs of her students. In the limited time provided, and with many of the students who struggle already receiving additional time for reading instruction, what is essential and what can be avoided? Is there an appropriate scope and sequence for instruction? At what grade or skill level should a specific concept be introduced for the first time? Do we focus primary attention on sentence skills or paragraph and essay writing? What defines competency?

Training instructors: One of the most challenging aspects of teaching students to write is arming tutors and teachers with the tools necessary to do the job effectively. I present on writing to thousands of teachers a year. Most work with struggling students. Many are trained in effective reading strategies. When I ask, as I often do, "who likes grammar?" if I'm lucky, ten percent of the instructors in the room raise their hands. I usually ask the follow-up question, "who is scared of grammar?" Often as many as half the teachers acknowledge their fear. On the one hand, I'm thrilled to see these reluctant learners in the room, ready to cover new material and incorporate it into their classrooms. On the other, it concerns me that so few teachers are comfortable with the basic elements of writing. Special education teachers, those responsible for a great number of struggling writers, often haven't seen grammar since they were teenagers, if then. When a teacher comes up at the conclusion of a workshop and says, "I'm not scared anymore," or "I feel better about teaching this," or even, "I finally understand how to teach writing," I'm heartened. But I'm also concerned. Why aren't direct and explicit strategies for teaching writing being taught across the board to all writing instructors, whether they teach six year olds or adults?

I don't do windows: Unfortunately, all too often I hear teachers of reading say, "writing isn't my department. I've got too much to do with this student. I simply can't add anything else." It is human nature to teach what we know, and reading teachers, who often spend their professional development and applied teaching time developing their reading repertoire, are overwhelmed by the notion of adding writing instruction to the mix. Teachers, then, often feel they lack the time and skills necessary to address writing beyond the simplistic (e.g., capitalization, periods, and spelling as it applies to reading). We teach writing not because it is easy, not because we have plenty of time to do so, but because we must. "Not my department" isn't a satisfactory response to a child who needs to learn to write. If not you, then who?

Why do many students find writing so difficult?

While there is a great deal of reading research at our disposal, precious little has been done in the area of writing. The research we do have can be useful and convincing, but it more often than not raises more questions than it answers. Certainly, most scientists on the cutting edge of writing research conclude their studies with suggested directions for further research. The advent of brain scans, conducted while children practice various reading-based tasks (rhyming, reading nonsense words, reading real words), is an open invitation to widespread study of brain activity during the act of writing. While a few brain studies have been conducted, most are focused on handwriting rather than idea generation, sentence or paragraph writing. Directions for further research are obvious.

As teachers, particularly if we are comfortable with writing ourselves, most of us find it difficult to put our feet in the shoes of a struggling writer. Nevertheless, we must recognize that writing coherent paragraphs and essays involves engaging in a number of activities simultaneously:

- **formation of letters:** whether students use manuscript, cursive, or a word processor, part of the brain is engaged with this process.
- **spelling of words:** even if students are not penalized for spelling, they must still sound out and spell the words they choose so that the reader can understand what is being written.
- **formation of sentences:** students must write coherent sentences, including mechanics (i.e., grammar, punctuation, usage) and structure (i.e., sentence quality and variety).
- **paragraph structure:** students must apply what they have learned regarding introductory, supporting, and concluding sentences/paragraphs.
- **content:** a topic chosen from students' own experiences is the most simple and direct content; eventually, students must write about topics assigned by content-area teachers.
- **audience:** students must determine the purpose of the assignment, the intended audience, and the approach to be taken in order to match written piece with that audience.

For a struggling writer, then, the amount of working memory devoted to tasks that a competent writer has already automatized prevents appropriate, typical dedication to the more cognitive acts: idea generation and organization. If a part of your mind is taken, for example, with spelling and handwriting, it becomes difficult to create coherent text for your audience.

The skills included in this skills development chart (*Figure 1*) involve knowledge in four categories. A student has achieved "mastery" only when he is able to engage with a category at all four stages.

Stages of Knowledge	Idea Generation	Parts of Speech	Sentence Parts	Paragraph/Essay Parts
Definition		learn definition	learn definition	be able to discuss/explain
Identification		recognize in text	recognize in text	recognize in text
Create in Isolation	generate/categorize list	provide examples in isolated sentences	provide examples in isolated sentences	create using known topic
Create in Application	generate/categorize list for content-based assignment	use in paragraphs	use in paragraphs	create using content-based topic

Figure 1

Handwriting & Spelling

Introduction

As an instructor considers the overall writing process, she must ponder the role of handwriting and spelling. This is not to say legibility, speed, and spelling should be emphasized when composition is taught or evaluated, but rather that difficulty in these areas will negatively impact a student's ability to produce writing commensurate with his intellectual ability. In large part this stems from processing issues.

Students who struggle with handwriting or spelling or a combination of both often take more time to complete these tasks. They are also more likely to be frustrated by the results of their efforts. Some children, even when they take an extraordinary amount of time and effort to produce letters on paper, still end up with an illegible or immature-looking product. Try as they might, struggling spellers are unlikely to spell correctly all or even most of the words they attempt. These surface concerns, however, dim in comparison to the role both of these skills play in conflicting with higher-level writing tasks. Mark Torrance and David

Galbraith, professors of psychology at Staffordshire University and authors of a chapter in *The Handbook of Writing Research* titled "The Processing Demands of Writing," argue that "spelling and handwriting, the two low-level processes that are most obviously required in written production but not in speech, are obvious candidates for automatization" (74). One study they reference in their meta-analysis shows that children recall more items when they are spoken than when they are written. Adding sentence production exacerbates that same discrepancy in facility with the spoken and written word. However, adults taking the same test score as well as or better on the written sections than the verbal sections, indicating that automatizing the lower level functions of handwriting and spelling allows performance in writing to improve significantly.

Torrance and Galbraith examined a number of studies concerned with retrieval as well. One indicates that "very low-level graphomotor processes are capable of interfering with retrieval from LTM [long term memory]" (75). Another suggests that "spelling retrieval interferes with processes involved in lexical retrieval, and/or that midword pausing in itself results in the loss of lexical items that are awaiting transcription but are less common and therefore have a lower level of activation" (75). Retrieving letter formations or spelling configurations, then, has the potential to prevent or slow down retrieval of words, concepts, and sentence structures. Steve Graham and Dolores Perin note that "effective writing instruction acknowledges that the smooth deployment of the higher-level writing strategies needed to plan, generate, and revise text depends on easy use of lower-level skills such as handwriting, keyboarding, spelling, [and] grammar and punctuation" (*Writing Next* 23). For a student who writes quickly and legibly and spells appropriately for her grade and age, this poses no problem. All too often, however, either handwriting, spelling, or a combination of both prove problematic for students.

Handwriting

At some point every instructor and/or school must make important decisions regarding handwriting:

- In what grade or at what age will manuscript be introduced?
  Cursive?
  Keyboarding?
- What emphasis will be placed on this area of instruction?
  How much daily instructional time?
  How often?
  How will follow-up be conducted as students get older?
- What curriculum will be used?
  What materials?
  What kind of training, both initial and follow-up, is required for teachers to implement the curriculum adequately?
- How will handwriting be assessed?

In an article entitled "Want To Improve Children's Writing? Don't Neglect Their Handwriting," published in the winter 2009/2010 edition of *American Educator,* Graham notes that "in dozens of studies, researchers...have found that, done right, early handwriting instruction improves students' writing. Not just its legibility, but its *quantity and quality*" (20). Maria Konnikova's June 2, 2014 article, "What's Lost As Handwriting Fades," appropriately located in the Science section of the *New York Times,* cites convincing research in favor of handwriting over typing. She explains that "children not only learn to read more quickly when they first learn to write by hand, but they also remain better able to generate ideas and retain information. In other words, it's not just what we write that matters -- but how" (Konnikova). While the Common Core mentions keyboarding as an important skill, its only mention of handwriting is for students in kindergarten and first grade. Though seven states still mandate cursive instruction, a number of states, often citing the omission of cursive in the Common Core, have eliminated it from their curricula. This decision ignores the fact that good, comfortable, legible writing is a precursor to any writing task demanded of students, including many of those outlined in the Common Core.

Some teachers incorrectly assume that handwriting instruction is about improving the attractiveness of the product. The impact of automatized handwriting is far more essential than that. Fluid handwriting unclogs a potential bottleneck so that children can direct appropriate attention towards idea generation and sentence and paragraph structure. Naturally, then, students who struggle with handwriting do not have the necessary processing space to develop their ideas, choose the correct spelling, or generate appropriate sentences and paragraphs (Coker 110). So, if for no other reason, students must be taught legible, fluent writing in order to free their available processing memory for the challenging task of developing coherent, grade-appropriate prose.

Diana King argues that "rapid, legible, and comfortable handwriting is important for success in all grades and for all students, but especially for young students beginning to write" (*Writing Skills - Teacher's Handbook* 119). Some research has even concluded that with "direct instruction and sufficient practice...handwriting can play a significant role in preventing the development of writing disabilities among younger students" (Schlagel 195). Just as phonemic awareness serves as a preventative measure for many reading difficulties, then, handwriting may decrease the number of students who struggle with writing. Unfortunately, research on handwriting with students above the third grade remains to be done (Graham and Perrin, *Writing Next* 42).

Currently, teacher education in handwriting is neglected. Graham also found that while 90% of 1st through 3rd grade teachers taught handwriting, averaging 70 minutes of instruction per week, only 39% claimed their students' handwriting was adequate. It should come as no surprise, then, that only 12% of teachers in Graham's study said they received "adequate preparation to teach handwriting in their college education courses" (21). Like any of us, teachers teach what they know. Inadequate professional development time for instructors will sabotage even the best-designed handwriting curriculum.

Kindergarten instruction usually includes recognition and formation of lower and uppercase manuscript letters. Such an approach is important as students first learn letter names and sounds and need the ability to recognize and pronounce them when they appear in text. Most schools continue with print through second grade, using the argument that the shift from print to cursive is too challenging and that students need the time to master one before continuing to the other. Unfortunately, this leaves third grade students learning a new mode of writing -- cursive -- at the same time that they begin taking notes and writing more significant paragraphs and even short essays. Cursive, like manuscript, requires isolated instruction so that students can both internalize and automatize its formations. Teachers provide models students can use to learn and practice formations through copying. Only when the formations are automatized is the student prepared to use the newly learned form of writing to create original text. A student who has three years of print under his belt and is only just learning to write in cursive will revert back to that with which he is most familiar -- manuscript -- to meet increased writing demands. It is no wonder, then, that many middle and high school students use a blend of both or revert to the print they were initially taught.

In particular, students with language-based learning difficulties need cursive instruction as soon as possible, and many schools for students with these struggles begin cursive in the first grade. Virginia Berninger found that students who struggle with dyslexia and dysgraphia, in particular, benefit from cursive instruction over print (Konnikova). King argues, "there is no reason why cursive writing should not be taught from the beginning to all students. However, in the case of dyslexics, there are several reasons for insisting on cursive" (*Writing Skills for the Adolescent* 3). Many have enumerated these reasons:

- In a proper lowercase alphabet, all formations begin on the baseline. These baseline alphabets include those in use by Montessori programs, Orton-Gillingham trained teachers, Wilson Reading, and King herself. (Interestingly, Catholic school nuns used similar teaching methodologies though they did not argue in favor of a backhand slant and paper positioning uniquely designed for left-handed writers.)
- Cursive decreases (and in some cases eliminates) reversals (e.g., b/d, p/q, m/w).
- It is difficult to discern where one word ends and another begins in some students' print because of inappropriate spacing. Cursive eliminates this issue.
- Though print does use some kinesthetic-tactile memory, this important pathway for learning is more strongly activated when students write in cursive. (As an example, skywrite a simple word, such as <u>mark</u>, in print, then in cursive. Notice how your arm feels as you write the word each time.) Activating this pathway is an important factor in developing student spelling.

For beginners and students who struggle, particular attention must be paid to the four key components of effective handwriting instruction: (1) letter and word formation, pencil grip, and paper positioning must be directly and explicitly taught and practiced; (2) assistive tools and effective and constructive support and criticism must be directed towards students learning to form letters; (3) students must develop the ability to assess their own handwriting; and (4) teachers must set as their goal *fluent* writing (Troia 331).

Since the primary goal of this text is sentence skills, I will mention a few appropriate sources for further instruction in handwriting. Both Diana King (*Writing Skills - Teacher's Manual* and her four handwriting texts) and Anna Gillingham (*The Gillingham Manual*) provide thorough explanations of appropriate positioning. Though I take issue with its support of "manu-cursive," the remainder of the chapter on handwriting in *Writing Assessment and Instruction for Students with Learning Disabilities* is thorough and useful. Those texts provide information regarding pencil grip, paper position, wrist position, and slant as well. These fundamental elements are essential to the automaticity of a student's writing, whether it is manuscript or cursive; moreover, they are challenging to correct once a student has cemented them incorrectly. Additionally, King, Gillingham, and Wilson (Wilson Reading) provide appropriate cursive alphabets, both for left- and right-handed students. King has both elementary (published by W.V.C.ED) and remedial (published by E.P.S.) workbooks for cursive instruction. If you or your school insist on print instruction, King's new manuscript text (soon to be published by W.V.C.ED) will prove useful. Also, the manuscript materials provided by *Handwriting Without Tears* are appropriate. (While the tactile materials *Handwriting Without Tears* provides for cursive instruction are well considered, their materials use a slantless alphabet, and some of the lowercase letters (e.g., a, c, d) do not begin on the baseline.) All the aforementioned resources are cited in Appendix IV.

Spelling

Just as a school must make decisions regarding handwriting, it must also make choices regarding spelling. Unlike handwriting, spelling remains an emphasis in most current elementary curricula and language arts texts:

- Will "invented spelling" play a role in the curriculum?
  If so, in which grades?
- Will patterns and rules (phonics) be a part of the instruction?
  If so, beginning and ending when?
- What techniques for learning patterns will be used?
  For individual words?
- How much curricular time will be committed to spelling instruction?
- What curriculum will be used?
  What materials?
  What kind of training, both initial and follow-up, will be established to assure proper implementation of the chosen curriculum?
- How will spelling be assessed?

Andrew Jackson said famously, "It is a damn poor mind indeed which can't think of at least two ways to spell any word." While spelling "variances" are indeed unrelated to intelligence, poor spelling is a visible indicator of a student's weaknesses. Entire books have been written about the supposed insanity of English despite the fact that some 85 percent of the language follows organized patterns. Teachers approach spelling instruction in a variety of ways, based on administrative expectations; the approved curriculum (in many cases); and their own training, experience, and philosophy.

Uninformed teachers who have spelling instruction foisted upon them by well-meaning school administrations but lack the training and perspective necessary to teach it well typically do more harm than good. These teachers often choose spelling words from a vocabulary list or the content areas in an effort to construct interdisciplinary studies. This is both illogical and inappropriate with a skills-based study such as spelling. Vocabulary and content area words are not grouped by recognizable pattern, and therefore struggling spellers must learn each word individually by rote memory. Additionally, since students do not use vocabulary words regularly in their writing because they are not familiar or comfortable with their meanings in applied context, long-term retention is low.

Teachers devoted to the weekly spelling unit, comprised of Monday pretest, various activities including sentence writing and repetitive writing of difficult words, and the dreaded Friday spelling test, often use basal spellers, which are organized appropriately by spelling concept (e.g., <u>ai</u> is used in the middle of a word to spell long <u>a</u> or use <u>ck</u> immediately following a short vowel in one syllable words). Typically, though, their students spell at different levels, and therefore the classroom text is only appropriate for the group spelling at or near grade level.

To address these concerns, researchers argue in favor of developmental spelling instruction. While such an approach might use basal spellers, students are given a spelling text to match their current spelling level rather than their grade. Many students may spell at or close to grade level and would therefore use the text that matches their grade.

Some students are strong natural spellers. They spell by sight and have internalized the generalizations that govern English, often without realizing it. It is this ability that enables them to construct a logical and appropriate spelling when asked to attempt a word they have never seen before. Such students rarely have difficulty learning words for the traditional spelling test, regardless of how those words are chosen or what curriculum is used. In the developmental model, an instructor would place them in a text above grade level.

Students for whom spelling does not come naturally should use a text below grade level and matched to their current spelling level. Putting them in a text at grade level leaves too great a discrepancy between their current knowledge of orthography and the words given each week. Though they might ace the Friday spelling tests, they are likely to utilize rote memory, and their long-term retention of the words in the lesson will be poor. Bob Schlagal's "Best Practices in Spelling and Handwriting," a chapter from *Best Practices in Writing Instruction*, mentions a significant research study in support of a developmental spelling instruction model. Students whose spelling abilities were beneath grade level, when placed into an at-grade-level curriculum, "made errors in spelling that were far poorer in quality than students working above grade level" and "poor spellers...did well on end-of-week tests, [but] their long-term retention and mastery of spelling concepts was poor in comparison with their instructional-level peers, who made significant strides in both areas" (Schlagal 191). More telling, however, when those same struggling students used lower-grade-level books, they made gains that paralleled their higher-achieving peers. In other words, when students are given words at their skill ability rather than their grade level, they are able reduce errors and also achieve retention of the material because the curriculum matches their skill level and ability (Schlagal 191).

Anna Gillingham, who co-developed the Orton-Gillingham Approach in an era when computers did not exist, counted and categorized words in order to tabulate percentages that would indicate which spelling choices were most common, which less common or rare, and which singular in the language. Good basal spelling programs use a similar method; in other words, they organize their lessons and exercises by concept and include spelling words that ask students to apply that concept. Gillingham's focus on the structure of the language, her attention to the needs of struggling readers and writers, and her sense that the patterns that govern the language are a necessity for those same struggling spellers align her with the tenets of developmental spelling. Most multisensory structured language methods originating from Orton-Gillingham would likewise argue in favor of an individualized, highly structured and patterned approach to studying spelling with the struggling student.

Since this text is not specifically devoted to spelling instruction, it is appropriate to mention several of the many resources that can help teachers understand the patterns that govern our language. Once again, *The Gillingham Manual* provides an excellent, if somewhat unwieldy, understanding not only of the way the language is organized but also effective teaching strategies for students who struggle. *How To Teach Spelling* provides an Orton-Gillingham based curriculum that many find useful. My own text, *Everything You Want To Know & Exactly Where To Find It*, an Orton-Gillingham based reference guide, and its newer companion guide, *Phrases & Sentences for Reading & Spelling*, also explore sound-to-symbol correspondence, kinds of syllables, syllable division patterns, and the rules and generalizations that govern the spelling of English. Any of these texts will prove beneficial, particularly to the tutor in a one-on-one or small group environment. The aforementioned resources are cited in Appendix IV. Most spelling series currently in use have a basal foundation. They may prove effective for a broader range of students in the classroom setting if (1) students are assigned texts based on their spelling ability rather than current grade level, (2) teachers emphasize and directly teach the patterns that govern each unit of study, and (3) various research-based techniques (such as simultaneous oral spelling) are put into place for all students, or at a minimum those who spell below grade level.

Vocabulary: Choosing Words That Are Specific and Vivid

My least favorite words in student writing are "very" and "fun;" together, they drive me over the edge. A sentence such as "The movie was very fun." will earn a reproving glance or an "opportunity" to redraft, and my students learn this lesson early on. A carefully chosen word can add substantial color and specificity to writing. Teach this lesson to your students in the early stages of writing instruction, and provide multiple opportunities for them to practice applying it when they write.

The word <u>very</u> puts a writer's lack of vocabulary on display, and there are always better alternatives. Study these examples, taken from thesaurus.com:

very fun	awesome, cool, incredible, wonderful, amazing, entertaining, unforgettable, rewarding, exciting, thrilling, pleasurable
very smart	adept, resourceful, knowing, clever, keen, alert, apt, astute, crafty, ingenious, sharp, on the ball, quick, quick-witted, shrewd, wise
very mean	bad-tempered, vile, callous, vicious, unpleasant, unfriendly, evil, ugly, cruel, shameless, snide, rotten, pesky, malicious, nasty, ill-tempered, infamous, dishonorable, dirty, difficult, despicable, contemptible, cantankerous

The word <u>walk</u> functions as noun, verb, adverb, and adjective. Examine a selection of the synonyms that www.thesaurus.com provides for <u>walk</u> as a verb:

lumber, advance, patrol, shuffle, trudge, amble, file, hoof it, march, perambulate, roam, wander, canter, escort, hike, meander, pace, pad, rove, plod, run, prance, saunter, parade, stroll, stride, strut, toddle, traipse, tread

More than mere alternatives, these synonyms provide nuances in meaning. In the sentences below, each of which includes an underlined verb replacement for <u>walked</u>, the choice not only enhances the sentence but provides its key meaning:

> The teen <u>bolted</u> when he saw the police.
> The teen <u>strolled</u> by the police officers.
> The teen <u>stormed off</u> in reaction to the police officer's comment.

The underlined verbs above are the only indication of the teen's attitude toward police officers in the above sentences. The first suggests a criminal who wishes to avoid being caught, the second a teen who by chance sees some police, and the third, a teen who has been warned or annoyed by a police officer's statement - and the verbs give us those different meanings.

Vocabulary choice is more complicated than this, though. Words with multiple meanings give our language its richness. Take, for example, the word <u>small</u>, which could be used in place of the underlined word in each of these sentences:

> The billionaire had <u>humble</u> beginnings.
> My <u>modest</u> salary barely pays my bills.
> She averted a <u>minor</u> catastrophe by catching the glass.
> He has always been a <u>slight</u> man.
> She is difficult to hear as she has a <u>little</u> voice.

Look at the different uses of the seemingly simple word <u>sad</u>, which could replace any of the underlined words in the sentences below:

> The obituaries brought the old woman some <u>sorrowful</u> news.
> The <u>tragic</u> deaths of the two youngsters brought tears from many at the funeral.
> While I loved the movie, I had a tough time getting through the <u>bittersweet</u> ending.
> The <u>pitiful</u> dog hobbled down the street on three legs.

These examples illustrate the richness of our language, the many words we have for expressing similar -- though not identical -- ideas, and the multiple meanings that some of our most-used words hold for us.

Each of us has both an *active* and a *passive* vocabulary (interchangeably called *expressive* and *receptive*). A person's active vocabulary is comprised of those words she is able to use actively -- either in writing or in speech. Her passive vocabulary is comprised of the words she comprehends when she reads or hears them. Naturally, a person's active vocabulary is included in her passive vocabulary though her passive vocabulary includes many words she does not use herself. The word <u>melancholy</u> illustrates this point. Since I understand its meaning (sad) from my study of Twain's *The Adventures of Huckleberry Finn*, it is in my passive vocabulary. I do not use the word in communication, however. Therefore, it is not my active vocabulary. The word <u>unhappy</u>, which I both understand and use, is in my passive and active vocabulary. A word I could not define or recognize is obviously in neither.

With this knowledge in mind, consider your students carefully. Some simply do not have the vocabulary necessary to write at grade level. Students who come to English as a second language often fall into this category. Struggling readers often do as well, because they are not exposed to the same amount of written text (and therefore vocabulary) as their classmates. Instructors should develop a vocabulary study plan for these students. A number of good sources for such a study exist.

Oftentimes, though, students have in their passive vocabulary a number of words that they cannot access and use actively. For these students, group list making (e.g., "List every word you can think of that means "funny.") can help. Word banks of good replacements for "dead" words (or words that students are no longer allowed to use when they write) can serve your students well. As they use the words from those lists in their writing, your students will, in turn, begin to move those words into their active vocabulary. Students who simply have difficulty generating words in general will also find such word banks of great benefit. Sometimes, I will create a "tombstone," writing the "dead" word at its top. Below, the students will help me generate good replacements. A teacher from one of my workshops uses retired sports jerseys instead.

For a classroom version of this activity that has year-long implications, divide your students into groups of three to five and arm them with a marker and a piece of butcher paper. In the middle of the paper, write a word you wish to retire. Examples include <u>said</u>, <u>went</u>, <u>fun</u>, and <u>nice</u>. Using a three minute timer or a stopwatch, get each group to generate as many replacement words for the dead word as they can. When time is up, have the groups rotate. Start the timer again, and this time each group must add to an existing list, but they are not allowed to repeat any of their classmates' words. Each group can use a different color so that author groups are easier to discern. Mount the finished products on the wall; some of them will have a hundred words or more. Refer to these word walls when students are using words that are supposed to be off limits.

With technology's ever-increasing impact on our writing, students have thesauri at their fingertips, on their computers, and even on their phones. These can be great tools, but only when used properly. Just the other day, I asked Mac, a ninth grader, to "find a good word to replace the word <u>great</u>," which he had used three times in a single paragraph. I turned to retrieve something from my tutoring bag and looked back to see him pulling up the thesaurus built into his MacBook. I glared at him, and he grinned impishly, reminding me that I had, indeed said *find*, and that he was only following instructions. I laughed. The nuances in meaning of the word <u>find</u> had been used against me! Mac has the intelligence and the vocabulary to use the thesaurus effectively. He found a replacement word for <u>great</u>, a word that fit the intended meaning of the sentence he had written, and solved his problem.

Many students are not as well-equipped. They will need guidance, and tombstone word lists or even longer, more thorough word banks can help them select proper words that are still within the boundaries of their vocabulary. Additional vocabulary instruction, either in isolation or in the context of a reading or writing lesson, will also help.

Sophisticated middle school students and most high school and college students will find the Visual Thesaurus (www.visualthesaurus.com - available at a cost) of interest. The developers describe it as "an interactive dictionary and thesaurus that creates word maps that blossom with meanings and branch to related words." It has a sophisticated interface that shows how words are interrelated and helps its user understand nuances in meaning.

Why Teach Grammar?

The debate over whether to teach grammar has continued for decades. Teachers and parents are passionate in their stances. Teachers who are comfortable with grammar often fight on its behalf; others, some of whom struggle with usage themselves, argue for its removal from the curriculum or remain quiet but in their silence avoid teaching it at all costs.

Steve Graham and Dolores Perrin, in *Writing Next*, cite research that "grammar instruction involving the explicit and systematic teaching of the parts of speech and structure of sentences" had a negative effect on students' writing abilities, albeit a slight one (21). Additional research, focused specifically on struggling writers, found similar results (Anderson, 1997; Saddler & Graham, 2005 as cited in Graham and Perrin 21). "'I Guess I'd Better Watch My English': Grammars and the Teaching of the English Language Arts," a chapter from the *Handbook of Writing Research* (264-6), cites other studies, all with similar results (2006). The argument against traditional, isolated grammar instruction is solid. Why, then, have I dedicated a significant portion of my teaching career to instructing students and teachers in grammar? Why was my empirical evidence -- visible and obvious improvement in student writing, success stories from attendees at my workshops, individual students' improved educational testing scores -- so convincing?

Good grammar instruction, the kind that improves student writing, prioritizes not definition and identification (prescriptive grammar), but rather the role of parts of speech and sentence parts in the context of student writing (*Figure 1*). *Writing Next* acknowledges two additional facts: (1) sentence combining has a significant, positive effect on student writing and (2) a study by Fearn & Farnan (2005) "found that teaching students to focus on the function and practical application of grammar within the context of writing (versus teaching grammar as an independent activity) produced strong and positive effects on student writing" (Graham and Perin 21). In "The role of grammar and the writing curriculum: A review of the literature" (2013), Myhill and Watson cite research that argues in favor of using grammar to "make conscious choices" (Myhill 46) and consider "'the interwoven relationship between what we say and how we say it'" (Miocchiche as cited in Myhill 46). Instead of a prescriptive "'set of structures which can be assessed as correct or incorrect'" (Derewianka and Jones as cited in Myhill and Watson 45), "rhetorical grammar is about explicitly showing young writers the repertoire that is available to them" (Myhill and Watson 46). In other words grammar taught in isolation both correctively and prescriptively yields poor results, but grammar applied to the act of writing has a positive effect.

Part of the process of developing sentence skills in student writers is helping those writers understand the structures of the sentences they analyze and then create. A natural extension of this work is in the area of reading comprehension. Students who understand the connection between subjects and their predicates; between adjectives, adverbs, and phrases and the words they modify; and between independent clauses and the clauses that depend upon them, for example, are logically better able to understand those structures when they read sentences that contain them. An understanding of the structure of a sentence shows the student the relationship between not just the words, phrases, and clauses within it, but also the relationship between the ideas that those elements convey. In essence when students work to develop their sentence skills, they are working on sentence-level comprehension at the same time.

Though the research in this area is minimal, what does exist is promising. In an older study, Willows and Ryan linked awareness of grammar in oral language to reading achievement (1986). With the very existence of this text, I argue in favor of teaching writing at the sentence level to improve students' overall writing. Cheryl M. Scott, in "A Case for the Sentence in Reading Comprehension," makes a parallel claim in the area of reading comprehension (Scott 2009). Additional studies support this claim (Cain 2007; Bouchafa, Potocki, and Magnan 2013). A recent study found "significant effects of syntactic knowledge and syntactic awareness on reading comprehension among adolescent students" (Brimo, Apel, and Fountain 1). A study currently being conducted at Tufts is specifically targeting the relationship between sentence writing and sentence comprehending.

Discouragingly, grammar books often teach parts of speech and sentence parts in isolation at the first two levels: definition and identification (*Figure 1* - page 6). Even successful students will find themselves only able to regurgitate a memorized definition and underline or circle the studied element in professionally written sentences. Teaching a student to say "action word" or to identify and circle "run" in an exercise about verbs does not teach the student to use verbs correctly and fluidly in sentence and paragraph writing. Knowing that "while I was eating" is a dependent clause and "Michael watched a good movie" is an independent one does not naturally transfer to the act of writing better sentences containing these elements.

What is Our Mission?

In a reading group, if a student misses a word or stumbles over a phrase, the moment of embarrassment is fleeting. The error lasts only until the next student is called upon, the next error recognized. This is not the case with writing, where the student creates a permanent record of both his abilities and his inabilities. Peer critiquing, portfolios, "final drafts," and classroom bulletin boards emphasize this permanence. While the advent of the computer and online writing certainly allows for a more fluid text and ease of revision, writing continues to provide students' most obvious record of skill level and achievement. One key indication of success in our culture is literacy level, and, increasingly, a college degree is expected for any work above minimum wage. At least in part, it is for these reasons that we must address writing fully and directly at all levels.

Part of the goal of designing a writing approach that is effective in one-to-one, small group, and classroom settings is to make it appropriate for students with broad educational needs. Obviously, students come from different socioeconomic backgrounds and attend different kinds of schools (e.g., public, private, charter, special needs). Those students also have access to different kinds of learning environments within their schools, and factors such as student-teacher ratio, teacher quality and training, and curriculum affect student performance.

In "'I Guess I'd Better Watch My English': Grammars and the Teaching of the English Language," Smith, Cheville, and Hillocks note that "current tests place a high emphasis on the standard of correctness that traditional school grammar is designed to provide" (264). This article is applicable to the Common Core State Standards (C.C.S.S. - www.corestandards. org). Designed at the state level, these Standards "provide appropriate benchmarks for all students, regardless of where they live," in reading, writing, language, and speaking and listening (www.corestandards.org/about-the-standards). Their goal is simple: to prepare students for higher education and the work force. As of July 2015, 43 states, the District of Columbia, and four territories have adopted them.

While the C.C.S.S. have become somewhat controversial of late, even those states that have opted to create their own Standards have developed writing guidelines remarkably similar to those established in the C.C.S.S. As such, it is important when designing a curriculum, whether it be for an individual student, a small group, a classroom, a school, or an entire district, to consider carefully the guidelines of these C.C.S.S. (or the adaptation or version your state has adopted). Overall, the C.C.S.S. provide a number of positive and grade-appropriate goals for instruction. The writing and language sections, in fact, cover many of the concepts introduced in this text, and I have matched data regarding the C.C.S.S. with specific concepts where appropriate. The A.C.T. and S.A.T. (including its 2016 revision), which are used by most colleges and universities as one determiner of preparedness, include required standard written English sections as well as optional essay sections. These standardized tests serve as yet another motivator for the development of writing skills for all students, or, at the very least, for those who intend to go on to college after high school.

More specific to students who struggle, Response to Intervention (RTI), the multi-level intervention model introduced as part of the Individuals with Disabilities Education Improvement Act of 2004 (IDEA, 2004), makes it important to provide successful teaching strategies to instructors in a variety of settings. RTI sets up a framework of a minimum of three tiers. The first argues for good classroom instruction at all grade levels coupled with regular screenings to identify both the skills expected of a typical student and those students who are struggling. Additional tiers provide increasingly intensive levels of intervention with the goal to put as many struggling students as possible back on track. Tier 2 recommends small-group instruction over a specific and limited period of time. Tier 3 argues for individualized instruction for those students whose skills do not improve enough through their work in Tiers 1 and 2. A writing approach such as the one outlined in this text can be used with success in the classroom setting; that said, RTI instructors and remedial tutors will find it useful in designing a more individualized approach as well.

In presenting workshops and seminars about teaching students to write, I have been asked with increasing frequency, "where is the book on this material?" While a number of excellent resources exist in the field, I became aware of the need for a text that captures both appropriate teaching practices for students and the reference information necessary to arm the instructor to teach her students effectively.

One function of this text, then, is as a teacher's course of action, which includes the following:

- skills to be studied
- strategies for instruction in one-to-one, small group, and classroom environments
- suggestions for and examples of meaningful assignments
- student-teacher dialogues that model effective instruction and review

Another key function this text serves is as a reference, comprised of the following components:

- an overview of each concept to enhance teacher understanding
- word lists both as the text unfolds and in the appendices
- potential sequences of skills, grouped by grade level

A final goal of this text is to alleviate the fears of teachers who have some uncertainties about teaching writing. Thus, there are three additional reference functions of this book:

- clear explanations of questions I often hear from teachers
- clarifications of commonly confused concepts with examples
- lists of recommended tools for teaching various elements of the writing process

There are three general categories into which we classify elements of study in written expression: parts of speech, sentence parts, and composition or paragraph/essay writing (*Figure 1* - page 6). All are essential, and while students often begin with parts of speech, instructors are not expected to work one category to completion before beginning the next. In fact the best kind of writing instruction involves moving fluidly between the three, spiralling back to assimilate previously covered concepts with new material. Students conduct ongoing review in conjunction with study of a new concept and ultimately apply that combination to the act of writing itself. Otherwise, a student might jump into paragraph writing before he has written an acceptable sentence or, just as bad, spend so much time practicing with the parts of speech that she never gets the chance to write a paragraph at all.

While it certainly makes sense to teach nouns before adverbs, to cover conjunctions before compound sentences, and to practice writing topic sentences before tackling a multi-page essay, some teacher discretion is advisable in choosing the correct concept for a given lesson or group of students. Mandated curriculum, standardized testing, content area writing assignments, and individual student strengths and weaknesses certainly influence the decisions we make regarding which concepts are most important, how much time we devote to them, and when they are to be taught. Nevertheless, we must keep our goal firmly in mind: solid, significant growth in applied writing skills for each of our students.

I hope you find this text useful. Writing matters!

William Van Cleave

May 2012; updated June 2014

(additional research added May 2015; updates to this chapter added August 2015)

At the Heart of the Matter:
Lesson Components Overview

Good sentence skills lessons are comprised of five components, briefly described here:

- **Warm-Up**: Since writing instruction is both skills-based and cumulative, each session should begin with a warm-up of previously learned concepts. Wherever possible, keep this fast-paced, interactive, and engaging. Students should review learned parts of speech and sentence parts. Typically a brief portion of the lesson, the warm-up usually involves definition and generation of examples of the reviewed concept or concepts. Where appropriate, this portion of the lesson may also include identification of examples from pre-written text.

- **Review of Previously Learned Concept**: Often, the instructor will follow the warm-up with review of a specific skill, usually one that the students have covered recently. Of particular interest might be a skill that has a strong and obvious connection to the new concept the instructor will introduce in the day's lesson. For example, the instructor might review adverbs in anticipation of a new lesson about adverbial phrases, nouns and verbs before beginning a study of gerunds, or subjects and predicates in preparation for a study of independent and dependent clauses.

- **Introduction of New Concept**: Where grammar is the area of study, mastery comes not when the terminology is memorized but rather when the concept is internalized and used automatically and unconsciously in applied writing. Not every lesson involves the introduction of a new concept. If students struggled with the previous concept or have difficulty recalling it during Review, this is a clear indicator that the instructor should delay introducing a new concept. Sometimes, "new" concepts are actually just spins on previously learned concepts. For example, one lesson might be devoted to adverbs while a follow-up lesson might cover those adverbs that do not end in -ly. Both the Review and Introduction of New Concept portions of the lesson follow the five-point strategy outlined at the end of this section.

- **Activities**: Where they will contribute to, rather than detract from, the lesson, activities can be built directly into the Review or New Concept portions of the lesson. As time permits, however, there are certain activities that genuinely enhance students' understanding of sentence structure in general though they may not apply directly to the concept of the day. In such a case, activities can accent the written expression lesson in an energizing, interactive, and yet productive way.

- **Wind-Down**: In the few minutes remaining, ask students rapid-fire questions concerning the day's lesson. This practice has three goals. It allows students to spiral back and recall the concepts of the day, furthers the chances they will remember those concepts for tomorrow's lesson, and helps them recognize the ground that has been covered in the session.

Recognize that the steps outlined above are for a full lesson of forty-five to sixty minutes. Some periods for writing instruction are shorter; portions of the recommended lesson will need to be shortened or eliminated altogether when this is the case. For instance, it may make sense not to cover a Review Concept during class sessions where a New Concept will be introduced. Alternatively, students may not have the chance to identify or create as many examples of the concept. If the sessions are shorter than a standard period of instruction, students will need more sessions to learn the material.

While this text concerns itself with sentence composition, a language arts period may include other aspects of language study, such as handwriting, spelling, decoding, oral reading, comprehension, and vocabulary. If this approach is included in an English curriculum, students will also be studying literature and working on expository and narrative writing. Clearly, priorities and time constraints will dictate commitment to the material as well as the rate at which the instructor and students can cover it.

As A Matter of Fact 1:
The Warm-Up

Introduction

The Warm-Up forms the first component of most lessons. To begin each lesson (whether one-to-one, small group, or classroom instruction), drill students with rapid-fire questioning concerning concepts previously covered. Like reading and math, writing instruction is a skills-based area of study. Using a spiraling technique that asks students to incorporate the new with the old is effective in strengthening writing skills.

While some instructors call on students only when they have raised their hands to volunteer, traditionally the Warm-Up works best when students know they will be called upon. Move around the room in a sequential order that the students expect. While they do not know the question that will be asked, they can predict when their turn will come. This increases comfort and also decreases the time the activity takes. Depending on the make-up of students in the class, the instructor may opt to call on students more randomly to motivate them to attend to the lesson. They need to understand that participation is mandatory and their attention improves their chances for success.

That said, students in a classroom setting can be provided with a "pass" option; if a question stumps a student, or she is not sure whether she will be right and is shy about taking the risk, then she may opt to "pass" for that question. Passing does not exempt the student from participation that day, however; it only takes the pressure off for that particular rotation. Typically, while the pass option does provide a safety net for tentative students, they rarely feel the need to use it. The comfort comes in the knowledge that it exists.

While the pace of questioning varies from group to group and certainly from individual to individual, as a general rule, this portion of the lesson should be lively and engaging. Encourage a certain amount of humor and create an energy that will engage the students in the lesson. During the Warm-Up the instructor should review both parts of speech and sentence parts. Typically a brief portion of the lesson, it always involves definition and generation of examples and often includes identification of examples in pre-written text.

Model Dialogue: Parts of Speech Review

The Warm-Up conversation might go something like this:

Teacher: Wes, what's a noun?

Wes: A noun names a person, place, thing, or idea.

Teacher: Good. [Places noun card in front of students.] And Logan, what's an example of a person noun?

Logan: <u>Logan</u>!

Teacher: Ha. Yes, Logan. And Charles, is <u>Logan</u> a proper or a common noun?

Charles: It's proper.

Teacher: Yes. How do you know?

Charles: Begins with a capital letter.

Teacher: Good. Nicolas, can you name a thing noun?

Nicolas: <u>Car</u>.

Teacher: And Martha, what about a place noun?

Martha: <u>New York</u>.

Teacher: Nice. Luke, what's a verb? [Places verb card to the right of noun card.]

Luke: It's an action word.

Teacher: Yes, and Will, can you name a verb besides <u>run</u> [since it has been given as an example a few times already in class]?

Will: Eat.

Teacher: Are you hungry, Will? Yes, <u>eat</u> is an excellent example. Is there another kind of verb, Taylor?

Taylor: Yes, verbs can link.

Teacher: Topper, what's an example of a linking verb?

Topper: <u>Is</u>?

Teacher: Yes, another?

Topper: <u>Am</u>.

Teacher: Sure. What's an adverb, Mac? [Places adverb card below verb card, allowing them to overlap slightly to show relationship.]

Mac: It usually describes a verb.

Teacher: Fine. And can you give me an example?

Mac: <u>Quickly</u>?

Teacher: Yes. [knowing that the students almost always think of <u>quickly</u> first] How about another?

Mac: <u>Enthusiastically</u>?

Teacher: Right. Ellie, can you give me an adverb that does not end in -ly?

Ellie: [after a pause] I'm not sure.

Teacher: It might help to think of a word that tells when.

Ellie: <u>Now</u>? <u>Never</u>?

Teacher: Both of those are fine adverbs.

The conversation continues in a similar fashion until the instructor has covered all review concepts. In one-to-one instruction, keep up a similar dialogue, with the one respondent. Remember to keep this fast-paced and relatively light. Typically, unless the instructor recognizes a confusion or problem with the previously learned material, the Warm-Up only takes a few minutes.

Each day, as the instructor covers the parts of speech, she should set up the concept cards in front of the students, always in the same pattern to show the relationships between the

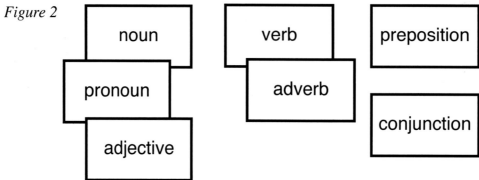

Figure 2

terms (*Figure 2*). Since pronouns replace nouns and both are described by adjectives, their cards overlap slightly. Adverbs most often describe verbs, and so they overlap. Though conjunctions and prepositions are not directly related, both help groups of words relate to one another. Therefore, they are together but not touching in this model. Students will start to group the parts of speech visually, providing yet another way to help them remember the vocabulary and relationships between terms and the words they identify. Eventually, ask a student volunteer to place the cards for each lesson. In a tutorial simply hand the student the seven cards, and he can place them on the table or desk; in a classroom, appoint a different student each day to create *Figure 3* on a whiteboard, chalkboard, Smartboard, or other surface. Since I typically identify articles as a particular kind of adjective and focus little attention on interjections, they are omitted from this figure.

Model Dialogue: Parts of Speech Error Correction

Good teaching involves eliciting a correct response from the student whenever possible. Simply saying, "no, it's actually a verb" corrects the error but does not teach the student how to find the answer for himself the next time around. The dialogue below models error correction:

Teacher: Cody, what's an adjective?

Cody: It describes a noun.

Teacher: What else can it describe?

Cody: Sometimes a pronoun.

Teacher: Good. Andrew, can you give me an example of an adjective?

Andrew: <u>Run</u>.

Teacher: Okay, Andrew, what's an adjective again?

Andrew: It describes a noun.

Teacher: Good. What does <u>run</u> describe?

Andrew: It describes what someone is doing.

Teacher: Ahhh, I see. But, because it's "what someone is doing," that's an action. What part of speech marks an action word?

Andrew: Oh, then <u>run</u> is a verb.

Teacher: Exactly. Adjectives often come right before the noun they describe. What word might I put in front of <u>boy</u> to describe him?

Andrew: <u>Ugly</u>?

Teacher: Yep. Can you think of another? Perhaps to describe this classroom?

Andrew: <u>Clean</u>.

Teacher: Yes. I'm going to put the word <u>door</u> on the board. Everybody, please write three adjectives on your papers that could describe <u>door</u>.

In the dialogue above, similar to one I had recently with a student, I come to understand why Andrew is confused and use it as an opportunity to clarify the definition of <u>verb</u> and also to help him come to a more accurate understanding of <u>adjective</u>. Then, I ask him to generate a few adjectives. Finally, I turn the activity over to the entire class. If Andrew is completely lost during the dialogue, which occasionally and regretfully does happen, I may turn the dialogue over to a student who understands the concept. This practice alleviates the pressure Andrew may be feeling but also models the process of self-discovery that I'm encouraging. Unless either student anxiety or restlessness in the room is high, I avoid providing the answer myself.

Model Dialogue: Sentence Parts Review & Subsequent Error Correction

The model dialogue for sentence parts review takes on a similar format to the one used for parts of speech (whether one-to-one, small group, or classroom instruction). I drill the students with rapid-fire questioning using concepts previously covered. The key difference is that the examples generated between questions are often written on paper and then shared with the class, largely due to their length. A typical review conversation for sentence parts might go something like this:

Teacher: Will, what's a clause?

Will: A clause is a group of words with a subject and its verb.

Teacher: Just for clarity, what is the term we use to discuss the verb and the words that follow it, Zach?

Zach: Predicate!

Teacher: Good. Jackson, what are the two kinds of clauses?

Jackson: Independent and dependent.

Teacher: Yes. How do you tell them apart?

Jackson: An independent clause can stand by itself as a sentence, and a dependent...

Teacher: Good. Rob, can you explain what a dependent clause is?

Rob: It cannot stand by itself.

Teacher: Everybody, take a moment and generate one of each kind of clause. Don't forget that the list of subordinating conjunctions is at the back of your binders. [The students take time to write dependent and independent clauses at their seats.]

Teacher: Okay, it looks like everybody has finished writing. Ethan, can you share your independent clause?

Ethan: <u>My mother served beets for dinner last night</u>.

Teacher: Good. What makes it independent, Ethan?

Ethan: It can stand by itself.

Teacher: Right. Eliza, what about yours?

Eliza: <u>Because dinner was served late</u>.

Teacher: That's a good clause, but not an independent one. We're going to come back to it. [Teacher writes it on the board for further study.] Zach, what about yours?

Zach: I sleep.

Teacher: Yes, Zach, that's correct though you didn't stretch yourself very much. [Class chuckles.] In the future, let's aim for independent clauses that have at least nine or ten words in them for exercises like this one. [The students continue to share their independent clauses until each student has had a turn. Rather than call on only two or three students to participate during sharing time, <u>all</u> students are both encouraged and expected to share their examples.] Good. Now, let's return to the example on the board. [Though Eliza is the author, the emphasis is away from her and instead on the clause.] Is "because dinner was served late" a clause? [The teacher searches for a raised hand.] Will?

Will: Yes.

Teacher: True. Why? [Always validate a student response when it is correct. Otherwise, a question such as "Why?" or "Explain your answer" is sure to have the student changing his response.]

Will: It has a subject and a verb.

Teacher: Ethan, what's the subject?

Ethan: <u>Dinner</u>.

Teacher: And the verb or predicate, Jackson?

Jackson: <u>Was</u>.

Teacher: What kind of verb is it?

Jackson: Linking.

Teacher: Nice. Why isn't this an independent clause? [A pause for hands.] Zach?

Zach: It can't stand by itself.

Teacher: Right, and what's the one word that keeps it from standing by itself?

Zach: <u>Because</u>.

Teacher: Excellent. Someone else, what part of speech is <u>because</u>? [A pause for hands.] Yes Eliza?

Eliza: It's a conjunction.

Teacher: Yes. What kind?

Eliza: Subordinating.

Teacher: Which makes the clause what kind?

Eliza: Dependent.

Teacher: What can we do to this clause to make it independent, then?

Eliza: Remove the <u>because</u> and just say, <u>dinner was served late</u>.

Teacher: Nice job, Eliza.

Above, I've woven correct and incorrect responses into one model dialogue. The dialogue shows that the instructor can explain an error without focusing on its creator. Additionally, it shows that eliciting a response in a group setting is sometimes best done by asking classmates for clarification.

The class continues in a similar fashion until the instructor has reviewed everything covered thus far. While asking students to write examples of each element discussed would slow the pace of the class too much, the instructor should have students write examples of *some* elements. Always provide adequate time for each student to share her example. In a one-to-one session, obviously, the student responds to each question posed by the instructor. Usually, the instructor can write an example as the student writes hers. This validates the assignment and also provides an additional sample for sharing and discussion.

As students review the sentence parts, set up the concept cards, always in the same pattern to show the relationships between the elements (*Figure 3*). The subject and verb (the predicate card can be substituted here with ease) come together to form the clause. Only two kinds of clauses exist -- independent and dependent -- and so they branch off from the clause in the layout in *Figure 3*. As they are covered, the different kinds of sentences (i.e., simple, compound, complex, compound-complex) can be placed below the two kinds of clauses. The students begin to recognize the terms and, more importantly, how they relate to each other.

Figure 3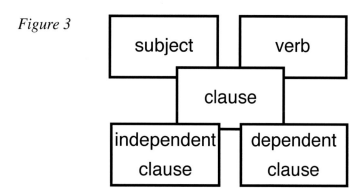

Though it is not necessary to create a written record of the Warm-Up each day, sometimes it can prove useful. On the following two pages are a blank record sheet and the same sheet with student responses. For each term, ask the students to provide a definition. Where appropriate, ask them to list the different kinds (e.g., verb - action, linking, helping). As the students provide the different kinds of nouns (i.e., person, place, thing, idea), the instructor writes each below the line. Then, he returns, prompting the students to generate examples for each kind. Keep the questioning language minimal and to the point. This written record can be created on a chalkboard, whiteboard, or Smartboard, either by the instructor or an appointed student scribe. Occasionally (though not too often as it significantly increases the time the Warm-Up takes), students can create versions of the written record at their seats. In small group or one-to-one instruction, the teacher and students can create the record together. The instructor might write the information below the line and then pass the paper to the students to include examples.

Name: _____ Date: _____

Parts of Speech Warm-Up Record Sheet

noun _____ _____ _____ _____

verb _____ _____ _____

pronoun _____ _____

adjective _____ _____

adverb _____ _____

conjunction _____ _____

Name: _____   Date: _____

Parts of Speech Warm-Up Record Sheet*
(with student responses)

noun**   _John_____   _Chicago_____   _table_____   _democracy___
          person   place   thing   idea

verb   _swing_____   _am_____   _was_____
          action   linking   helping

pronoun*** _he_____   _they_____
            singular   plural

adjective   _turquoise____   _intelligent___
            color/number   other

adverb   _selfishly____   _often_____
            ending in -ly   not ending in -ly

conjunction _yet_____   _until_____
             coordinating   subordinating

*   The instructor can require multiple examples of each term as well.

**   Depending on the concept the instructor is covering, the students could also list
     concrete/abstract, singular/plural, common/proper, or animate/inanimate nouns
     rather than person/place/thing/idea.

*** Instead of singular/plural, the students could list subject/object.

As A Matter of Fact 2:
Five-Point Instructional Strategy

Introduction

The core of any lesson is the time devoted to focused study of a particular skill. Whether it is the introduction of something new or review of a familiar concept, instruction is quite similar. Below, I've identified and explained the steps to include in covering a concept in detail and the reasons behind those steps; at the conclusion of this section, there is a one-page summary that can be photocopied for the teacher's ready reference.

Steps

1. Choose either a or b or, if time allows, include both:

   a: **Review of Previously Learned Concept**: Often, the instructor will follow the warm-up with review of a specific skill, usually one that the students have covered recently. Of particular interest might be a skill that has a strong and obvious connection to the new concept the instructor will introduce in the day's lesson or in the near future. For example, the instructor might review adverbs in anticipation of a new lesson about adverbial phrases, nouns and verbs before beginning a study of gerunds, or subjects and predicates in preparation for a study of independent and dependent clauses.

Students explain concept, proving understanding. The emphasis here is on information your students have learned and can share. With most concepts this will take only a few minutes. Students should begin by verbalizing what they know from memory and then use the concept vocabulary card to elaborate on their understanding.

b. **Introduction of New Concept**: Where grammar is the area of study, mastery comes not when the terminology is memorized but rather when it is internalized and used automatically and unconsciously in applied writing. Not every lesson involves the introduction of a new concept. If students struggled with the previous concept or have difficulty recalling it during Review, this is a clear indicator that the instructor should delay introducing a new concept. Sometimes, "new" concepts are actually just spins on previously learned concepts. For example, one lesson might be devoted to compound sentences while a follow-up lesson might cover those that use <u>yet</u> as the coordinating conjunction.

Teacher introduces concept and then asks students to explain it, proving understanding. In most instances, introducing a part of speech or sentence part to your students should take just a few minutes. Students should create (or you should provide) a vocabulary card with term on front, definition and examples on back; explain the term and its definition; and have them explain it back to you or, in the case of large group instruction, to each other. Students can illustrate their cards as well.

2. **Students identify examples of the concept in context.** Have students sort words, sentence parts, or sentences to help them recognize the concept you are teaching. Have them identify examples of the studied element in a larger context. Professionally written sentences, from both textbooks and good literature, sometimes serve this purpose well and also offer material for further discussion.

3. **Students create their own examples in isolation**. Students must focus primary attention on creating examples of the concept, in isolation and in applied context. Keep the emphasis on student-generated work.

4. **Students share their examples with the instructor and their classmates**. When the students complete independent practice of a concept at their desks, always allow time to share results. This does the following:

    (a) validates the students' writing

    (b) encourages them to write at a more sophisticated level since they anticipate an audience

    (c) allows the instructor to check for competence

    (d) provides student-generated examples (whether correct or not) for further discussion and analysis

5. **Teacher uses examples, both correct and incorrect, for clarification and further instruction**. As the students share, the teacher writes any incorrect examples as well as any examples that show a new or interesting development that warrants discussion. Since the examples come from the students' own writing on the day in question, the teacher is able to target student difficulties immediately and strengthen class understanding. Using student examples rather than prefabricated, professionally written sentences does the following:

    (a) connects students to the assignment

    (b) provides immediacy and relevance

    (c) gives the teacher valuable information about where the students are and what they need next in order to further their writing.

On the next page is a summary of the Five-Step Instructional Strategy for easy reference.

Five-Point Instructional Strategy

New Concept	Review Concept
a. **Teacher introduces concept and then asks students to explain it, proving understanding.** In most instances, introducing a part of speech or sentence part to your students should take just a few minutes. Students should create (or you should provide) a vocabulary card with term on front, definition and examples on back; explain the term and its definition; and have them explain it back to you or, in the case of large group instruction, to each other. Students can illustrate their cards as well.	a. **Students explain concept, proving understanding.** The emphasis here is on information your students have learned and can share. With most concepts this will take only a few minutes. Students should begin by verbalizing what they know from memory and then use the concept vocabulary card to elaborate on their understanding.

b. **Students identify examples of the concept in context.** Have students sort words, sentence parts, or sentences to help them recognize the concept you are teaching. Have them identify examples of the studied element in a larger context. Professionally written sentences, from both textbooks and good literature, sometimes serve this purpose well and also offer material for further discussion.

c. **Students create their own examples in isolation.** Students must focus primary attention on creating examples of the concept, in isolation and in applied context. Keep the emphasis on student-generated work.

d. **Students share their examples with the instructor and their classmates.** When the students complete independent practice of a concept at their desks, always allow time to share results. This (a) validates the students' writing, (b) encourages them to write at a more sophisticated level since they anticipate an audience, (c) allows the instructor to check for competence, and (d) provides student-generated examples (whether correct or not) for further discussion and analysis.

e. **Teacher uses examples, both correct and incorrect, for clarification and further instruction.** As the students share, the teacher writes any incorrect examples as well as any examples that show a new or interesting development that warrants discussion. Since the examples come from the students' own writing on the day in question, the teacher is able to target student difficulties immediately and strengthen class understanding. Using student examples rather than prefabricated, professionally written sentences connects students to the assignment, provides immediacy and relevance, and gives the teacher valuable information about where the students are and what they need next in order to further their writing.

As A Matter of Fact 3:
The Wrap-Up

Introduction

The Wrap-Up forms the final component of most lessons. In essence, its format is a repeat of the Warm-Up, but the content is the material covered in the day's lesson rather than review of previously learned material. This practice has three goals:

1. It allows students to spiral back and recall concepts they have covered during the day's lesson. Spiralling allows students to see how the specific concepts of today's lesson fit into the larger context of how their writing is developing.

2. It furthers the chances they will remember those concepts for tomorrow's lesson. Some research indicates that the first and last few minutes of instructional time are often a teacher's best chance for long-term retention of material. Asking students to re-cap what has been covered increases chances that the material will be remembered in the future.

3. It also helps students recognize the ground that has been covered in the session. This validates the time they've committed to being in class and the focus they've put into the material you've been covering. Often, during the Wrap-Up, students are surprised at just how much they've learned in a very short period of time.

The Matter at Hand 1:
Parts of Speech for Instruction

Introduction

The information you choose to teach is determined by the age, grade, and skill level of your students as well as the time you can commit to the writing process. A good rule of thumb is this: do not teach a concept unless it has a direct application to the act of writing for your students. That said, each concept in this section of *Writing Matters* has three components:

1. an overview of the concept, including background information and points of clarity for teacher understanding

2. concept introduction and application for the student in as clear and succinct a manner as possible

3. examples of activities and assignments to help students understand, learn, and review the concept

Where appropriate, I have interspersed model dialogues to demonstrate effective teaching strategies.

No one ever became a better writer by underlining nouns or drawing arrows from adverbs to the verbs they modify. This activity is merely the first, brief step in understanding a particular concept. Immediately follow it by having students generate examples and use them in their own sentences; otherwise, the task develops an isolated sub-skill with no relevance to the writing process. Use parts of speech terminology merely as a language to introduce, discuss, and practice with different structures in English.

Core Concept

Part of speech involves the *job* a word is doing, its *function* or *role*. The only way to know, without a shadow of a doubt, a word's part of speech is to see it as it relates to other words in a phrase, clause, or sentence. With the most basic students, <u>oil</u> is a noun, plain and simple. However, as students mature, it is important to realize that context determines its function:

noun: Your car needs <u>oil</u>.

verb: I will <u>oil</u> that squeaky hinge before we leave.

adjective: The <u>oil</u> painting is worth over a million dollars.

Another good example is the word <u>rock</u>:

noun: I threw the <u>rock</u> into the lake.

verb: If you <u>rock</u> the boat, I will become seasick.

adjective: We built a <u>rock</u> wall in our backyard.

<u>Table</u> is more challenging; it is usually a noun but can also serve as a verb:

noun: I sat at the <u>table</u>.

verb: We will <u>table</u> that issue until the next meeting.

<u>Orange</u> serves as both a noun and an adjective:

noun: I always have an <u>orange</u> with my breakfast.

adjective: The boy had <u>orange</u> hair and freckles.

Consider <u>only</u>, which can serve as both an adjective and an adverb:

adjective: The <u>only</u> car in the parking lot is a Mazda.

adverb: Mary was <u>only</u> joking.

A number of conjunctions, including <u>after</u> and <u>since</u>, can also serve as prepositions:

conjunction: <u>After</u> the game is over, we will grab some dinner.

preposition: <u>After</u> dinner you must do your homework.

conjunction: I have had a headache <u>since</u> we finished lunch.

preposition: I have not wanted to go dancing <u>since</u> the party.

Consider <u>canned</u>:

adjective: I prefer not to eat <u>canned</u> vegetables.

(participle = verb used as adjective)

verb: I <u>canned</u> the beans for the long winter ahead.

As the English language evolves, its users embrace new words and even new meanings and usages of existing words. Recently, for example, the word <u>text</u> has gained a new part of speech, for example. It has always been a noun. With the expanded use of cell phones, however, we use it more often as a verb:

noun: The <u>text</u> is difficult to understand.

verb: I will <u>text</u> you when I land in Washington.

There are literally thousands of words that can serve as more than one part of speech. Many serve as both nouns and verbs:

Word	As A Noun	As A Verb
drink	Have a <u>drink</u> of water.	<u>Drink</u> this.
run	The next <u>run</u> will clinch the game.	I will <u>run</u> with you tomorrow.
spit	We will roast the pig on a <u>spit</u>.	Llamas <u>spit</u> frequently.
fan	The <u>fan</u> cooled the room.	I will <u>fan</u> myself with this book.
wash	I did a load of <u>wash</u> before we ate.	Jake can <u>wash</u> the jerseys before the game.
thought	I had a <u>thought</u> about dinner tonight.	I <u>thought</u> we could buy some sodas at the corner store.
shield	The knight wielded his <u>shield</u> against his attacker.	Good suntan lotion will <u>shield</u> you from the sun.

Figure 4

Activities That Ask Students To Apply Their Knowledge of Parts of Speech to Writing

Classroom Lab:

Use the classroom as a lab for the study of parts of speech. Have students list nouns in the classroom. Write the items they name on index cards, which they can then attach to the items themselves with tape. Verbs and eventually adjectives and even adverbs can be added using this technique. For example, during noun study *floor* might be taped to the floor; students might add *walk*, *run*, and *slide* to the floor when the instructor covers verbs. *Beige, dirty,* and *slippery* might be adjectives the students consider while *quickly, dangerously,* and *haphazardly* could be added to the verbs *walk, run,* and *slide* when adverbs are addressed.

Living Noun Builders:

- What would you like to do for 24 hours?:
    1. Vertically list five jobs you would like to have for twenty-four hours (e.g., *pilot*).
    2. Add a verb to the right of each job noun (e.g., pilot *flies*).
    3. Next, add a different adjective to each job noun and a different adverb to each job verb (e.g., *dangerous* pilot flies *quickly*).
    4. Finally, add a prepositional phrase to the end of each job expansion (e.g., dangerous pilot flies quickly *above the clouds*).
- Here's a spin on the above activity. (See *Figure 5* with model and blank template.):
    1. Write a career or a living creature (common noun) in the box.
    2. To the left of this, write five adjectives that could describe him/her.
    3. To the right of this, write five action verbs that he/she could do.
    4. To the right of each verb write an adverb that could describe that verb.
    5. To the right of each adverb write a prepositional phrase that could tell more about the action verb you chose.

adjectives		action verbs	adverbs	prepositional phrases
safe	pilot	flew	quickly	through the dark cloud
dangerous		sat	uncomfortably	beside the loud co-pilot
crazy		ate	rudely	in the dirty cockpit
female		dodged	skillfully	between enemy fighters
alien		dives	stupidly	into danger

adjectives		action verbs	adverbs	prepositional phrases
_____	⬜	_____	_____	_____
_____		_____	_____	_____
_____		_____	_____	_____
_____		_____	_____	_____
_____		_____	_____	_____

Figure 5

- Ask students to list five places that would be interesting to live for a month. You can allow proper names (e.g., Paris, New York, Cairo, etc.) or only common nouns (e.g., a castle, the moon, a cottage, the coast). Have the students list adjectives to describe their locations. Then, using the pronoun I, have the students list verbs that they would like to do there (e.g., cave: *I explore.*) Then, have them add adverbs to their verbs (e.g., I explore *nervously.*). Finally, have them add prepositional phrases to their groups of words (e.g., I explore nervously *through the tunnels.*).

- Ask students to choose a person (e.g., grandmother, baby, etc.). Have them list five adjectives to describe that person (e.g., baby - *ugly, whiny, happy*). Then, they should list five verbs that express actions that person might do (e.g., ugly baby - *wails, burps, laughs*). Have them add adverbs to their list of verbs (e.g., ugly baby wails - *loudly, obnoxiously, despairingly*). Finally, have them add prepositional phrases to their groups of words (e.g., ugly baby wails loudly - *in the crib, at our dinner table, on the airplane*).

- The card game *Sentence Stretch* provides an excellent version of this activity (wvced.com).

Using Word Lists For Sentence Development:

For students who struggle with word retrieval or need a stronger and broader vocabulary, provide lists of words grouped by part of speech. Put lengthy adjective, noun, and verb lists in a section of the student's binder, and assign sentences using words from those lists. Have the students check off words they have used once so that they will use different words each time they complete one of these assignments. As the list of "unchecked" words narrows, some of the remaining words can be chosen as vocabulary words as the students are most likely to leave unfamiliar words unchecked. (Lists of words grouped by part of speech appear in Appendix I of this text on pages 284-295)

Grammar Charts:

At wvced.com a variety of charts like *Figure 6* are available at different levels (free download). Make this activity an interactive one. Students can pair up, each with their own form. They fill in their own verbs, trade papers to add adverbs to their partners' verbs, and so on. In a one-on-one tutorial, you are the partner in this pairs activity.

Verb Expander

verb	adverb	prepositional (adverb) phrase
sleep	*soundly*	*through the storm*

Figure 6

Writing From Pictures:

Establish an envelope or box to store scene pictures, loaded with characters and action. Successful pictures include an active farm (with farmers, animals, etc.), a castle (with guards, knights, king, queen, and even a dragon), a pirate ship (with pirates, prisoners, and a ship's parrot), an airport (with planes taking off and landing, cars, utility vehicles, pilots, and passengers), a quaint village (with multiple labeled shops and dwellings, various villagers, and maybe some marauders), and a circus (with performers, animals, and crowds). Some of the more complicated built Lego sets can be substituted for pictures as well. For younger students, pictures in a Richard Scarry book might prove an excellent resource. David Macaulay's *Castle* works with older students. Use these and other pictures you discover for student-generated word and sentence lists of all kinds.

Sentence Combining:

Provide students with sentences to be combined. If the focus is on parts of speech, locate the essential information in each of the short sentences that you will combine into one, more descriptive sentence. A few examples follow. More of these can be found in the Sample Assignments sections of Adjectives and Adverbs and throughout the Sentence Parts section of this text.

The man bought a house.

The house was new. (adjective)

He did this quickly. (adverb)

The man was elderly. (adjective)

one answer: *The elderly man quickly bought a new house.*

The picnic happened.

A party happened the same day. (noun)

It was Tuesday. (adverb)

The party was charming. (adjective)

The picnic was messy. (adjective)

one answer: *The messy picnic and the charming party happened on Tuesday.*

Sentence Writing:

Provided the students have the capability, the culmination of any writing lesson must be generating actual sentences. Only with this activity can competence be assessed and measured. Only with this activity do students begin to internalize and apply the concepts their instructor has introduced.

Venn Diagrams For Parts of Speech:

This activity is useful for helping students explore multiple meaning words as they work on their understandings of parts of speech. Generate a list of terms in advance and ask the students to place each term, one at a time, on the diagram in the correct location. A simple, two-circle diagram works for adjective/noun or verb/noun (See *Figure 7.*). For more sophisticated thinkers, a three-circle diagram can include adjective/noun/verb.

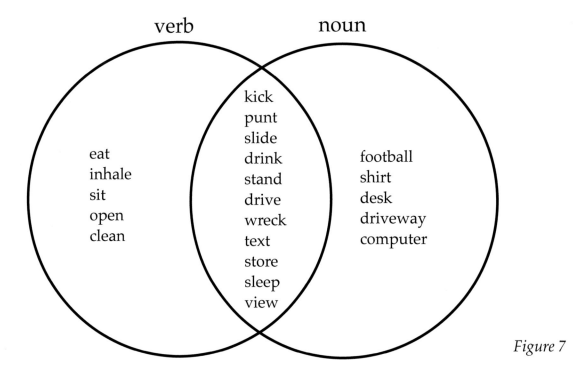

Figure 7

Jennifer Hasser of Kendore Learning has an interesting spin on this: she uses lists of words grouped by phonetic concept (e.g., <u>ai</u> = long a) for parts of speech analysis.

Concepts & Lessons

Students should build personal stacks of vocabulary cards representing the terms below (*Figure 8*). They should only have cards for terms the instructor has introduced. More advanced parts of a term's definition can be added once students have covered them. For example, a student may initially learn that nouns name people, places, and things; her concept card would represent that fact. Later, when she has learned that nouns can also name ideas, she (or her instructor) would add that fact to her concept card. Following this strategy, her cards are a stack of concepts she has actually covered. Sample cards are included with the discussion of each individual concept. (Concept cards are available for purchase from wvced.com.)

A Brief Overview

Part of Speech	Basic	Advanced
noun	names person, place, thing	names idea
verb	action	state of being/linking; helping/auxiliary
pronoun	replaces noun (subject)	replaces noun (object, etc.)
adjective	describes noun (or pronoun)	
adverb	describes verb	describes adjective or another adverb
preposition	begins phrase (concrete - anything a plane can do to a cloud)*	begins phrase (abstract)
conjunction	coordinating (joins two words or two groups of words)	subordinating (joins dependent and independent clauses)
interjection	expresses strong emotion	

* *over* a cloud, *through* a cloud, *beside* a cloud   *Figure 8*

Figures 9 and *10* (next page) are charts that show relationships between parts of speech. An arrow pointing from one term to another shows that the first describes or supports the second. A two-ended arrow shows that the two terms can be switched in a sentence. A dotted line shows a relationship that is less important (adverb to adjective) or less strong (preposition and conjunction) than the other relationships in the chart. The parts of speech are arranged exactly as term cards would be laid out during Warm-Up.

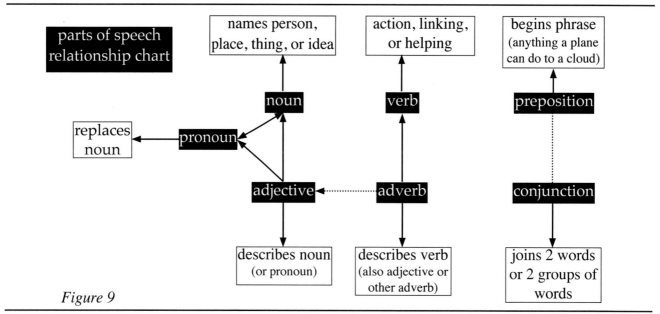

Figure 9

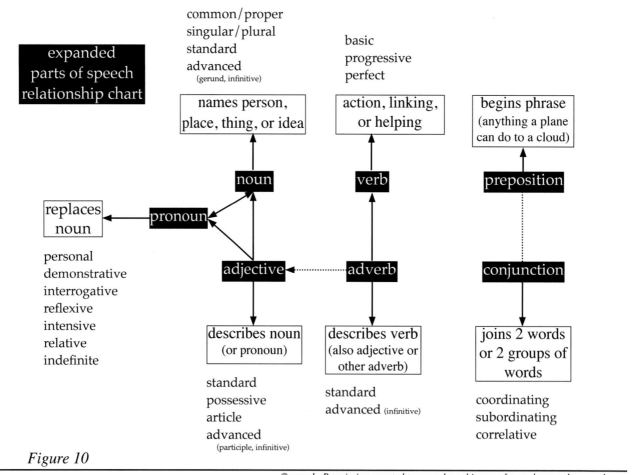

Figure 10

Nouns

Overview: A noun *names* a person, place, thing or idea. In other words, <u>table</u> is the name in English for "an article of furniture consisting of a flat, slablike top supported on one or more legs or other supports" (www.dictionary.com). The Spanish word for this same object, <u>mesa</u>, is different from our word for it. Students can discuss the fact that different languages usually have different names for the same person, place, thing, or idea. In other words, the object is the same, but the *name* is different.

Latin Origin
nomen = name
derivatives:
nominate
nominal
nomenclature

Often, sentences contain more nouns than any other individual part of speech. Typically, they are taught first though some have argued convincingly in favor of teaching verbs first instead as it is sometimes easier to locate the action and then locate its actor.

Nouns can serve as subjects or objects in a clause or sentence.

See page 284 for a page of useful nouns.

Kinds & Categories: Discussions of some of these more specific categories

of nouns may prove useful as the study unfolds. Maintain your primary focus, though. Students need to be generating nouns, and lots of them. The act of *writing* produces better writers. The act of labeling or identifying does not.

1. common: names generally (e.g., boy, gym, pillow, rage)

   proper: names particular people, places, things (e.g., Abe Lincoln, Rome, I-Pod)

2. singular: one (e.g., grandmother, park, table)

   plural: more than one (e.g., brothers, zoos, lamps)

3. concrete: names nouns you can experience with your senses (e.g., Bob, chair, flame)

   abstract: names ideas or feelings (e.g., love, curiosity, patience)

Verbals are verbs used as other parts of speech. These are discussed in the Sentence Parts section of this text, but the two verbals that can serve as nouns are mentioned below. Even students with more basic skills will use these structures in their writing:

1. gerund: -ing verb used as a noun:

    <u>Skiing</u> is enjoyable. I love <u>walking</u> in the afternoon.

2. infinitive: to + a verb used as a noun (also can be adjective or adverb):

    I love <u>to swim</u> after a long day. <u>To eat</u> is what I want most right now.

Common Core: The Common Core State Standards provide the following grade-level guidelines regarding nouns:

- Use singular/plural nouns. (K)

- Use singular/plural nouns with matching verbs. (1)

- Use collective nouns. (2)

- Form and use frequently occurring irregular plural nouns. (2)

- Form and use regular/irregular plural nouns. (3)

- Use abstract nouns. (3)

- Ensure subject-verb and pronoun-antecedent agreement. (3)

- Explain the function of nouns in general and their functions in particular sentences. (3)

noun

names a person, place, thing, or idea

examples: Logan, school, table, anger

noun

names a person, place, thing, or idea

Jane, city, table, hunger

advanced: *kinds of nouns*
common: names generally turkey, tree, house
proper: names particular people, places, things
    Sam, Porsche, Chicago
concrete: names nouns you can experience with
    your senses Bob, chair, flame
abstract: names ideas or feelings anger, curiosity

Introduction:

- Define the term, writing it on the board. Include several examples.

- Hand students concept cards or have them create their own.

- List examples from their everyday lives.

Initial Application:

- Have students generate their own examples, using items in the classroom, pictures, trips around the school, or even an outing to a nearby supermarket or zoo. Older students may be stimulated by a good list topic, such as historical figures (people), vacation spots (places), or sports equipment (things).

- Have students identify nouns from written sentences (if they are readers).

- Have students categorize nouns.

- If they have the ability, have students generate their own sentences and locate their own nouns. (Steer students away from pronoun usage at this point.)

Model Dialogue: Noun Introduction

The teacher begins the lesson by placing the term and its definition in front of the students. Where appropriate, the teacher can elicit the definition from students, particularly when the concept has probably already been introduced at some point in their schooling.

Teacher: *Does anyone know the definition of a noun?*

Eliza: *A person, place, or thing?*

Teacher: *Well, Eliza, yes, a noun **names** a person, place, or thing. Martha, can you come up with an example of a noun? [Already, the teacher is moving the discussion from the simple definition to an application activity.]*

Martha: *Chicken?*

Teacher: *Yes, Martha, chicken is a perfectly good noun. [Teacher writes the definition on the board and, underneath it, Martha's example, chicken.] Will, do you have another noun?*

Will: *Horse?*

Teacher: *Yes, Will. And what do horse and chicken have in common?*

Will: *They're both animals. Barn animals.*

Teacher: *Good, Will. Look at the definition of a noun. Which of the three things that nouns can name fits best for horse and chicken?*

Will: *They're things.*

Teacher: *Good. Who has a noun that is not a thing?*

Luke: *What about Luke?*

Teacher: *[Smiling.] Yes, Luke, your name is definitely a noun because it names a person.*

Luke: *Yes, me!*

Teacher: *That's right. [Adds Luke to the list of examples on the board.] We don't have a place noun yet.*

Charlie: *I'm going to Chicago for Spring Break. What about Chicago?*

Teacher: *Yes, Charlie, that's an excellent choice. [Adds Chicago to the list of examples.] Are there some places that are a bit smaller than cities?*

Rob: What about school? Or the police station?

Eliza: Or even this classroom?

Teacher: Excellent. [Adds these to the list.] These are all good examples of nouns. Okay, there is
            another kind of noun -- not a person, place, or thing. Does anybody know what else nouns
            can name?

Chris: Ideas. They name ideas.

Teacher: Yep, that's right. Some of those ideas are feelings or emotions. Who can think of one?

Jeb: _Anger._

Teacher: Good. Who has another?

Logan: _Sad._

Teacher: Well, Logan, that is certainly an emotion. But that one is an adjective. It isn't a thing.
            You can say, "Anger can tire you out." Can you say, "Sad can tire you out?"

Logan: No.

Teacher: Also, you can say, "the sad girl," which means _sad_ is describing _girl_. Do nouns describe?

Logan: No.

Teacher: What's the ending I'd need to put on _sad_ to make it fit that sentence?

Logan: _-ness._ _Sadness_ can tire you out.

Teacher: Good. You've changed the adjective, _sad_, into the noun, _sadness_. Are there some idea
            nouns that are not feelings? (Silence.) Okay, what about _war_ and _peace_? _Democracy_?
            Activity? [Adds these to the list on the board.]

At this point, the teacher hands concept cards to the students. Each student creates a
card like the model. If the cards are pre-made, each student is asked to read the contents
silently, and then a volunteer is asked to read his aloud to the class. Whether the students
make their own cards or the teacher provides them, each student is asked to read her
concept card to a classmate. Then, the classmate reciprocates. In either case, the cards can
be illustrated with pictures of appropriate example nouns.

Subsequent Lessons:

For students in grades one and two or those who are developing their sense of grammar for the first time, limit the Initial Lesson to "person, place, or thing." Instruction of noun as "idea" should wait until students are in at least 3rd grade. These students with more basic skills might benefit from subsequent, individual lessons distinguishing between common and proper as well as singular and plural nouns. Also, the collective noun is a sophisticated element that might warrant individual attention. For older students who have covered nouns before and are in the remedial setting, most of the noun categories can be explored together in the same lesson.

Identification: Before students begin generating their own nouns, some brief

identification exercises are useful.

One format looks like this:

- Which word can function as a noun: of not bank

A slightly more sophisticated activity is this one:

- Underline the words that can function as nouns from the list below:

   ugly now tree shirt printer eat

When they are ready, students should do several activities like these:

- Underline the noun in the phrase: on the boardwalk
- Underline the noun in the clause: if Mary finds the shop with the handbags in it
- Underline the nouns in the sentence: The robber stored his loot in the back of a closet.

Sorting: Categorizing is not only a higher level thinking skill but also a preliminary step

to writing essays of more than one paragraph. These tasks, then, serve a dual purpose -- to
extend knowledge of nouns and to encourage higher level thinking:

- Person/Place/Thing/Idea:

   peace truck doctor wallet curiosity tree
   pilot Georgia shopper democracy playground zoo

person	place	thing	idea
_____	_____	_____	_____
_____	_____	_____	_____
_____	_____	_____	_____

60

- Animate/Inanimate:

lion	table	shirt	falcon
mother	eel	book	chalkboard

inanimate   animate

_____   _____

_____   _____

_____   _____

_____   _____

- Common/Proper:

chicken	Farmer Joe	Kentucky	Nike
ice	lamp	Lizzie	suitcase

common   proper

_____   _____

_____   _____

_____   _____

_____   _____

- Singular/Plural:

men	book	geese	bicycle
wall	beds	pens	sidewalk

singular   plural

_____   _____

_____   _____

_____   _____

_____   _____

Matching:
Matching nouns with other words encourages students to participate in the higher-level thinking involved in context. Activities such as these encourage students to think about the relationships nouns have with other words. Students can be asked to match nouns in a variety of contexts:

- match concrete noun to action verb:

lion	whispered		ball	flew
librarian	fired		airplane	rolled
gunfighter	roared		radio	blared

- match adjective to concrete noun:

enormous	sun		wooden	package
red	apple		glowing	cabinet
bright	lion		heavy	embers

- match pronoun to noun:

he	Chris and Bob		it	my family and I
us	Jake		we	Cindy
they	Jane and I		her	table

- match noun to prepositional phrase:

eagle	in the north pasture		antique	at the restaurant
cow	on the moon		dinner	in France
man	with a huge wingspan		chicken	with broccoli

Fill In The Blanks:
Like the matching exercises above, these fill-in-the-blanks activities encourage students to think about nouns in a broader context, but with one subtle difference. For the first time here, students are asked to generate their own nouns for each blank. (Items in parentheses are optional.)

- adjective - noun:

| ugly _____ | challenging _____ |
| red _____ | considerate _____ |

- preposition - (adjectives) - noun:

  on the _____   under the old _____

  beside her _____   through the _____

- (article) - noun - verb:

  _____ slept   _____ fell

  _____ shines   _____ will eat

- noun - conjunction - noun

  _____ and _____

  _____ and _____

  _____ but _____

- sentences:

  _____ and _____ went bowling this afternoon.

  The farm had _____ and _____.

  The doctor, who was also a _____, flew planes on the weekends.

Adding & Changing Endings: Endings often represent a word's part of speech. Adding or changing the ending of a word will usually shift its part of speech or its application. Activities like these can be followed by asking students to use the newly formed words in sentences.

- Add -hood to the following individual person nouns to make them groups or general states:

  brother _____   adult _____

  neighbor _____   boy _____

- Add -ness to these adjectives to make them general nouns:

  dark _____   calm _____

  ill _____   wet _____

- Drop the silent-e and add -ion to make these -ate verbs into -ation nouns:

  duplicate _____   aggravate _____

  generate _____   locate _____

- Add -ion to these verbs to make them into nouns:

  erupt _____   instruct _____

  elect _____   inspect _____

- Make these words into -sion nouns. You will need to drop the silent-e for all of them; for some, the final d in the stem will need to change to an s:

  persuade _____   decide _____

  invade _____   conclude _____

  confuse _____   infuse _____

- Drop the final silent-e, and change these action or process verbs ending in -ize into nouns about these processes, ending in -ism:

  metabolize _____   optimize _____

  hypnotize _____   terrorize _____

- Drop the final silent-e and add -ism to these basewords to create general nouns:

  race _____   alcohol _____

  tour _____   skeptic _____

- Add -ity to these adjectives to make them into general nouns. Sometimes, you will need to drop a final silent-e before adding the -ity:

  real _____   hostile _____

  objective _____   original _____

- Add -or to these verbs to make them people nouns. Sometimes, you will need to drop a final silent-e before adding the -or:

  instruct _____   operate _____

  audit _____   visit _____

- Change the y to -ist or merely add the suffix -ist in these words to make them into people nouns.

  column _____   nutrition _____

  panel _____   biology _____

List Generation:
Students often create a list before beginning to write a longer piece, such as a paragraph. The noun-centered lists below ask students to generate their own nouns, but within certain categories:

- places to visit

  _____

  _____

  _____

  _____

  red things

  _____

  _____

  _____

  _____

  furniture in your house

  _____

  _____

  _____

  _____

- good restaurants

  _____

  _____

  _____

  _____

  equipment for football

  _____

  _____

  _____

  _____

  worthwhile sports

  _____

  _____

  _____

  _____

- people I admire

  _____

  _____

  _____

  _____

  good pet names

  _____

  _____

  _____

  _____

  types of cars

  _____

  _____

  _____

  _____

Sentence Generation:
Ultimately, students must generate sentences containing every element they study. When they turn to sentence writing, you can engage them and develop their writing by providing parameters, including (a) minimum word count, (b) specific element required and/or located in particular position, and (c) specific content:

- Write a sentence with at least two nouns.   e.g., *Andrew* bought a dozen *eggs*.

- Write a sentence of at least ten words that contains at least three nouns.

    e.g., My *cousin* lives in *Chicago* near the *airport*, and we visit her each *Thanksgiving*.

- Write a sentence with a noun in the third position.

    e.g., The ugly *dog* barked ferociously at me whenever I came home from school.

- Write a sentence with a proper noun that is not a place.

    e.g., *Mark* saw his *Reeboks* behind the couch.

- Write a sentence of at least fifteen words with at least two nouns that are plural.

    e.g., The *trees* in the *woods* near my house are over one hundred *years* old, and we are worried that they may be chopped down to make way for new *stores* in the nearby mall.

- Write a sentence with at least three nouns about a favorite activity.

    e.g., *Taylor* and *Joseph* play *lacrosse* in *rain* or *shine* because they love the *sport*.

- Write a sentence with one proper and one common noun about Mark Twain.

    e.g., *Mark Twain*, who wrote *The Adventures of Huckleberry Finn*, is read in most *schools* around the *country*.

- Write a sentence with two proper nouns, one common noun, and at least twenty words about the Civil War.

    e.g., In the *war* between the *North* and the *South*, *brother* often fought *brother*, *governments* were created and destroyed, and a *country* was divided and then reunited.

Verbs

Overview:

Even the simplest of sentences requires a verb. The strongest verbs (action) show what the subject is doing. While nouns are more concrete, it is sometimes simpler to locate the verb in a sentence. Verbs either convey action (e.g., <u>run</u>) or state of being (e.g., <u>am</u>).

Latin Origin
verbum = word
derivatives:
verbal
verbose
reverberate

Typically, verbs in the infinitive (e.g., <u>to run</u>) are considered to be pure or base verbs. Every verb can be put into this form, and sometimes that fact is useful when identifying them.

Note that infinitives, which are verbals -- or verbs functioning as other parts of speech, never act as verbs in a sentence. In other words, any time in writing where to + a verb appears (e.g., to run, to eat), that construction is serving as a noun, adjective, or adverb, *not* a verb.

See pages 285-287 for useful lists of verbs.

Kinds & Categories:

Teachers need to understand the general ways verbs are organized to help students with proper usage but also to be able to address concerns and complications as they arise.

1. There are three major categories of verbs:

    action: shows the action of the subject (e.g., run, eat, sleep, consider)

    linking: links the subject to the rest of the sentence (e.g., was, am, is, are, feels)

    helping: helps a main action or linking verb (e.g., was, am, is, are, be, been)

2. Both action and linking verbs are also organized by tense, and the helping verbs help convey that tense. Tense means "time:" *Figure 11* contains an extensive verb tense chart for reference. Typically, a basic understanding of the fundamental concepts will

be sufficient for the student:

past: happened before the current moment (e.g., turned, was running)

present: happens or happening now (e.g., eats, is sleeping)

future: has not happened yet (e.g., will clean, will be packing)

The tenses (past, present, future) can further be organized into these groups:

basic: yelled, watches, will paint

progressive (continuous): was jumping, is studying, will be driving

perfect: will have eaten, has climbed, had rained

3. Though this is usually unnecessary lingo for students, verbs are sometimes identified as transitive (takes a direct object) and intransitive (does not take a direct object).

Common Core: The Common Core State Standards provide the following grade-level guidelines regarding verbs:

- Use frequently occurring verbs. (K)

- Use singular/plural nouns with matching verbs. (1)

- Use verbs to convey a sense of past/present/future. (1)

- Form and use the past tense of frequently occurring irregular verbs. (2)

- Form and use regular/irregular verbs. (2)

- Form and use the simple verb tenses. (3)

- Ensure subject-verb and pronoun-antecedent agreement. (3)

- Explain the function of verbs in general and their functions in particular sentences. (3)

- Form and use the progressive tense. (4)

- Use modal auxiliaries. (4)

- Form and use the perfect tenses. (5)

- Use verb tense to convey various times, sequences, states, and conditions. (5)

- Recognize and correct inappropriate shifts in verb tense. (5)

- Form and use verbs in the active and passive voice. (8)

- Form and use verbs in the indicative, imperative, interrogative, conditional, and subjunctive mood. (8)

Figure 11

Verb Conjugation:

Notice the helping verbs in front of the main verbs in these two examples. The first helping verb always carries the tense. The top example is the regular verb "to work." The bottom example is the irregular verb "to buy." The continuous tense is also called progressive.

The website http://conjugator.reverso.net/conjugation-english.html can be useful to check verb conjugations.

Person	Present Perfect	Present (Continuous)	Present Perfect (Continuous)	Past Perfect	Past (Continuous)	Past Perfect (Continuous)	Future	Future Perfect	Future (Continuous)	Future Perfect (Continuous)
I	have worked	am working	have been working	had worked	was working	had been working	will work	will have worked	will be working	will have been working
you	have worked	are working	have been working	had worked	were working	had been working	will work	will have worked	will be working	will have been working
he/she/it	has worked	is working	have been working	had worked	was working	had been working	will work	will have worked	will be working	will have been working
we	have worked	are working	have been working	had worked	were working	had been working	will work	will have worked	will be working	will have been working
you	have worked	are working	have been working	had worked	were working	had been working	will work	will have worked	will be working	will have been working
they	have worked	are working	have been working	had worked	were working	had been working	will work	will have worked	will be working	will have been working

Person	Present Perfect	Present (Continuous)	Present Perfect (Continuous)	Past Perfect	Past (Continuous)	Past Perfect (Continuous)	Future	Future Perfect	Future (Continuous)	Future Perfect (Continuous)
I	have bought	am buying	have been buying	had bought	was buying	had been buying	will buy	will have bought	will be buying	will have been buying
you	have bought	are buying	have been buying	had bought	was buying	had been buying	will buy	will have bought	will be buying	will have been buying
he/she/it	has bought	is buying	have been buying	had bought	was buying	had been buying	will buy	will have bought	will be buying	will have been buying
we	have bought	are buying	have been buying	had bought	was buying	had been buying	will buy	will have bought	will be buying	will have been buying
you	have bought	are buying	have been buying	had bought	was buying	had been buying	will buy	will have bought	will be buying	will have been buying
they	have bought	are buying	have been buying	had bought	was buying	had been buying	will buy	will have bought	will be buying	will have been buying

verb – action

action word

examples: run, jump, laugh, skate

verb

action word

jump, run, laugh

Jane ran in a race.

I drink milk with
my dinner.

Introduction:

- Put <u>noun</u> on the board and review its definition and an example or two.

- Define the term <u>verb</u>, putting it on the board. Include several examples.

- Hand students concept cards or have them create their own.

- List examples from their everyday lives. Use an action-packed picture for this activity if you like.

Initial Application:

- Have students generate their own examples of action verbs, listing activities they enjoy or connecting their verbs to nouns you provide, or both.

- Have students identify verbs from written sentences (if they are readers).

- If they have the ability, have students generate their own sentences and locate their own verbs. (Steer students away from linking verbs at this point. You can do this by asking them to generate a list of verbs first and then having them use those verbs in sentences.)

Suggested Exercises & Activities

Identification: Briefly have students identify verbs either in isolation or in context

at the word, phrase, sentence, and paragraph levels. Move as quickly as possible to those

activities that involve generating text, however. The simplest format looks like this:

- Underline the word that can function as a verb: from   jump   computer
- Underline the words that can function as verbs from the list below:

   sleep   of   computer   grumpy   ran   laugh

When they are ready, have students try several of these kinds of exercises:

- Underline the verb in the phrase: reads on grade level
- Underline the verb in the clause: while I swept the porch
- Underline the verbs in the sentence: We ordered our food and ate just in time.

Sorting: Sorting requires students to think at a higher level about verbs. The most

common way to sort verbs is by tense (time) though there are other ways that can be effective:

- Past/Present/Future:

run	will sleep	shot
burped	finish	will eat
drove	swim	will pass

past	present	future
_____	_____	_____
_____	_____	_____
_____	_____	_____

- Body Verbs / Mind Verbs:

| run | jump | consider | ate |
| enjoy | think | paint | decide |

body verbs   mind verbs

_____   _____

_____   _____

_____   _____

_____   _____

Matching:
Asking students to match verbs to other words requires that they explore the relationships verbs have with other words in particular contexts. Here, students can match each verb with an appropriate partner word:

- match concrete noun to action verb:

window	cleaned	farmer	darted
janitor	leads	fish	danced
general	broke	ballerina	planted

- match verb to adverb:

jumped	quietly	finished	thoroughly
sleeps	dangerously	examines	yesterday
climbed	carefully	eats	now

- match verb to prepositional phrase:

runs	with gusto and bravery	topples	harshly
yelled	in the quiet room	punishes	over
fights	across the finish line	stood	here

Fill In The Blanks: With this type of exercise, students are asked for the first time to generate language. Here, they are to put an appropriate verb in each blank:

- noun - verb:

    doctor _____   chair _____

    waiter _____   lightning _____

- verb - adverb:

    _____ fitfully   _____ harshly

    _____ kindly   _____ strategically

- verb - conjunction - verb

    _____ and _____

    _____ or _____

    _____ but _____

- sentences:

    Sue _____ and _____ this weekend.

    The farmer _____ the stalls in the barn.

    The doctor _____ last night, but the patient _____ anyway.

Conjugation: While asking students to conjugate verbs can appear somewhat archaic, where time permits, conjugating a verb a day or a verb a week has positive consequences that surpass mere proper form. Students will learn to understand tense (time) not just as form for consistency but also as a narrative device. Verbs from a science or social studies text or even a novel give teachers the opportunity to introduce new vocabulary or secondary meanings of known words. Further, if students are asked to generate sentences using their newly conjugated verbs, the activity has a direct writing application. Students who use non-standard verb forms in everyday speech outside of school will find verb conjugation particularly fruitful.

to jump - present

I	_____	we	_____
you	_____	you	_____
he/she/it	_____	they	_____

to turn -

	present	past
I	_____	_____
you	_____	_____
he/she/it	_____	_____
we	_____	_____
you	_____	_____
they	_____	_____

Adding & Changing Endings:
Endings often represent a word's part of speech. Adding or changing the ending of a word will usually shift its part of speech or, in the case of verbs, its tense.

- Using the appropriate spelling changes, add the suffix -ed to the following verbs to change them from present to past tense:

jump	_____	turn	_____
climb	_____	nap	_____

- Using the appropriate spelling changes, add the suffix -ing to the following verbs to move them into the progressive (continuous) tense:

eat	_____	run	_____
push	_____	drive	_____

- Add -s to these verbs to move them from 1st/2nd person to 3rd person. For example:

run: I run. She runs.

sleep	She _____	clean	She _____
kick	He _____	shine	It _____

- Add -ize to these nouns and adjectives to turn them into verbs meaning "to make:"

vandal _____   alphabet _____

visual _____   ideal _____

List Generation: List generation, a pre-cursor to paragraph and essay writing,

serves a purpose here as well. Students are asked to generate verbs that apply to other words.

Below, they must come up with several different choices for the same scenario.

- List verbs to go with specific locations:

airport	school	park	restaurant	space station
_____	_____	_____	_____	_____
_____	_____	_____	_____	_____
_____	_____	_____	_____	_____

- or activities:

getting ready for school	playing a soccer game	cooking a meal	playing a video game	travelling to a foreign land
_____	_____	_____	_____	_____
_____	_____	_____	_____	_____
_____	_____	_____	_____	_____

- or animals and people:

alligator _____   swimmer _____   soldier _____

_____   _____   _____

_____   _____   _____

Sentence Generation:

Ultimately, students must generate sentences containing every element they study. When they turn to sentence writing, you can engage them and develop their writing by providing parameters, including (a) minimum word count, (b) specific element required and/or located in particular position, and (c) specific content:

- Write a sentence with one verb in the past tense.   e.g., I *ran* down the street.

- Write a sentence that has at least ten words with one verb in the fifth position.

  e.g., My crazy aunt suddenly *announced* her candidacy for president to her stunned family.

- Write a sentence with a compound verb.

  e.g., The elephant *trampled* the tall grass and *sprayed* water all over her baby.

- Write a sentence with at least two verbs about your trip to the dentist.

  e.g., The dentist *examined* my teeth and *reported* to my mother that I *had* three cavities.

- Write a sentence with one good action verb about your favorite baseball player.

  e.g., Roy Halladay *pitched* an extraordinary game last night.

- Write a sentence about photosynthesis with a verb in the second position.

  e.g., Plants *convert* carbon dioxide into organic compounds using energy from sunlight.

verb - linking
(also called state of being)

links subject to the rest of the sentence
(can be replaced with an "=")

examples: am, is, are, was, were,
be, being, been, become, seem,
feel, appear, smell, taste

verb

action word	*advanced*
jump, run, laugh	*linking:* This <u>seems</u> obvious.
Jane ran in a race.	
I drink milk with my dinner.	examples: am, is, are, was, were, be, being, been, have been, has been, had been, will be

Introduction:

- Put <u>noun</u> and <u>verb</u> (action) on the board and review their definitions and an example or two of each.

- Define the new kind of verb (linking), writing it on the board. Include several examples. Make sure to clarify how linking verbs are different from action verbs.

- Hand students concept cards or have them create their own. (It may be best to add this new kind of verb to the existing verb concept card that was created when you taught action verbs. The sample card above includes both the original action verb information and the new information to be added for linking verbs.)

- Conjugate the verb "to be" on the board with student assistance. Begin with present tense. When the students are ready, expand to past and future. Have students copy the conjugations onto their cards or into their notebooks. (Eventually, ask students to generate the conjugations from memory.)

- Share with them the other common linking verbs. Explain to them how linking verbs can be replaced with an "=" sign or the word "is" or "are" and still retain meaning.

John is a pilot. (John = pilot.)

John feels tired. (John = tired. or John is tired.)

This tastes good. (This = good. or This is good.)

Initial Application:

- Have students identify linking verbs from written sentences.

- Advanced: Explore the verbs that can serve as both linking and action.

- Advanced: Conjugate other common linking verbs.

Notes:

- The most common linking verb by far is the verb "to be" in its various forms:

Person	Past	Present	Future	Past Perfect	Present Perfect	Future Perfect
I	was	am	will be	had been	have been	will have been
you	were	are	will be	had been	have been	will have been
he/she/it	was	is	will be	had been	have been	will have been
we	were	are	will be	had been	have been	will have been
you	were	are	will be	had been	have been	will have been
they	were	are	will be	had been	have been	will have been

Conditional tenses exist only in the present:

Person	Conditional Present	Conditional Present Perfect
I	could/would/should be	could/would/should have been
you	could/would/should be	could/would/should have been
he/she/it	could/would/should be	could/would/should have been
we	could/would/should be	could/would/should have been
you	could/would/should be	could/would/should have been
they	could/would/should be	could/would/should have been

- Besides the verb "to be," there are two other verbs that are always linking: "to become" and "to seem." Their forms are listed in *Figure 12*. The other linking verbs can also be action verbs, depending on context. Note these examples:

look   linking: It *looks* wonderful in here.

           action: *Look* at that robin!

taste   linking: This *tastes* awful.

           action: I *taste* chocolate in this recipe.

get   linking: It will *get* cold when the sun goes down.

           action: We should *get* her from soccer practice.

Common Linking Verbs Besides *to be*	
"to become"	other common linking verbs
become	
becomes	grow
became	look
has become	prove
have become	remain
had become	smell
will become	sound
will have	taste
become	turn
	stay
"to seem"	get
	appear
seemed	feel
seeming	
seems	
has seemed	
have seemed	
had seemed	
will seem	

Figure 12

Suggested Exercises & Activities

Identification: Identify verbs either in isolation or in context at the word, phrase, sentence, and paragraph levels. A few examples follow:

- Underline the words that can function as linking verbs from the list below:

  run   am   seems   friendly   felt   marks

- Underline the linking verb in the phrase: becomes loud around lunchtime

- Underline the linking verb in the clause: if Susan is unhappy with the job

- Underline the linking verb in the sentence: This tastes like burnt rubber!

- Write an "=" sign above each linking verb and then read the sentence aloud, replacing the verb with the word "is" or the word "are" as appropriate:

  It seems quite hot outside today.   Today, you become a man.

  It feels like spring in the park.   I hope the meeting stays friendly.

Matching: Match each noun with the linking verb (plus other words) it best matches:

- concrete noun - linking verb:

chicken	smells refreshing	stain	remains on the blouse
daisy	tastes delicious	problem	grows more significant
silk	feels	music	sounds awful

- linking verb - adjective (predicate adjective):

tastes	beautiful	grows	attractive
looks	delicious	smells	difficult
sounds	easy	appears	stinky

- linking verb - prepositional phrase:

appears	inside because of weather	was	in the store
stays	in another world	stay	here
seems	in three films	grows	in a cast

Sorting: Place the following linking verbs into appropriate categories:

- Past/Present/Future of *to be*:

was	will be	are	am
were	is		

past	present	future
_____	_____	_____
_____	_____	
	_____	

Conjugation: Conjugating linking verbs helps students recognize some of the most common verbs as well as their proper usage in various circumstances.

to be - present

I _____   we _____

you _____   you _____

he/she/it _____   they _____

to become - present   past

I _____   _____

you _____   _____

he/she/it _____   _____

we _____   _____

you _____   _____

they _____   _____

Sentence Generation:
Ultimately, students must generate sentences containing every element they study. When they turn to sentence writing, you can engage them and develop their writing by providing parameters, including (a) minimum word count, (b) specific element required and/or located in particular position, and (c) specific content:

- Write a sentence with one linking verb in past tense.

  e.g., I *felt* sick after I ate the seafood chowder.

- Write a sentence with a linking verb in the fifth position.

  e.g., The new chicken recipe *tasted* delicious after I spent a long day at work.

- Write a sentence with a compound linking verb.

  e.g., Our dinner *smelled* delicious but *tasted* horrible.

- Write a sentence about a parent and child with a linking verb in the future tense.

  e.g., You *will be* in your room when I get home.

- Write a sentence about Abraham Lincoln where a linking verb is in the second position.

  e.g., Lincoln *was* one of our greatest presidents.

82

verb - helping

helps the main verb

examples: am, is, are, was, were, be,
being, been, have, has, had

verb

action word	*advanced*
jump, run, laugh	*linking: link subject to rest of sentence* This <u>seems</u> obvious. *helping: help the main verb* Liz <u>is</u> sleeping.
Jane ran in a race.	
I drink milk with my dinner.	examples: am, is, are, was, were, be, being, been, have, has, had, have been, has been, had been, will be

Introduction:

- Put <u>noun</u> and <u>verb</u> (action, linking) on the board and review their definitions and an example or two of each.
- Define the new kind of verb (helping), writing it on the board. Include several examples.
- Hand students concept cards or have them create their own. (It may be best to add this new kind of verb to the existing verb concept card that was created when you taught action and linking verbs. The sample card above includes both the original action and linking verb information and the new information to be added for helping verbs.)
- Review the verb "to be" in past, present, and future tenses, explaining that it is not only the most common verb but also the most common *helping*

The 23 Helping Verbs

am	does
is	did
are	will
was	would
were	shall
be	should
being	can
been	could
have	may
has	might
had	must
do	

verb. For more advanced learners, explain that the verb "to be" + -<u>ing</u> verb forms the continuous or progressive tense (ongoing action) while the verb "to be" + -<u>ed</u> verb forms the perfect (ongoing but completed action).

Initial Application:

- Ask students to help conjugate a regular verb (e.g., *jump*) through all the tenses, paying particular attention to the helping verbs.
- Have students identify helping verbs from written sentences.
- Have students recognize that words that are *not* verbs can be inserted between parts of the verb. For example...

I have **not** studied for the test.   You should **really** be more careful.

I have **never** seen that movie before.   We are **still** going to dinner tonight.

Tenses for Reference:

am working	(present progressive = the work is happening now and is ongoing)
was working	(past progressive = the work is completed but happened over a limited period of time)
have worked	(present perfect = completed action extended from a point in the past to either the present or near present)
had worked	(past perfect = past action completed before another action in the past)
have been working	(present perfect progressive = past action continuing into the present)
had been working	(past perfect progressive = continuing past action completed before another action in the past)
will work	(future)
will have worked	(future perfect = future action completed before another future action)

Suggested Exercises & Activities

Identification: Identify helping verbs either in isolation or in context at the word,

phrase, sentence, and paragraph levels. A few examples follow:

- Underline the words that can function as helping verbs from the list below:

  is   am   inhale   black   felt   will be

- Underline the helping verbs in the phrase: is walking on the sidewalk next to me

- Underline the helping verbs in the clause: when the monster was eating his snack

- Underline the helping verbs in the sentence: I will be sitting here when you get out.

Sorting: Place the following helping verbs before the correct form of the verb "to walk"

in the appropriate column. (Eliminate from the exercise forms students have not covered.):

- Past/Present/Future:

had been	had	am	was
have been	were	is	are
will have been	will be	will	will have

past	present	future
_____walking	_____walking	_____walking
_____walking	_____walking	_____walking
_____walking	_____walking	_____walk
_____walked	_____walking	_____walked

Matching: Match each helping verb with the appropriate word:

- pronoun - helping and main verb:

she	am walking	it	were walking
we	is walking	I	was walking
I	are walking	you	was walking

Conjugation:

- progressive (continuing):

past progressive		present progressive	
I	_____ walking	_____ walking
you	_____ walking	_____ walking
he/she/it	_____ walking	_____ walking
we	_____ walking	_____ walking
you	_____ walking	_____ walking
they	_____ walking	_____ walking

Fill In The Blanks: For fill-in-the-blank exercises with helping verbs, it is most often useful to have the student select the proper choice from two or three. Put the appropriate helping verb in each blank:

- Eliza _____ (will be, would have been, has been) studying when we finally get home from the movies.

- The general and his men (are landing, will be landing, was landing) next Tuesday.

- Marcia (had been dancing, will be dancing, could be dancing) when the rain started.

Sentence Generation: Ultimately, students must generate sentences containing every element they study. When they turn to sentence writing, you can engage them and develop their writing by providing parameters, including (a) minimum word count, (b) specific element required and/or located in particular position, and (c) specific content:

- Write a sentence with one helping verb in past tense.

  e.g., The tortoise *was* crossing the street when the truck ran it over.

- Write a sentence with one helping verb in the third position in the future tense.

  e.g., The cabinets *will be* arriving on Tuesday.

- Write a sentence with one helping verb in the past progressive.

  e.g., The family *was* eating when Dad's cell phone began ringing.

- Write a sentence about a relative in the present progressive:

  e.g., We *are* spending Thanksgiving with my Aunt Harriett this year.

- Write a sentence about F. Scott Fitzgerald in the past progressive tense.

  e.g., F. Scott Fitzgerald *was* not still living when he became famous.

Adjectives

Overview:

Adjectives describe nouns (and pronouns). They make nouns more vivid and accurate.

Colors and numbers are some of the simplest adjectives.

Grammar books often use the term "modifies" instead of "describes." While "modifies" more precisely defines this category of words, it is a term that conveys little actual meaning to most students; therefore, "describes" is used throughout this text.

Latin Origin
jacere = to throw
ad = to, toward
derivatives:
project
reject
interjection
(think of the adjective throwing meaning to its noun)

After students have grown comfortable with adjective role and function, they can attend to word placement. Even the youngest students and those with the most basic skills can probably tell a teacher that adjectives come right before the nouns they describe. This makes them easy to locate and identify on worksheets and easy to add to barebones sentences:

> The <u>scary</u> man had a <u>hairy</u> wart on his nose.
>
> I stained the <u>hardwood</u> floors with a <u>walnut</u> stain.

The more advanced student is ready to investigate less traditional and more sophisticated adjective placement. Study these sentences carefully:

> The <u>broken, hobbled, weary, old</u> man shuffled aimlessly down the street.
>
> <u>Broken</u> and <u>weary</u>, the <u>hobbled old</u> man shuffled aimlessly down the street.
>
> The <u>hobbled old</u> man, <u>broken</u> and <u>weary</u>, shuffled aimlessly down the street.

Though these three sentences impart identical meanings, the first is cumbersome and simplistic in structure, relying on a standard series of adjectives preceding the noun. The second and third sentences, however, show sophistication and individual style. Thanks to adjective placement and the addition of the conjunction <u>and</u>, the adjectives sound intentional. These two sentences "work" in the best sense of the word.

Commas between adjectives: When two or more adjectives come before the noun or pronoun they describe, use commas to separate them only if they will still make sense if their order is switched (coordinate adjectives). "John ate the juicy, delicious burger in three bites." works as well as "John ate the delicious, juicy burger in three bites." Therefore, the adjectives need a comma between them. Inserting <u>and</u> between adjectives in a series is also an effective test; if <u>and</u> works, then the series should contain commas: "John ate the delicious and juicy burger in three bites." sounds fine. Therefore, the series needs commas. If a series of adjectives does *not* pass this test, do not use commas. "His impressive red sports car was kept in the garage." cannot be "His sports red impressive..." or "Sports red his impressive" or "His red impressive sports..." The order cannot be changed; hence, the list does not take commas.

See pages 290-291 for useful lists of adjectives. http://simple.wiktionary.org/wiki/Category:Adjectives has an extensive list of over 2000 adjectives for vocabulary development and expansion.

Kinds & Categories:

Adjectives are conceptually straightforward, though some of the sub-classifications bear further consideration. Recognize that the term <u>adjective</u> refers to an entire family of words used to describe nouns and pronouns. Students first learn it as a term that applies to single words; eventually, they will understand that it applies to a broader classification of words:

1. adjective - single word describing noun/pronoun:

    The <u>rocky</u> path made walking dangerous.

2. adjective phrase - phrase describing noun/pronoun:

    The woman <u>at the counter</u> bagged my purchases.

3. adjective clause - clause describing noun/pronoun:

    The doctor, <u>who always wore a white lab coat at the office</u>, took lunch at noon.

Participles and infinitives, both of which are covered in the Sentence Parts section of this text, have adjective functions. Even students with more basic skills will use these structures in their writing:

1. participle: one of three verbals (verbs used as other parts of speech)

    participial verb (often ending in -ing or -ed) used as an adjective:

    His <u>busted</u> lip bled profusely.

    The <u>sleeping</u> baby woke during the storm.

2. infinitive: one of three verbals (verbs used as other parts of speech)

    to + verb used as an adjective (also adverb or noun)

    almost always located directly after the noun it describes

    The boy <u>to beat</u> just passed Kris on the track. (describes boy)

    You have a difficult decision <u>to make</u>. (describes decision)

The predicate adjective, explained in the Sentence Parts section of this text, refers to an adjective positioned after the subject it describes and a linking verb. Students at the basic level may have a difficult time identifying these words as adjectives because of their location. If this is the case, reword the sentence to show struggling students that the word does, indeed, describe a noun -- most often the subject:

    She is <u>hungry</u>.

    Andrew felt <u>anxious</u> about his upcoming exam.

    My grandmother was <u>red</u> with embarrassment.

    He is <u>ugly</u>.

I stumbled because it was <u>dark</u> on the basement staircase.

After her hospital visit, she seemed much <u>better</u>.

Grandmother's dinner tasted <u>delicious</u>.

There are three forms of adjectives. Typically, one-syllable adjectives use -er to form the comparative and -est to form the superlative. Two-syllable adjectives ending in -y, -er, -le, or -ow will also use -er and -est:

1. *positive*	2. *comparative*	3. *superlative*
nice	nicer	nicest
dark	darker	darkest
thin	thinner	thinnest
happy	happier	happiest
narrow	narrower	narrowest

In most multisyllabic words, <u>more</u> usually replaces -er and <u>most</u> usually replaces -est:

1. *positive*	2. *comparative*	3. *superlative*
attractive	more attractive	most attractive
thoughtful	more thoughtful	most thoughtful

A few common adjectives use irregular comparative and superlative structures:

1. *positive*	2. *comparative*	3. *superlative*
good	better	best
bad	worse	worst
far	farther	farthest
little	less	least
many / much / some	more	most

Note: Standardized testing often includes questions that ask students to choose between the comparative and superlative forms of an adjective. Remember that the comparative is used for two:

> correct: He took the <u>larger</u> of the two pieces of cake.
>
> incorrect: My grandfather was the <u>friendliest</u> of the two.

The superlative can only be used for three or more:

> correct: He was the <u>eldest</u> of the three brothers.
>
> incorrect: Of the eight goldfish, Marcie is the <u>larger</u>.

Model Dialogue – Generating Adjectives:

Students often have difficulty generating good adjectives. Examine this model eliciting dialogue:

Teacher: Picture your ideal car in your head.

Drew: Okay, I've got it.

Teacher: What color is it?

Drew: <u>Blue</u>.

Teacher: Which blue? Is it light blue or navy or?

Drew: It's <u>metallic blue</u>.

Teacher: That's good, Drew. [Teacher heads a list entitled "Drew's Dream Car" and puts <u>metallic blue</u> directly under it.] Is it an older car or a new car or...

Drew: It's not old.

Teacher: If it were, what word could we use to describe it?

Drew: <u>Broken</u>?

Teacher: Yes, but what if it were old and valuable?

Drew: <u>Antique</u>.

Teacher: Good. Or vintage. Now, you said it's new. What's a word for new that works with cars?

Drew: <u>Modern</u>.

Teacher: [Adds <u>modern</u> underneath metallic blue.] Good. That describes **time**. Do you have a brand in mind?

Drew: Yep, it's a <u>Ferrari</u>.

Teacher: Nice. Do you know what country Ferraris come from? We could use that as another adjective.

Drew: They're from Italy.

Teacher: That's right. What is the adjective form of Italy?

Drew: Not sure.

Teacher: Well, what do we call people who are from Italy?

Drew: Oh, Italians.

Teacher: Good, so this car is <u>Italian</u>. That is its **origin**. [Adds it to the list.] What condition is it in? Has it been in any accidents? Is it dirty or scratched?

Drew: No, it's <u>mint</u>.

Teacher: Another great adjective. That one tells its **condition**. [Adds it to the list.] What shape is it?

Drew: Well, it's shaped like a car.

Teacher: Yes. [Smiles.] Is it like a mini-van? Or an S.U.V.? Maybe a station wagon.

Drew: [Rolling his eyes.] Noooooo, it's more -- sleek. And it's a sports car.

Teacher: Good, two more adjectives. <u>Sleek</u> tells its shape. (Adds it to the list.) It's kind of a **size** adjective. [A more advanced lesson might identify sports as a qualifier, but size is a good way to think about it for this lesson.] It really tells us what group it fits into. <u>Sports</u> puts your car into a category that includes other cars. When you run your hand along it, how does your car feel?

Drew: It's <u>smooth</u>.

Teacher: Good, I'm adding that as a **feel** adjective. [Adds it to the list.] How does the engine run?

Drew: It's <u>powerful</u>.

Teacher: Perfect. Does it make any sound?

Drew: Yep, it's <u>roaring</u>.

Teacher: Good. How do you feel about it?

Drew: It's <u>incredible</u>.

Teacher: Good. <u>*Incredible*</u> and <u>*powerful*</u> are both **opinions** about the car. <u>*Roaring*</u> is its **sound**. *[Adds all three to the list.]*

In just a few short minutes in this dialogue, the teacher elicits eight adjectives about the student's ideal car as well as a few additional adjectives. He also introduces several general categories: color, time, origin, condition, shape, size, feel/touch, observation, and sound. Here again are those categories with additional examples included:

color: silver, black, transparent, white, cherry-red, sky-blue, orange

time: late, early, brief, drawn out, short, vintage, antique, speedy

origin: European, Kentuckian, Jewish, Christian, Buddhist, Navaho

condition: alive, exhausted, stubborn, mushy, dry, dead, wrong, inferior, superior

shape: angular, square, circular, wide, narrow, oblong, broad, flat, deep

size: enormous, colossal, miniature, teeny, scrawny, mammoth, microscopic

feel/touch: grimy, dusty, dirty, rough, unbroken, glass-like, bristly, sensitive

Determiner	Observation	Size	Shape	Age	Color	Origin	Material	Qualifier	Noun
a	stunning	grand	squat	immortal	turquoise	Egyptian	wooden	diving	pool
an	breathtaking	tiny	oblong	ancient	apple-red	English	gold	umbrella	stand
the	hideous	miniscule	circular	retired	opaque	American	rayon	football	jersey
many	broken down	expansive	box-like	mortal	beige	Jewish	concrete	care	package
eight	scrumptious	enormous	lumpy	antique	coal-black	South American	cotton	hair	products
this	valuable	wide	billowy	young	magenta	Ethiopian	leather	marker	box
my	humorous	heavy	cylindrical	modern	transparent	Martian	copper	card	game
our	peaceful	big	dwarf-like	new	wheat-colored	French	plastic	library	book
a few	uninteresting	narrow	flat	middle-aged	brown	Spanish	nylon	grandmother's	recipe

Figure 13

observation:	incredible, awe-inspiring, curious, undervalued, mediocre
taste/touch:	lemony, delicious, bland, sour, yummy, fresh, burnt, sticky, gooey
quantity:	more, plenty, few, enough, abundant, scattered, full

Sometimes, it is helpful to think of categories of **feelings**, particularly when it comes to describing a person, whether it be someone the student knows, an historical figure, or a fictional character. Feelings can be sorted into "good" and "bad." Some examples are below:

bad feelings:	distraught, drained, thoughtless, mean, grumpy, nervous, defeated
good feelings:	faithful, gentle, proud, brave, peaceful, excited, happy, victorious

A good rule of thumb is that no noun should have more than three adjectives in a series describing it. There is an order of placement that native English speakers not only expect but naturally apply when they use adjectives. This order is best described using the Royal Order of Adjectives, a version of which is in *Figure 13* (preceding page). Students who are ready for a more sophisticated categorizing system than the one I outlined using the model dialogue about the car may find these categories useful. No attempt has been made on the chart provided to have the words read "correctly" across except in the case of the qualifier and noun (as qualifiers taken out of context often do not make sense). Use the categories as a means of stimulating students to generate adjectives. Combine words from up to three categories (excluding the noun) to create vivid images. Always work from left to right. Here are some examples:

determiner	*observation*	*size*	*noun*
the	stunning	grand	piano
an	avoidable	big	mistake

determiner	size	shape	age	noun
my	huge	box-like	old	car
the	tiny	round	antique	footstool

determiner	shape	origin	qualifier	noun
an	oblong	Egyptian	burial	chamber
several	hulking	American	basketball	players

determiner	size	color	material	noun
seven	enormous	blue	silk	tapestries
many	squat	Spanish	end	tables

Students can use these groupings creatively as well. Here are several mythical creatures, for example:

determiner	size	color	qualifier	noun
two hundred	gigantic	blue	burping	bandarks
a	miniscule	violet	shoe	eater

Most students can come up with eight to ten basic colors, but to energize writing, students should expand their color choices. Often, they enjoy choosing colors from a large Crayon box. If Crayons are not readily available, Wikipedia has the Crayola colors -- both names and samples (en.wikipedia.org/wiki/List_of_Crayola_crayon_colors).

Another rewarding activity involves building color adjectives from nouns. Choose a color, and ask students to list three things that frequently come in that color. Under red, for example, students might list fire engine, apple, and blood. Any of these can be placed, with a hyphen, before the word <u>red</u> to make a more vivid adjective. Students now can use <u>fire-engine-red</u>, <u>apple-red</u>, and <u>blood-red</u>. If a student put <u>emerald</u> under green, she can now describe her best friend's eyes as <u>emerald-green</u>. Your car might be eggplant-purple, a room's new paint job ocean-blue, or a villain's cloak obsidian-black.

Common Core: The Common Core State Standards provide the following grade-level guidelines regarding adjectives:

- Use frequently occurring adjectives. (1)

- Use adjectives and adverbs and choose between them depending on what is modified. (2)

- Form and use comparative and superlative adjectives and adverbs, and choose between them depending on what is to be modified. (3)

- Order adjectives within sentences according to conventional patterns. (4)

- Use a comma to separate coordinate adjectives. (7)

- Explain the function of adjectives in general and their functions in particular sentences. (3)

Initial Lesson

adjectives

describes noun (or pronoun)

examples: three, ugly, blue, tall

---

adjectives

describes noun (or pronoun)

green, angry, wooden

three chairs   rough ground   blue sky

adjectives include colors and numbers

articles (a category of adjectives) limit or clarify nouns: a, an, the

---

Introduction:

- Put <u>noun</u> and <u>verb</u> (action, linking, helping) on the board and review their definitions and an example or two of each.

- Define the new term, <u>adjective</u>, putting it underneath the term <u>noun</u> to show their relationship. Include several examples.

- Hand students concept cards or have them create their own.

noun   verb

adjective

Initial Application:

- Have students name nouns in the classroom and then generate adjectives to describe those nouns. Have students do the same things with nouns that are not in their classroom.

- Provide a photograph, painting, or interesting object and ask students to come up with adjectives to describe its various elements.

- Help students discover that numbers and colors are generally adjectives.

- Have students identify adjectives from written sentences (if they are readers).

- Provide students with barebones sentences that require them to add adjectives (if they are readers).

Subsequent Lessons

- Basic: Though some grammar texts introduce articles as an entirely separate part of speech, a, an, and the should be studied with adjectives since they precede nouns and serve to clarify them. At the bottom of the adjective concept card, add the following:

article: a special category of adjective - a, an, the

Described this way, the article becomes merely one kind of adjective rather than an entirely separate part of speech to study and understand. Most native English speakers inherently know when and where to use articles. Books that specifically address non-native speakers teach rules for article usage. At any rate, a, an, and the typically precede any other adjectives that come before a noun. Look at these examples:

an elderly gentleman	an unusual story
the weathered front porch	the last thing I need to hear
a difficult problem to solve	a bright and beautiful day

While students need to know what to call a, an, and the when they are examining sentences and determining part of speech, a quick introduction and a short exercise aimed at finding and labelling them will usually suffice. Some struggling writers may need to learn that an is used before a vowel sound while a precedes consonant sounds. Conduct this practice on a need-to basis so that students iron out confusions early.

- Advanced: The words my, your, his, her, its, our, and their can be used to describe the nouns they precede. Though they might at first glance be called possessive pronouns, remember that this study focuses on function or job. By function, these words are adjectives (or possessive adjectives). For example...

I love *my* job.   The doctor told *her* patient about *his* cold.

My family goes to *our* grandparents' house for Thanksgiving.

Because of their function, these words should be identified by students as possessive adjectives. That said, errors concerning antecedent (a word replaced by a pronoun later) are covered in the Pronouns section. Some of these errors concern possessive adjectives.

Identification:
Identify adjectives either in isolation or in context at the word, phrase, sentence, and paragraph levels. A few examples follow:

- Underline the words that can function as adjectives from the list below:

  green   under   witty   friend   angry   eight

- Underline the adjectives in the phrase and draw an arrow to the noun they describe:

  under the rocky, old table

- Underline the adjectives in the clause and draw an arrow to the noun they describe:

  when the tall man stooped to walk under the low door

- Underline the adjectives in the sentence and draw arrows to the nouns they describe:

  The sweet lemonade quenched my thirst on the dry, hot day.

Sorting:
Place the following adjectives into appropriate categories:

- positive/comparative/superlative:

ugly	thirstier	coldest
serious	more considerate	brightest
lowest	evil	hungrier

positive	comparative	superlative
_____	_____	_____
_____	_____	_____
_____	_____	_____

- see/hear/taste-smell/touch

rough	stinky	sweet	slippery
bright	beautiful	loud	deafening
bitter	blue	squishy	whistling

see	hear	taste/smell	touch
_____	_____	_____	_____
_____	_____	_____	_____
_____	_____	_____	_____

Matching: Match each adjective with the appropriate word:

- match adjective to common noun:

new	monster	difficult	beverage
scary	car	rushing	problem
cold	ice cream	cold	river

- match linking verb to adjective (predicate adjective):

tastes	dark	grows	huge
looks	bitter	smells	impossible
sounds	loud	appears	delicious

Fill In The Blanks: Put an appropriate *word* in each blank:

- **adjective   noun**

  red _____

  _____

  _____

  adjective   noun

  _____ car

  _____

  _____

- **color adjective   noun**

  blue _____

  pale _____

  fire-engine-red _____

  sea-blue _____

  beige _____

  color adjective   noun

  _____ sky

  _____ T-shirt

  _____ ocean

  _____ eggplant

  _____ money

size adjective	noun
humongous	_____
deep	_____
miniature	_____
wide	_____
skinny	_____

size adjective	noun
_____	street
_____	S.U.V.
_____	elephant
_____	mouse
_____	football player

sense adjective	noun
attractive	_____
smelly	_____
delicious	_____
cold	_____
piercing	_____

sense adjective	noun
_____	trunk
_____	telephone
_____	pizza
_____	locker room
_____	water

note: Charts like these can be created for a single sense as well.

feeling adjective	event noun
miserable	_____
joyful	_____
excited	_____
curious	_____
exhausted	_____

feeling adjective	event noun
_____	funeral
_____	party
_____	roller coaster
_____	argument
_____	graduation

quantity adjective	noun
several	_____
a few	_____
twelve	_____
seven	_____
all	_____

quantity (article) adjective	noun
_____	eggs
_____	socks
_____	friends
_____	geese
_____	lions

- **shape adjective   noun**   **shape adjective   noun**

  oblong _____   _____ hat

  oval _____   _____ room

  cylindrical _____   _____ edge

  box-like _____

- **sentences:**

  The _____ mountain stood before the _____ travellers.

  My _____ grandmother always laughed while she was cooking us _____ _____ meals.

  Christopher has a _____ headache and may not be able to finish his _____ homework.

Adding & Changing Endings: Endings often represent a word's part of speech. Adding or changing the ending of a word can shift its part of speech.

- Using the appropriate spelling changes, add -y to these verbs and nouns to create adjectives:

  mess _____   sleep _____

  run _____   gum _____

- Add -ward to these basewords to form adjectives. (They can also be adverbs.):

  back _____   after _____

  to _____   north _____

- Add -ful to these nouns to form adjectives:

  harm _____   use _____

  pain _____   hope _____

- Add -less to these words to form adjectives:

  name _____   use _____

  pain _____   worth _____

- Add -ish to these basewords to form adjectives. Drop the silent-e as needed:

  small   _____   style   _____

  baby   _____   impish   _____

- Add -ive to these basewords to form adjectives. Drop the silent-e as needed:

  offense   _____   recluse   _____

  secret   _____   innovate   _____

- Add -ous to these nouns to form adjectives:

  hazard   _____   joy   _____

  rigor   _____   danger   _____

- Add -al to these nouns to form adjectives:

  critic   _____   magic   _____

  ethic   _____   politic   _____

- Add -ial to these nouns to form adjectives. Drop the silent-e as needed. All of your new adjectives will end in -cial or -tial:

  part   _____   office   _____

  race   _____   president   _____

- In the first column, add -er to the base adjective to form a comparative form. In the second column, add -est to the base adjective to form the superlative form. Make changes to the base word endings where appropriate. All three forms are adjectives:

adjective	comparative adjective (+er)	superlative adjective (+est)
large	_____	_____
great	_____	_____
loud	_____	_____
noisy	_____	_____

104

List Generation: Generating lists of adjectives helps students move beyond tired, overused words in their writing.

- List some examples of adjectives that fall under certain categories:

size	shape	good feelings	bad feelings	time
_____	_____	_____	_____	_____
_____	_____	_____	_____	_____
_____	_____	_____	_____	_____

taste	feel (touch)	sound	quantity	color
_____	_____	_____	_____	_____
_____	_____	_____	_____	_____
_____	_____	_____	_____	_____

- List nouns that are **usually** these colors:

black	blue	green	red	yellow
_____	_____	_____	_____	_____
_____	_____	_____	_____	_____
_____	_____	_____	_____	_____

Any of these nouns can now be attached to their adjectives to create more vivid adjectives: obsidian-black, sea-blue, emerald-green, brick-red, and sunset-yellow are just a few examples.

Sentence Combining: Students can be asked to consolidate the noun elements in two or more sentences to create a single, more sophisticated sentence:

- single adjectives

Jonah found the jacket. The jacket was leather.

answer: Jonah found a leather jacket.

The girl had juice. The juice was fresh-squeezed.

answer: The girl had fresh-squeezed juice.

We bought a house. The house was brick.

answer: We bought a brick house.

- two or more adjectives

The girl and the boy went to the mall. The girl was short. The boy was tall. The mall was huge.

answer: The short girl and the tall boy went to the huge mall.

Sentence Generation: Ultimately, students must generate sentences containing

every element they study. When they turn to sentence writing, you can engage them and develop their writing by providing parameters, including (a) minimum word count, (b) specific element required and/or located in particular position, and (c) specific content:

- Write a sentence of at least ten words with at least two adjectives.

  e.g., The *ugly* car pulled up to the curb in the *heavy* rain.

- Write a sentence of at least fifteen words with a color adjective in it.

  e.g., While I was studying the constellations in the sky outside my house, a *blue* motorcycle roared past and broke the peacefulness of the evening.

- Write a sentence of at least ten words containing one adjective about the football game.

  e.g., *Our strong* opponents dominated the game in the *first* half, but we were able to come back to win after halftime.

- Write a sentence using the adjective "delicious" about a favorite food you ate recently.

  e.g., My aunt's lemon pie is *delicious*, and she serves it each Sunday when we join her for lunch.

- Use the adjective "brave" in a sentence about Karana (the protagonist of Scott O'Dell's *Island of the Blue Dolphins*).

  Karana, the protagonist in Scott O'Dell's *The Island of the Blue Dolphins*, is particularly *brave* when she finds herself stranded on the island alone.

- Write a sentence about Martin Luther King that uses two adjectives with a proper noun.

  Martin Luther King, a *peaceful* and *wise* man, did a great deal for the Civil Rights Movement.

Pronouns

Overview:

Pronouns replace nouns. A pronoun stands *for* the *naming* part of the sentence. There are only a few pronouns to represent all the nouns. This is why <u>he</u> can stand for Chuck or father, and <u>it</u> can stand for table, window, Alabama, or rocket ship. Pronouns keep our writing from sounding monotonous and repetitive. As a general rule, native English speakers are relatively comfortable with pronoun use.

Latin Origin
nomen = name
pro = for
derivatives:
proverb
projectile
promise

One struggle they sometimes have is with agreement and clear antecedent references. An antecedent is a word that is replaced later on in a piece of writing. Consider this sentence: John is a great guy, but he needs to be more punctual. <u>John</u> is the antecedent of <u>he</u>.

See page 292 for lists of useful pronouns.

Confusions Addressed:

1. Most of the pronoun categories are defined with examples in Kinds & Categories, but *possessive pronouns* and *possessive adjectives* warrant special attention. Consider these sentences:

   The book is <u>mine</u>.   The problem is <u>hers</u>.   The present is <u>yours</u>.

Possessive pronouns used like this, including <u>mine</u>, <u>yours</u>, <u>his</u>, <u>hers</u>, <u>ours</u>, and <u>theirs</u>, are sometimes called *absolute* possessives, and there is no debate as to their identity or function.

That said, sometimes possessives describe nouns. Consider these sentences:

   <u>Your</u> friend arrived today.   I have a pain in <u>my</u> toe.   <u>Her</u> shoe fell off in the mud.

These *might* be seen as possessive pronouns, and like pronouns, they replace nouns, but by function, since they describe the nouns they precede, they are possessive adjectives. In this manual, they are covered as possessive adjectives in a Subsequent Lesson in the Adjectives section. That said, both pronoun and possessive adjective confusions are addressed here as these usage difficulties are intertwined.

2. Some pronouns are easily confused with similar looking contractions:

   a. it's is always a contraction:

it's = it is	its = possessive
It's time to go. I think it's fine.	Its tires need changing.

   b. who's is always a contraction:

who's = who is	whose = possessive
Who's that? I don't know who's here.	Whose shirt is that anyway?

3. Most *indefinite pronouns*, including the following, are singular:

anybody, anyone, anything	everybody, everyone, everything
no one, nobody, nothing	somebody, someone, something
whoever, whichever, whatever	each, neither, either

Standardized test writers love questions concerning indefinite pronouns. Consider these sentences. On the left the subject and verb are both in the singular. On the right, the antecedent is in the singular while the verb is in the plural:

correct	*incorrect*
Anybody <u>is</u> welcome!	*Anybody* <u>are</u> welcome!
We know that *everybody* <u>is</u> in trouble.	We know that *everybody* <u>are</u> in trouble.
Nobody in these houses <u>is</u> home.	*Nobody* in these houses <u>are</u> home.
Each of you <u>is</u> a friend of mine.	*Each* of you <u>are</u> friends of mine.

Indefinite pronouns can serve as antecedents for possessive adjectives as well:

correct   *incorrect*

Everybody should drink <u>his</u> or <u>her</u> juice.   *Everybody* should drink <u>their</u> juice.

Nobody should look at <u>her</u> test yet.   *Nobody* should look at <u>their</u> test yet.

4. <u>Eli and me or Eli and I, who/whom, and other confusions</u>:

a. To a true grammar nut, there is nothing more painful to witness than a public speaker, attempting to be precise and proper, who says, "my friend and I" when he means "my friend and me." When we compound a noun, we do not want to change its form. The rules are straightforward, but many confuse or over-generalize their application. To replace a noun as subject, use a pronoun in the *subject* form.

Jane and <u>I</u> are going to the movies tonight.   Carol and <u>I</u> should get home now.

To replace a noun as object, use a pronoun in the *object* form.

The storm blew debris at Jane and <u>me</u>.   Mom grounded Carlos and <u>me</u>.

An easy trick that can help is to delete the noun and the word <u>and</u> from a pair and read the sentence with just the pronoun. Consider the following sentence:

The coach sent Mac and I/me to get water.

Eliminate the noun and conjunction before the questionable pronoun:

The coach sent *I* to get water. *or* The coach sent *me* to get water.

Without the words "Mac and," *me* becomes the obvious answer, and therefore the original sentence should read as follows: The coach sent Mac and *me* to get water.

b. Who/whom: In some circles <u>whom</u> is seen as somewhat archaic, but unless it becomes extinct, this is how things work. <u>Who</u> is the subject form; <u>whom</u> is the object form.

who: *Who* is that? (subject - interrogative)

        Who will take the next problem? (subject - interrogative)

        Jason, who is a smart guy, aced the recent test. (subject - relative)

whom: I don't know *whom* we should get. (direct object)

        The senators, four of whom gathered for dinner, discussed the upcoming vote. (object of preposition)

Kinds & Categories:

Pronouns are grouped by number, person, and case.

number	singular/plural
case	subject/object
person	1st (I, me, we, us)
	2nd (you)
	3rd (he, him, she, her, it, they, them)

Students who study a foreign language, such as Spanish or French, will often have a good understanding of person in that language. Making the transition to English becomes easier if this is the case. Also, discussing person for pronoun usage is often a good way to introduce person in narrative. First person narrative is using "I" to tell the story; in other words, the narrator is *in* the story. Third person narrative uses "he" and "she;" the narrator views the story from the outside.

The most commonly used pronouns are <u>personal</u> and fall into three categories:

as subject	*as object*	*possessive* (absolute possessive) (stands alone without noun)
I	me	mine
you	you	yours
he/she/it	him/her/it	his/hers

we	us	ours
you	you	yours
they	them	theirs

Other common categories of pronouns include the following, useful for the teacher to understand:

demonstrative:	points to nouns
	this, that, these, those e.g., *This* is the book I wanted.
interrogative:	used in questions
	who, which, what e.g., *Who* are you?
reflexive:	ends in -<u>self</u> or -<u>selves</u> and refers to another noun/pronoun in sentence
	myself, yourself, himself, themselves, ourselves
	e.g., I have to find the way *myself*. We should get *ourselves* indoors.
intensive:	identical in form to reflexive; immediately follows subject; can be omitted without loss of meaning
	myself, yourself, himself, themselves, ourselves
	e.g., I *myself* consider this to be a concern.
	The singer *himself* wrote those lyrics.
relative:	relates groups of words to nouns (or pronouns)
	who (including whom and whose), which, that, where
	e.g., The teacher, *who* seemed to be in a bad mood, marked papers quickly at her desk.
indefinite:	functions as noun; refers to something unspecified
	everybody, anybody, some, several, anyone, many
	e.g., *Everybody* needs to sit down now. *Many* died in the Civil War.

Common Core: The Common Core State Standards provide the following grade-level guidelines regarding pronouns:

- Use the pronoun I. (K)

- Use personal, possessive, and indefinite pronouns. (1)

- Use reflexive pronouns. (2)

- Use relative pronouns (and relative adverbs). (4)

- Ensure that pronouns are in the proper case. (6)

- Use intensive pronouns. (6)

- Recognize and correct inappropriate shifts in pronoun number and person. (6)

- Recognize and correct vague pronouns. (6)

- Explain the function of pronouns in general and their functions in particular sentences. (3)

pronoun

replaces a noun

examples: I, you, he, she, it, we, they
me, him, her, us, them

pronoun

stands for a noun

I, you, he, she, it, we, they, me, him, her, us, them, mine, yours, hers, its, ours, theirs (personal pronouns)

advanced:
demonstrative - points to nouns:
    this, that, these, those
relative - relates groups of words to nouns (or pronouns): who, which, that
indefinite - functions as noun; refers to something unspecified:
    everybody, anybody, somebody

Introduction:

- Put <u>noun</u>, <u>verb</u>, and <u>adjective</u> on the board and review their definitions and an example or two of each.

- Define the new term, <u>pronoun</u>, putting it with the terms <u>noun</u> and <u>adjective</u> to show their relationship. (See diagram.) Include several examples.

- Hand students concept cards or have them create their own.

- Explain that <u>pro</u> means *for*. If you are pro-Yankees (or whatever an important local sports team is), you are *for* the Yankees.

- Read aloud a paragraph from a source, but use nouns in place of all pronouns. Here is an example:

Andrew got home from school late today. Andrew rushed to change for the soccer game. Andrew's mom called to Andrew, and Andrew rushed down the stairs and jumped in the car. Andrew rode to the game nervous that Andrew would be late. Andrew arrived just in time and ended up scoring the winning goal in Andrew's game.

Ask students what is wrong with the paragraph above, and they will most likely point out that the word <u>Andrew</u> appears far too often. Use this as a springboard to discuss the reason pronouns are so essential to writing.

- Draw the family tree of a well known figure, either fictional or non-fictional, or use your own family tree if you like. (The Simpsons and the current president are just two examples.) Have class members describe the relationships between people in the family, using pronouns. For example, [pointing to Homer and then his sister on the family tree] "how would Homer describe his sister? (Answer - "she" or "her.") "How would Marge describe everybody in the family, *including* herself? (Answer - "we" or "us.")

Initial Application:

- Have students name nouns in the classroom and then generate pronouns to replace those nouns.
- Have students identify pronouns from written sentences (if they are readers).
- Provide students with sentences that require them to write follow-up sentences containing pronouns. For example, write, "The man went to the store." (Appropriate follow-up sentence might be "He got some milk.")

Subsequent Lessons

- Basic: Spend significant time on *subject/object pronouns* because they are the most common and also sometimes confused. Provide plenty of activities so that students learn to recognize them and also grow comfortable using them.

  Struggling writers often overuse and repeat nouns, perhaps because they take such time and effort to craft each individual sentence that they lose track of the flow from sentence to sentence.

  Likewise, novice writers often begin short answer responses, isolated sentences, and paragraphs with pronouns, leaving the reader to guess (or read a prompt or question to discern) to whom the pronoun refers.

- Advanced: Kinds & Categories lists the various *other kinds of pronouns*. An entire semester of teaching time could be spent covering and mastering them -- to little benefit. Certainly, for students who have already learned the basics, a little practice is advisable, but do not overdo the teaching time devoted to this study, and make sure it is focused on student application. A little work with identifying is useful, but then move your students to generating examples in their own sentences. Unless required by curriculum or assessment tool to identify by name, do not add these different kinds to the pronoun concept card.

Suggested Exercises & Activities

Identification: Identify pronouns either in isolation or in context at the word, phrase, sentence, and paragraph levels. A few examples follow:

•   Underline the words that can function as pronouns from the list below:

I   tree   mushroom   they   we   under

•   Underline the pronouns in the phrase: with Jake and me

•   Underline the pronouns in the clause: while I was sitting next to her on the seat

•   Underline the pronouns in the sentence:

Mark and I saw a mouse in the dining room, and it was moving fast along the baseboard.

Sorting: Place the following pronouns into appropriate categories:

•   subject / object / possessive

mine	him	theirs
he	yours	they
them	I	us

as subject	as object	possessive
_____	_____	_____
_____	_____	_____
_____	_____	_____

Matching: Match each pronoun with the word it would replace:

•   common noun - pronoun:

tree	she	sidewalk	they
grandmother	he	queen	it
uncle	it	girl and boy	her

- proper noun - pronoun:

Mr. Jones	she		President Lincoln	it
Mrs. Jones	them		McDonald's	they
Nike shoes	he		Capt. & Mrs. Jones	he

Fill In The Blanks: Put an appropriate word in each blank:

as subject	as object		noun	pronoun
I	_____		_____	him
you	_____		_____	they
he	_____		_____	she
she	_____		_____	we
it	_____		_____	it
we	_____		_____	us
they	_____		_____	I

noun	pronoun		pronoun	noun
chicken	_____		_____	street
Mary	_____		_____	S.U.V.
Jake	_____		_____	elephant
Mary and I	_____		_____	mouse
cars	_____		_____	football player

- sentences:

Jane was a fine person. _____ always had time for a kind word.

Mark and Bob played tennis each Saturday morning. _____ really got a great workout trying to beat each other.

Sue and I like taking walks in the park. _____ really enjoy the chance to talk together.

The ferocious dog pulled at his chain whenever Sue walked by. _____ was really scared of _____.

Sentence Generation:
Ultimately, students must generate sentences containing every element they study. When they turn to sentence writing, you can engage them and develop their writing by providing parameters, including (a) minimum word count, (b) specific element required and/or located in particular position, and (c) specific content:

- Write a sentence of at least twelve words with at least one pronoun.

  e.g., *We* couldn't find Mark's shoe, and *he* was late getting to school.

- Write a sentence with a pronoun in the third position.

  e.g., Charlotte and *I* are headed to the mall after lunch.

- Write a sentence using the pronoun "mine" about something you keep in your room.

  e.g., Though my brother often borrows it, that Lego kit is *mine*.

- Write a sentence about Edgar Allen Poe, and include the pronoun "him."

  e.g., Edgar Allen Poe, the original horror story writer, has had a number of biographies written about him.

- Use at least one pronoun in a sentence that describes a female relative.

  e.g., My Aunt Alice, the funniest person *I* know, makes all of *us* laugh when *we* get the chance to see *her*.

- Write a sentence that uses one adjective, a present progressive verb, and a pronoun.

  e.g., The hideously *ugly* lizard *is crawling* on *me* right now!

Adverbs

Overview:

Adverbs describe verbs, adjectives, and even other adverbs. Initial instruction should be limited to those that describe verbs. They are by far the most common, and they serve the best chance of enhancing a student's writing. Adverbs that describe adjectives and other adverbs are far less frequently used, and developing a student's ability to use them will not impact his writing ability substantially.

Latin Origin
verbum = word
ad = to, toward
derivatives:
verbiage
adverbial
verbally

Many instructors, particularly those who work with younger children, use "adverbs end in -<u>ly</u>" as a way to make this difficult part of speech more concrete and understandable. Though an instructor might ease the introduction of adverbs with this generality, be aware that many adverbs, particularly those that involve time, often do *not* end in -<u>ly</u> (e.g., <u>now</u>, <u>soon</u>, <u>never</u>, <u>not</u>, <u>always</u>). There are other words, most of them adjectives, that end in -ly as well: That sweater is rather <u>ugly</u>. Lest you think that when -<u>ly</u> is a suffix, it always generates an adverb, consider this sentence: The *friendly* gentleman bought his wife flowers. If students are instructed merely to mark any word that ends in -<u>ly</u> as an adverb, teachers are not asking them to understand the relationships adverbs have with other words in the sentence. The exercise is one of rote memory rather than an understanding of the relationships between words.

See pages 293-294 for useful lists of adverbs.

Kinds & Categories:

Adverbs are conceptually straightforward, though some of the sub-classifications bear further consideration. Recognize that the term adverb refers to an entire family of words used to describe verbs (as well as adjectives and other adverbs). Students first learn it as a term that applies to single words; eventually, they will understand that it applies to a broader classification of words:

1. adverb - single word describing verb (also adjective or other adverb):

   The firefighter stepped <u>carefully</u> through the debris in the burning house.

2. adverb phrase - phrase describing verb (also adjective or other adverb):

   The doctor ran <u>into the house</u> to get her keys.

3. adverb clause - dependent clause describing verb inside an independent clause (also adjective or other adverb):

   <u>While I was taking my afternoon nap</u>, an owl flew through my window.
   The pilot looked desperately for an airport <u>since he was low on fuel</u>.

Adverb phrases and clauses are covered more extensively in the Sentence Parts section of this text.

Adverbs are usually categorized by what question they answer about the verb. There are four categories of adverb. The first three primarily describe (or modify) verbs, and students should focus primary attention on those. The fourth, adverbs of degree, can modify verbs, adjectives, and other adverbs. Advanced students can spend some time with them, but they are not worth much when it comes to developing writing.

1. adverbs of manner: answer the question <u>how?</u>

   I yelled <u>loudly</u> to get my neighbor's attention.
   Clark mixed the ingredients <u>thoroughly</u> before baking the pie.

2. adverbs of place: answer the question <u>where?</u>

>   Mike and Adrian are going <u>there</u> tomorrow.
>
>   Go <u>outside</u> and play while it's sunny.

3. adverbs of time   answer the question <u>when?</u>

>   <u>Soon,</u> you will have to get a new car.
>
>   Murdoch found that cat <u>yesterday</u> before I got home from work.

4. adverbs of degree   answer the question <u>how much?</u> or <u>to what degree?</u>

>   It is <u>very</u> likely that we will not be home before dinner.
>
>   On the soccer field, Quentin is <u>really</u> good at sweeper.

Verbals are verbs used as other parts of speech. Infinitives, which are covered in the Sentence Parts section of this text, have adverb functions. Even students with more basic skills will use these structures in their writing.

infinitive: to + verb used as an adverb (also adjective or noun)

>   usually located directly after the verb it describes
>
>   I ran <u>to win</u> the race. (describes ran)
>
>   The pirates attacked <u>to get</u> the treasure. (describes attacked)

There are three forms of adverbs, though the comparative and superlative are used far less frequently than their adjectival counterparts. Adverbs ending in -<u>ly</u> use <u>more</u> to form the comparative and <u>most</u> to form the superlative:

1. positive	2. comparative	3. superlative
quietly	more quietly	most quietly
loudly	more loudly	most loudly

Adverbs that keep the same form as their adjectival counterparts use -er for the comparative and -est for the superlative:

1. positive	2. comparative	3. superlative
hard	harder	hardest
early	earlier	earliest

A few common adverbs use irregular comparative and superlative structures:

1. positive	2. comparative	3. superlative	4. adjective form
well	better	best	good
badly	worse	worst	bad
far	farther	farthest	far

Common Core: The Common Core State Standards provide the following grade-level guidelines regarding adverbs:

- Use adjectives and adverbs, and choose between them depending on what is modified. (2)

- Form and use comparative and superlative adjectives and adverbs, and choose between them depending on what is to be modified. (3)

- Explain the function of adverbs in general and their functions in particular sentences. (3)

adverb

describes verb (adjective, or adverb)

examples: quickly, soon, always

adverb

describes a verb	*advanced*
often ends in -ly; *tells how, when, where*	*describes an adjective*
happily, soon	*very* ugly duckling
runs *quickly*	*describes an adverb*
sneezed *loudly*	wrote *rather* rapidly

Introduction:

- Put previously learned terms on the board and review their definitions and an example or two of each.

- Define the new term <u>adverb</u>, putting it underneath the term <u>verb</u> to show their relationship. (See diagram.) Include several examples.

- Hand students concept cards or have them create their own.

- Generate verbs and attach adverbs to them.

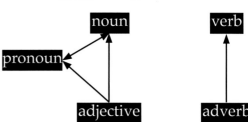

Application:

- Have students add adverbs to verbs you provide.

- Have students watch a video, look at an action-laden photograph or drawing, or watch kids on a playground or people on a busy street. Have them list the verbs that are occurring as well as the adverbs that might describe those verbs.

- Have students identify adverbs from written sentences (if they are readers).

- Provide students with barebones sentences that require them to add adverbs.

Subsequent Lessons: (advanced)

- Advanced: Students should first understand what adverbs do, how to describe verbs using adverbs, and what a simple sentence is before covering this material. Once they are comfortable with these concepts, conduct a lesson explaining to students that adverbs can shift location in a sentence to increase sentence variety. Consider the following example:

  > The teenager backed his car into the garage door.

  The word <u>accidentally</u> could be inserted in any of the locations indicated by an X:

  > X The teenager X backed his car X into the car door X.

  Once students understand this concept, provide sentences like the sample and have them experiment with inserting adverbs in different locations.

- Advanced: Immediately following the above lesson, teach students this guideline for comma usage. Adverbs that begin sentences (and those that begin independent clauses) are followed by commas:

  > Sometimes, I drink a glass of juice before heading to school.

  > Occasionally, I have trouble sleeping the night before a big test.

  > Hurriedly, the teacher explained the homework assignment to her students.

- Advanced: Only when mandated by testing or school curriculum should students pay attention to adverbs that describe adjectives and other adverbs.

Identification: Identify adverbs either in isolation or in context at the word, phrase, sentence, and paragraph levels. A few examples follow:

- Underline the words that can function as adverbs from the list below:

  now   slowly   closet   chew   suddenly   until

- Underline the adverbs in the phrase and draw an arrow to the verb they describe:

  runs regularly and often

- Underline the adverbs in the clause and draw an arrow to the verb they describe:

  because Jane sometimes slept through a storm and awoke suddenly in the morning

- Underline the adverbs in the sentence and draw an arrow to the verb they describe:

  The angry boss spit fiercely onto the floor as he stormed loudly from the room and quickly slammed the door.

Sorting: Place the following adverbs into appropriate categories:

- *Adverbs:* when / where / how:

now	nowhere	outside
eagerly	yesterday	smoothly
softly	soon	here

when?	where?	how?
_____	_____	_____
_____	_____	_____
_____	_____	_____

Matching: Match each adverb with the appropriate word:

- verb - adverb:

burp	soundly	ponder	gratefully
eat	loudly	thank	skillfully
sleep	voraciously	dodge	carefully

Fill In The Blanks: Put an appropriate *word* in each blank:

- Adverbs:

verb	*how adverb*	verb	how adverb
sleep	_____	_____	quickly
run	_____	_____	amusingly
burp	_____	_____	soothingly
argue	_____	_____	joyously
fight	_____	_____	curiously

verb	*when adverb*	verb	when adverb
juggle	_____	_____	soon
arrive	_____	_____	immediately
wake up	_____	_____	often
serve	_____	_____	frequently
grow	_____	_____	anytime

verb	*where adverb*	verb	where adverb
toss	_____	_____	nowhere
walk	_____	_____	anywhere
shovel	_____	_____	somewhere
discuss	_____	_____	here
laugh	_____	_____	there

- sentences:

I ran _____ to my car so that I would not be _____ late for my appointment.

The athlete stepped _____ onto the path before running _____ towards the shore.

List Generation: Generating lists of adverbs helps students move beyond tired, overused words in their writing.

- List some examples of adverbs that describe certain verbs:

yell	cry	laugh	kick	score
_____	_____	_____	_____	_____
_____	_____	_____	_____	_____
_____	_____	_____	_____	_____

- List adverbs that answer the following questions:

when?	where?	how?
_____	_____	_____
_____	_____	_____
_____	_____	_____

Adding & Changing Endings: Endings often represent a word's part of speech. Adding or changing the ending of a word can shift its part of speech.

- Add -ly to these adjectives to form adverbs. (Sometimes, -ly turns words into adjectives as well.):

brave _____   immediate _____

real _____   final _____

Placing Adverbs in Sentences:
Sentences can be made more interesting if the writer relocates the adverb:

- *Move the adverb to another appropriate location in the sentence:*

  My aunt sat <u>obnoxiously</u> snoring.

  The doctor yelled <u>loudly</u> for his patient to stop smoking.

  I tiptoed <u>quietly</u> out of the room to avoid waking my sleeping grandfather.

  You should consider the problem <u>carefully</u> to avoid making an error.

  I go to bed by midnight <u>usually</u>.

- With an arrow indicate each point where the given adverb could be placed to show one method of varying sentences:

quickly:	The man's headache was considered in light of the other illnesses.
often:	I see a movie on Saturday night.
smoothly:	The skater glided across the ice.
energetically:	The woman cooked after a long day at work.
naturally:	I understand your concern.

Sentence Combining:
Students can be asked to consolidate the noun elements in two or more sentences to create a single, more sophisticated sentence:

- single adverbs

  The crocodile snapped his jaws. He did this loudly.

  possible answers: The crocodile snapped his jaws loudly. The crocodile loudly snapped his jaws. Loudly, the crocodile snapped his jaws.

  The boy drank the juice. He did this hastily.

  possible answers: The boy drank his juice hastily. The boy hastily drank his juice. Hastily, the boy drank his juice.

  You need to go to your room. You need to do this now.

  possible answers: You need to go to your room now. Now, you need to go to your room. You now need to go to your room.

- two or more adverbs

  I studied. I did this carefully. I did this quietly.

  possible answers: I studied carefully and quietly. Carefully and quietly, I studied. I carefully and quietly studied.

Sentence Generation: Ultimately, students must generate sentences containing every element they study. When they turn to sentence writing, you can engage them and develop their writing by providing parameters, including (a) minimum word count, (b) specific element required and/or located in particular position, and (c) specific content:

- Write a sentence of at least eleven words that includes one adverb.

  e.g., The police officer *firmly* questioned the teenager about the broken window.

- Write a sentence with an adverb in the sixth position.

  e.g., If you don't get home *soon*, you won't have enough time to study for the test.

- Write a sentence with an adverb that answers the question "how" in it.

  e.g., My mother *fiercely* slammed the door to prove her point to me.

- Write a sentence of at least thirteen words containing one adverb about how you played in the game today.

  e.g., My coach thought I played *well* in today's lacrosse game because I scored a hat trick.

- Use at least two adverbs in a sentence about "The Tortoise and the Hare."

  e.g., The tortoise moved *slowly* but *steadily* to win a race against the hare, who moved *quickly* but *inconsistently*.

- Write a sentence with at least one adjective, one compound subject and one adverb.

  e.g., The *elderly woman* and her *husband quietly* sat underneath the oak tree in the shade.

Conjunctions

For The Teacher:

Overview:

Conjunctions join two words or two groups of words. The word conjunction literally means "to join together."

Latin Origin		

Latin Origin

jungere = to join
con = together
derivatives:
(train) junction
adjunct
juncture

> joins single words: AJ <u>and</u> Robert grabbed some food on the way to the game.

> joins phrases: I looked for my keys in the yard <u>and</u> in the car.

> joins clauses: Mark picked up his clothes, <u>and</u> his mother washed them.

> The actor left the show, <u>but</u> he was quickly replaced.

> You can drink from the can, <u>or</u> I can find you a glass.

> The janitor mopped the floors <u>while</u> the students were in class.

> <u>After</u> the President spoke to the nation, others responded.

While the last two examples may be less familiar to you, they contain <u>subordinating</u> conjunctions.

The lists of conjunctions in this section are reproduced on page 288 (bottom) for copying. A reference chart for middle and high school students can be found on 296.

Kinds & Categories:

There are three kinds of conjunctions:

1. coordinating: joins 2 words or groups of words
   <u>equal</u> standing; can join individual words, phrases, or clauses

Coordinating Conjunctions of

for	but
and	or
nor	yet
	(so)

> Eliza <u>and</u> Sophie bought prom dresses from a local vendor.

> Marcus lost his keys, <u>but</u> Elijah found them again.

> Our friends could go with us, <u>or</u> we could go alone.

When studying coordinating conjunctions, I often omit <u>so</u>, a decidedly weak, overused, and confusing conjunction. This leaves only six coordinating conjunctions.

Taking the first letter of each forms the mnemonic fanboy (for, and, nor, but, or, yet), which is useful to help students remember them.

Subordinating Conjunctions		
after	even though	so that
although	if	though
as	if only	till
as if	in case	unless
as long as	in order that	until
as much as	just as	when
as soon as	lest	whenever
as though	now that	where
because	once	whereas
before	only if	wherever
by the time	provided that	whether
even if	since	while

Figure 14

2. subordinating: only used to join a dependent clause to an independent one; begins the dependent clause and makes it subordinate to the independent one (see *Figure 14*)

While we have the time, we should pack our bags for the trip.

He can bench press over 100 pounds although he wants to lift more.

Without while in the first example and although in the second, these sentences would be run-ons, and the reader would have no sense of which parts were primary (the independent clauses) and which were secondary or subordinate (the dependent clauses). Since subordinating conjunctions are only used to begin dependent clauses, they will be discussed further in the Sentence Parts section of this text.

Correlative Conjunctions
both...and
either...or
neither...nor
not only...but also
whether...or
not...but

Figure 15

3. correlative: paired conjunctions that join 2 words or groups of words of equal standing (see *Figure 15*)

Both Robert and Jack want to win the soccer championship.

Neither Susan nor Heidi knew what his car looked like.

Not only do you have to clean your room, but you also must feed the dog.

Note: The word <u>so</u> can be used as both a coordinating *and* a subordinating conjunction. See the notes after each Initial Lesson for further discussion.

Common Core: The Common Core State Standards provide the following grade-level guidelines regarding conjunctions:

- Use frequently occurring conjunctions. (1)

- Use coordinating and subordinating conjunctions. (3)

- Use correlative conjunctions. (5)

- Explain the function of conjunctions in general and their functions in particular sentences. (5)

conjunction – coordinating

joins two words or groups of words
of equal value

for, and, nor, but, or, yet, (so)

---

coordinating conjunction

joins 2 words or 2 groups of words of equal value (only 6 of them)

for, and, nor, but, or, yet

Tim *and* Drew   lions *and* tigers

It started to rain, *but* we still went to the park.

I do not like liver, *nor* do I like mushrooms.

Introduction:

- Put previously learned terms on the board and review their definitions and an example or two of each.

- Define the new term, <u>coordinating conjunction</u>. Include several examples. With primary students

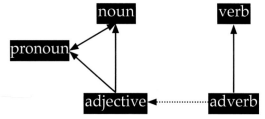

and those with basic skills, teach <u>and</u>, <u>but</u>, and <u>or</u>. Other students can learn all six. (Do not include <u>so</u>.) If you are teaching all six, show students the mnemonic <u>fanboy</u>: <u>f</u>or, <u>a</u>nd, <u>n</u>or, <u>b</u>ut, <u>o</u>r, <u>y</u>et. Younger students enjoy this mnemonic, and older students will tolerate it because it's effective and easy to remember.

- Hand students concept cards or have them create their own. Include some examples in context on the card:

  Rob <u>and</u> Isabelle went dancing yesterday.

  I bought birthday cards for Jack <u>and</u> Andy.

  Will hurried down the street <u>but</u> missed his bus.

  Christopher shouldered the heavy boxes <u>and</u> carried them to his car.

Initial Application:

- Have students name pairs of nouns and then join them with "and." For example, they might come up with boys/girls, table/chairs, fork/knife, work/play, socks/shoes.

- Have students identify coordinating conjunctions from written sentences (if they are readers).

- Provide students with some example sentences and have them choose the appropriate conjunction. For example, you might write...

    John _____ Mike played tennis. (and)

    Mary closed the windows _____ forgot to shut the door. (but)

    Do you want tea _____ lemonade with dinner? (or)

Notes:

- Most people know that <u>and</u> and <u>but</u> are conjunctions. Of the six coordinating conjunctions, <u>and</u>, <u>but</u>, and <u>or</u> are most commonly used and recognized. That said, <u>nor</u>, <u>yet</u>, and <u>for</u> appear in published text and therefore are useful for text comprehension.

- The word <u>so</u> functions as a coordinating conjunction only when you could insert the word <u>and</u> in front of it and retain meaning (e.g., Soto has always been nervous in large gatherings, (and) so it is no surprise that he avoids crowds of his adoring fans.). It isn't the strongest of transition words when used as a coordinating conjunction, and most student writers overuse it anyway; hence, I rarely teach it directly with coordinating conjunctions. (For more about <u>so</u>, see the sentence section of this text.)

- See the section on compound sentences for examples of each of the six core coordinating conjunctions in action and an explanation of the difference between compound subjects/predicates and compound sentences, all of which use coordinating conjunctions.

134

Suggested Exercises & Activities

Identification: Identify coordinating conjunctions either in isolation or in context at the word, phrase, sentence, and paragraph levels. A few examples follow:

- Underline the words that can function as conjunctions from the list below:

  and   mind   forever   for   but   understand

- Underline the conjunction in the phrase: beside Mary and me

  feast or famine

  on the table or in the cabinet

- Underline the coordinating conjunctions in the sentence:

  Our neighbor's ferocious poodle barked, but she calmed after midnight.

  Jackson and Zach are cousins, but they are as close as brothers.

Sorting: Place the following phrases into appropriate categories:

- *Conjunctions:* Place the following compounds into appropriate categories:

  John and Sue   ran and skipped   studied and passed

  kicked and screamed   the doctor and the nurse   my lawyer and his friend

  noun-conjunction-noun   verb-conjunction-verb

  _____   _____

  _____   _____

  _____   _____

Fill In The Blanks: Put an appropriate conjunction in each blank:

- sentences:

  Jake _____ Martin enjoyed the movie immensely.

  We got back home, _____ the sun had set.

  My tutor was late, _____ I still had a full session.

  Lila does not like broccoli, _____ does she like brussel sprouts.

List Generation: Generating lists of conjunctions helps students move beyond tired, overused words in their writing.

- List the six coordinating conjunctions:

  _____

Sentence Generation: Ultimately, students must generate sentences containing every element they study. When they turn to sentence writing, you can engage them and develop their writing by providing parameters, including (a) minimum word count, (b) specific element required and/or located in particular position, and (c) specific content:

- Write a sentence of at least eleven words that includes one coordinating conjunction.

  e.g., My dad loaded the car, *and* my mom locked up the house.

- Write a sentence with a coordinating conjunction in the eighth position.

  e.g., The boy quickly typed his English essay, *and* then his mom proofread it.

- Write a sentence with a coordinating conjunction, but do not use <u>but</u> or <u>and</u>.

  e.g., Jessie found her wallet, *yet* she decided not to go to the mall anyway.

- Write a sentence using the conjunction "yet" about one of the leaders you are studying.

  Winston Churchill led Great Britain through World War II, *yet* he struggled along the way.

- Write a sentence with one adjective, one adverb and a coordinating conjunction.

  The *fierce* lion roared *angrily and* leaped across the stream.

- Write a sentence of at least eight words that uses a conjunction to join two proper nouns.

  Harry and Hermione are two of the main characters in the Harry Potter series.

136

conjunction - subordinating

joins a dependent clause to an
independent clause

examples: although, since, until
even if, since, whenever

subordinating conjunction

joins a dependent clause to an independent clause

because, although, if, as

We canceled the picnic *when* the storm started.

While I ride the bus, I often listen to music.

Introduction:

- Put previously learned terms on the board and review their definitions and an example or two of each.

- Define the new term, <u>subordinating conjunction</u>. Include several examples. Define the term, writing it on the board. Include several examples.

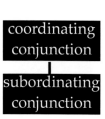

- Hand students concept cards or have them create their own.

- Provide students with a more thorough list of subordinating conjunctions for future reference and sentence writing.

- Note: Do not teach students subordinating conjunctions until they are ready to study complex sentences. Teaching them in isolation beforehand will serve no purpose. See page 236 for complex sentences.

Initial Application:

- Have students identify subordinating conjunctions from written sentences (if they are readers).

- Provide students with some example sentences and have them choose an appropriate conjunction. For example, you might write...

  John swept up the mess ____ Mary made it. (possible answers: although, even though)

  You may go to the movies ____ you finish your homework. (possible answers: if, when, after)

  ____ I was washing the car, it started to rain. (possible answers: When, While)

Notes:

- When <u>so</u> functions as a subordinating conjunction, it could be followed by <u>that</u>, and the meaning would remain the same (e.g., We packed the night before so (that) we could depart in the morning without delay.). (For more about <u>so</u>, see the sentence section of this text.)

- Since subordinating conjunctions are used exclusively with complex sentences, Suggested Activities and Exercises are located in the Sentence Parts section of this text.

Prepositions

Overview:

Prepositions are words used to begin phrases. They can appear quite abstract, particularly to the novice. Introduce them in as concrete a manner as possible: anything you can do to a box, anything a plane can do to a cloud, or anything a bee can do to a jar will introduce students to about two thirds of the common prepositions. More abstract examples can be introduced at a later point, once students are comfortable with the concrete ones.

Latin Origin
positio = placing
pre = before
derivatives:
<u>pre</u>game (show)
<u>pre</u>view
de<u>positio</u>n

Remember that our study of part of speech concerns function or job. A few years ago, I spent three one-to-one tutoring sessions helping a student memorize an alphabetical list of prepositions. Why? Because the activity was worth three quiz grades for the ninth grade English class he was taking. This kind of activity is pointless. Most prepositions can serve other functions as well, and memorizing a list of words like this does nothing to develop writing in a student.

Keep in mind that prepositions begin phrases as there will be noun following the preposition. In these examples the prepositions are underlined, and the phrases, which will be discussed in more detail in the Sentence Parts section of this book, are in parentheses:

(<u>On</u> the cover of the magazine), I found the name (<u>of</u> the article).

The coach yelled a lot (<u>during</u> the game).

We shouldn't eat (<u>at</u> McDonald's) again this week.

The young woman jogged (<u>in</u> the park) each morning before she went (<u>on</u> the subway) to work.

If a word that is often a preposition appears outside of a phrase, it is serving another function:

> We eat <u>out</u> all the time. (Eat out is a phrasal verb.)
>
> We climbed <u>out</u> the window. (Out is a preposition in the phrase out the window.)
>
> You should shut <u>up</u> before you make me mad. (Shut up is a phrasal verb.)
>
> He climbed <u>up</u> the mountain. (Up is a preposition in the phrase up the mountain.)

One way to determining whether a word is a preposition, then, is by determining whether it begins a phrase.

For a discussion of adverb and adjective phrases (the two different kinds of prepositional phrases), see the sentence parts section of this text.

The lists of prepositions in this section (*Figure 16* and *Figure 17*) are reproduced on page 295 for copying. A reference chart for middle and high school students can be found on 296.

Concrete Prepositions

above	by	out of
across	close to	outside
ahead of	down	outside of
alongside	far from	over
among	from	past
amongst	in	through
around	in front of	throughout
at	inside	to
atop	into	toward
behind	near	towards
below	near to	under
beneath	next to	underneath
beside	on	up
between	on top of	upon
beyond	onto	within

Figure 16

More Advanced Prepositions

aboard	due to	on account of
about	during	on behalf of
according to	except (for)	out
after	for	prior to
against	in addition to	subsequent to
along	in case of	to
aside from	in place of	with
because of	in spite of	with regard to
before	instead of	
besides	of	without
despite	off	

Figure 17

Kinds & Categories:

Different writers have tried to cluster prepositions into categories based on the kinds of questions they answer. These categories vary widely from author to author. That said, three categories that include a lot of prepositional phrases are time, place, and movement. Before focusing attention on categorizing, though, keep in mind that our goal is to improve and develop student writing. If there isn't a reason to focus attention on these specific categories, then don't do it.

Common Core:

The Common Core State Standards provide the following grade-level guidelines regarding prepositions:

- Use the most frequently occurring prepositions. (K)

- Use frequently occurring prepositions. (1)

- Form and use prepositional phrases. (4)

- Explain the function of prepositions in general and their functions in particular sentences. (5)

preposition

begins a phrase
(often shows position or location)

in, on, under, around, through, beside

---

preposition

begins a phrase
(hint: anything a plane can do to a cloud)

in, on, under, around, through, beside

under the tree   *next to* the river

Introduction:

- Put previously learned terms on the board and review their definitions and an example or two of each.

- Define the new term <u>preposition</u>, writing it on the board. Include several examples.

- Hand students concept cards or have them create their own.

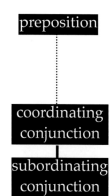

- Provide a drawing of a cloud and a plane dangling from a string that can be maneuvered. Show students that the plane can fly over, under, through, next to, around (and so on) the cloud. Younger students can use themselves and a chair as well. In other words, they can walk *around* the chair, step *on* the chair, crawl *under* the chair, sand *next to* the chair, etc.

Initial Application:

- Have students identify prepositions from written sentences (if they are readers).

- Provide students with some example sentences and have them choose an appropriate preposition. For example, you might write...

  John stood ___ me. (possible answers: beside, next to, in front of)

  The house you want is ___ the corner. (possible answers: around, on)

- Provide a drawing of a box with no prepositions written on it, and have students fill in as many prepositions as they can remember. Here is a chart that can be duplicated and given to students when they are writing prepositional phrases or expanding sentences with prepositional phrases (*Figure 18*):

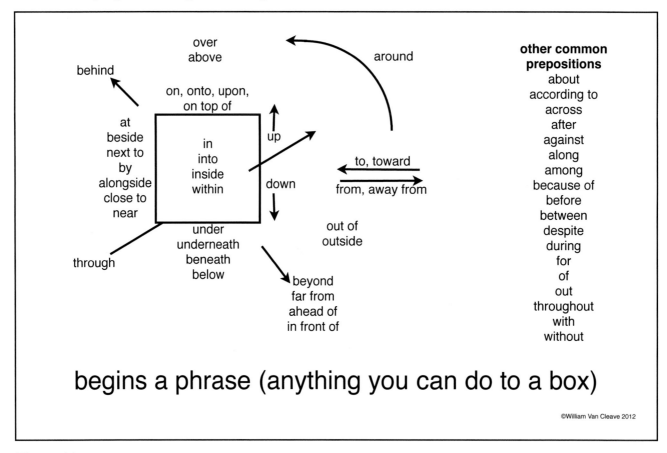

Figure 18

Identification:
Identify prepositions either in isolation or in context at the word, phrase, sentence, and paragraph levels. A few examples follow:

- Underline the prepositions from the list below:

  in   very   table   through   next to   eat

- Underline the preposition in the phrase: under the wooden table

- Underline the prepositions in the clause:

  while Jane climbed under the table and Mark stepped over the fallen toy

- Underline the prepositions in the sentence:

  At the ice skating rink, the children made sharp turns on the smooth ice and giggled about the silly songs on the sound system.

Sorting:
Place the following prepositions into appropriate categories:

- Position the listed prepositions correctly on the box* below. Two have been done for you:

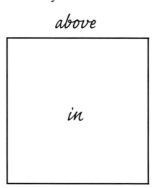

in	on	around	next to	beside	under
above	below	under	over	into	within
inside	beneath	by	underneath		

This can be done with a plane and cloud or a bee and jar as well.

Matching: Match each preposition with the appropriate word:

- preposition - rest of phrase:

under	the covers	beside	the night
around	the dark woods	by	William Faulkner
through	the sharp corner	into	the loud boy

- noun - prepositional phrase:

boy	with Valentine's candy	seat	in high tide
astronaut	on the long space mission	sports car	on the packed flight
girlfriend	in the back of the classroom	waves	at the car show

Fill In The Blanks: Put an appropriate preposition in each blank:

- prepositions:

preposition	rest of the phrase	preposition	rest of the phrase
_____	the broken bridge	_____	the boring day
_____	my upset friend	_____	a rocket ship
_____	Mark Twain	_____	the whole team
_____	my dearest friend	_____	the table
_____	the little tricycle	_____	a loaded gun

- sentences:

I jumped _____ my car and sped _____ the road so that I could reach the store before it closed.

She wept _____ the movie after the character was killed _____ _____ his arch enemy.

_____ the rainy day, they chose to stay _____ the house and watch their favorite movie _____ the flat screen television.

List Generation: Generating lists of prepositions helps students move beyond tired, overused words in their writing.

- List some examples of nouns/pronouns that could go with the following prepositions:

under   beside   next to   around   inside

_____ _____ _____ _____ _____

_____ _____ _____ _____ _____

_____ _____ _____ _____ _____

- In each column, list prepositions that could come before the words listed below:

_____

_____

_____

the rickety chair   the newly paved street   the dark and scary cave

Sentence Generation:
Ultimately, students must generate sentences containing every element they study. When they turn to sentence writing, you can engage them and develop their writing by providing parameters, including (a) minimum word count, (b) specific element required and/or located in particular position, and (c) specific content:

- Write a sentence of at least ten words that includes one preposition.

  e.g., The mountain climber stepped *onto* the ledge and took a sip *from* his water bottle.

- Write a sentence with a preposition in the eighth position.

  e.g., The doctor sat down with the patient *in* his office to discuss her illness.

- Write a sentence that uses a preposition as its first word.

  e.g., *During* the night the shutter fell into the front yard.

- Write a sentence using the preposition <u>under</u> about a magical castle.

  e.g., The magical castle *under* the purple mountain sparkled in the morning sunlight.

- Use the preposition <u>in</u> in a sentence about Franklin Delano Roosevelt.

  e.g., FDR remains the longest serving President though he spent most of his adult life *in* a wheelchair.

- Write a sentence with at least one adjective, one adverb and one preposition.

  e.g., The *antique* car turned the corner *sharply* and avoided an accident *with* a large truck.

Interjections

Overview:

An interjection is a word or phrase that shows strong emotion. It can stand alone but is often contained within a sentence. They are almost never used in expository writing. In narrative writing or fiction, the user is unlikely to benefit from extensive study of interjections. I spend as little instructional time as possible on them and would not encourage extensive study or practice.

Latin Origin
jacere = to throw
inter = between
derivatives:
interject
projection
interactive

interjection

expresses strong emotion

examples: Ouch! Oh! Gosh!

interjection

expresses strong emotion

Ouch! That hurts.

Oh! You're here!

Gosh, it's hot in here.

Introduction:

Define the term, writing it on the board. Include several examples.

Hand students concept cards or have them create their own.

Explain carefully that interjections are not a part of the sentence or its flow but rather "interject" a surprise emotion.

Have students identify interjections from written sentences (if they are readers).

Application:

Provide students with some example sentences and have them choose an appropriate interjection. For example, you might write...

_____, that hurt! (possible answers: Ouch!, Darn!, Yow!)

_____, you're impossible. (possible answers: Gosh!, Honestly!, Holy Cow!)

Note:

• Interjections are rarely found in expository writing. While a brief introduction can't hurt, repeated practice with these rare elements is likely to be a waste of time. As a result, except for those listed above, no sample activities are included here.

The Matter at Hand 2:
Sentence Parts For Instruction

Introduction

Like the study of parts of speech, each concept in this section has three components:

1. an overview of the concept, including background information and points of clarity for teacher understanding

2. concept introduction and application for the student in as clear and succinct a manner as possible

3. examples of activities and assignments to help students understand, learn, and review the concept

There are several model dialogues to demonstrate instruction as well. What you choose to teach is determined by the age, grade, and ability level of your students as well as the time you can commit to the writing process. Remember, a good rule of thumb is this: do not teach a concept unless it has a direct application to the act of writing for the students you teach.

Follow instruction with direct application. Students should be generating examples of each concept almost from the very beginning. Otherwise, they may be able to identify a particular element, but they will not be able to produce it naturally in their own writing.

A word of caution: I have seen a number of good teachers of writing, who truly "know their stuff" and teach it well. Bound by curriculum and an enormous amount of material to cover, however, they do not stick with the application long enough. While a concept might take just minutes to introduce, practicing it properly takes days, weeks, and even months. Sporadic return to previously taught concepts serves as review and, more importantly, applied practice. Most students I teach can produce in isolation any kind of sentence I have taught.

Some, however, continue to work towards automatic application in their own paragraphs and essays. Unfortunately, only time will address their need.

Core Concept

The core of this unit of study is the clause. Except for coordinating conjunctions between independent clauses, in a sentence each word exists in a clause. Learning to create and manipulate clauses is at the core of varying the sentences a student uses in writing.

Often, when I teach writing workshops, teachers are familiar with nouns and verbs, subjects and predicates. They may even be able to explain that a compound sentence is made up of two smaller sentences and a conjunction. Too often, though, the most important concept in sentence writing, the clause, eludes them. Some have a vague recollection of a lesson from grammar school, and others believe it to be an independent thought, capable of serving as a sentence. While some clauses indeed *can* stand alone as sentences, many can*not*. The clause, a group of words with a subject and its predicate, serves as the fundamental building block for all sentence construction. Again, with the exception of coordinating conjunctions, every word in every complete sentence in the English language exists in a clause. Each sentence in English contains at least one independent clause. Independent and dependent clauses are combined to form the wide variety of sentence kinds we use to express ourselves. They give writing its variety and its interest. Without knowledge of their structure and an understanding of their potential, a struggling writer hits a wall, writing simplistic sentences in rapid repetition, struggling with developing an idea past a single sentence or two, or writing paragraphs replete with fragments and run-on sentences.

Activities That Ask Students To Apply Their Knowledge of Sentence Parts and Sentences to Writing

After each concept in this section, I have listed a number of different sentence-building activities. Though Sentence Generation is included in these individual sections, I've also chosen to list some plausible sentence-writing activities here. Generating good sentences is the single best way to develop writing skills. The Sentence Generation suggestions listed with each concept include sample responses. Here, I have just listed plausible assignments.

Arlene Sonday has a handy rule of thumb: the number of words in a child's sentence should at least equal her age. In other words ten-year-olds should have at least ten words in their sentences, and fifteen-year-olds should have at least fifteen words in theirs.

Sentence Generation:

- *Specify content.*

  with a particular word or words (can be spelling or vocabulary word)

  Write a sentence including the word <u>bridge</u>.

  Write an 8 word sentence including the word <u>bridge</u>.

  Write a sentence containing <u>bridge</u> in the second position.

  Write a sentence using <u>tree</u> and <u>park</u>.

  Write a 12 word sentence using <u>tree</u> and <u>park</u>.

  Write a sentence containing <u>tree</u> in the third position and <u>park</u> in the eighth position.

  about a particular topic

  Write a sentence about something blue.

  Write a sentence about your recent soccer game.

  Write a sentence about the local park.

  about a particular topic using a word other than the one provided

  Write a sentence about something fun without using the word <u>fun</u>.

  Write a sentence about a goalie but do not use the word <u>goalie</u>.

about more than one topic

Write a sentence about an elderly woman and a race car.

Write a sentence about a thunderstorm and a fight.

Write a sentence about a doctor and an airplane.

- *Specify number of words in a sentence that contains a particular sentence part or type.*

single element

Write a simple sentence with at least 12 words.

Write a compound sentence with at least 14 words.

Write a sentence of at least eight words that begins with a prepositional phrase.

Write a complex sentence with the dependent clause first that contains at least 13 words.

Write a complex sentence with the dependent clause last that contains at least 11 words.

kind of sentence and specific part of speech

Write a compound sentence with at least 3 adjectives.

Write a compound-complex sentence with at least 2 prepositional phrases.

Write a complex sentence containing a compound verb.

Write a simple sentence with at least one adverb that does *not* end in -ly.

with a specific combining technique

Write a compound sentence of at least 12 words. Use *yet* as the coordinating conjunction.

Write a complex sentence of at least 10 words. Use *since* as the subordinating conjunction.

Write a complex sentence of at least 10 words with an adjective clause. Use *which* as the relative pronoun.

Write a compound sentence with at least 12 words. Use a semi-colon and a conjunctive adverb.

- *Push students to broaden their vocabulary by specifying minimum number of letters in a particular word or requiring them to avoid a specific word or words. (These can require a minimum number of words as well.)*

Write a sentence about soccer. Avoid the words <u>fun</u> and <u>cool</u>.

Write a sentence with one adverb in it. Avoid the word <u>very</u>.

Write a compound sentence. Join it with <u>for</u>, <u>nor</u>, or <u>yet</u>. (Avoid <u>and</u>, <u>but</u>, and <u>or</u>.)

Write a complex sentence. Use a subordinating conjunction other than <u>although</u>.

Write a sentence containing two adjectives. Neither can have fewer than six letters.

- *Specify content and number of words.*

  Describe why you like skiing in a sentence of 14 words.

  Write a sentence of 12-15 words about the way a tiger hunts its prey.

  Write a 10 word sentence about Huckleberry Finn (the boy).

  Describe Richard Nixon in a compound sentence of 16 words.

  Describe this picture (provide picture) in a sentence of 16 words.

Sentence Expanding Using Question Words: Begin with a barebones sentence; pages 300-304 contain many of them. Teach students to expand this type of sentence using question words:

to expand the predicate (action - verb): use adverbs, adverb phrases, and adverb clauses
answer the questions when? where? how? why?
or use a concession (e.g., <u>although</u>, <u>in spite of the fact that</u>, etc.)

to expand the subject (doer): use adjectives, adjective phrases, and adjective/relative clauses
answer the questions what kind? which one? whose? or how many?

As students respond to these questions -- either verbally or in writing -- encourage them to use single word, phrase, and clause responses, assuming they have learned the appropriate concepts to do this effectively:

- *Expand the predicate (verb) using <u>**when**</u>: The hikers will rest.*

single word	*phrase*
The hikers will rest soon.	After dinner the hikers will rest.
The hikers will rest tomorrow.	The hikers will rest throughout the night.

The hikers will rarely rest.

Daily, the hikers will rest.

Before the rain the hikers will rest.

The hikers will camp next week.

clause

Once they find a good spot, the hikers will rest.

The hikers will rest after it heats up.

Whenever they hear an animal growl, the hikers will rest.

The hikers will rest as soon as they can.

- *Expand the predicate (verb) using __where__: The boy jumped.*

single word

The boy jumped nearby.

The boy jumped outside.

Somewhere, the boy jumped.

The boy jumped up.

phrase

The boy jumped at his school.

The boy jumped down the street.

The boy jumped into a car.

The boy jumped in the antique shop.

clause

Where he could find the space, the boy jumped.

The boy jumped wherever he was told not to jump.

The boy jumped where you might not think to look.

- *Expand the predicate (verb) using __how__: The musician practiced.*

single word

The musician practiced enthusiastically.

The musician practiced fanatically.

Speedily, the musician practiced.

The musician practiced regularly.

phrase

The musician practiced without a care.

With great purpose, the musician practiced.

The musician practiced with glee.

The musician practiced in fine rhythm.

clause

The musician practiced as though she were preparing for a major recital.

As if she had never touched an instrument, the musician practiced.

The musician practiced exactly as you would expect her to.

- *Expand the predicate (verb) using <u>why</u>: The farmer hunts.*

single word	*phrase*
why is usually a phrase or clause	For the fun of it, the farmer hunts.
rather than a single word	The farmer hunts because of deer overpopulation.
	The farmer hunts for food for the table.
	The farmer hunts to share tradition with his sons.

  clause

  The farmer hunts because he wants venison.

  The farmer hunts so that he can relax and become one with nature.

  The farmer hunts hoping that he will be rewarded with a kill.

  Only when he has nothing better to do, the farmer hunts.

- *Expand the predicate (verb) using a **concession** (suggests the opposite of the main part of the sentence). Often uses <u>though</u>, <u>although</u>, <u>even though</u>, etc.: The couple relaxed.*

single word	*phrase*
not possible	Against the wishes of their parents, the couple relaxed.
	In spite of the hour, the couple relaxed.
	Although overextended, the couple relaxed.

  clause

  Although I couldn't imagine why, the couple relaxed.

  The couple relaxed though they knew that something was amiss.

  In spite of the fact that they heard a scary sound, the couple relaxed.

  Though their children tried to prevent them from doing so, the couple relaxed.

- *Expand the subject using <u>what kind</u>, <u>which one</u> or <u>whose</u>: The boats collided.*

single word	*phrase*
The Union ships collided.	The ships on the Potomac collided.
The new ships collided.	The ships in dock collided.
The British ships collided.	The ships covered in rust collided.
The attack ships collided.	The ships from Portugal collided.

clause

The ships, which were in relatively good shape, collided.

The ships that we are most ashamed of collided.

The ships, whose captains were brothers, collided.

- *Expand the subject using <u>how many</u>: The flights were delayed.*

single word	*phrase*
The three flights were delayed.	*not possible*
All the flights were delayed	
Some flights were delayed.	*clause*
No flights were delayed.	*not possible*

- *Below are 2 barebones sentence expansions. Clearly, all the parts could not be used in one sentence.*

  The ghost haunted the mansion.

when?	for hundreds of years
where?	on the corner of the deserted street
how?	by wandering the halls late into the night
why?	because her death had not been avenged
concession	despite the fact that few people noticed her presence
what kind?	young, female
which one?	of Andrea Longhorn
how many?	the (word already included in the basic sentence above)

  The teams competed.

when?	twice each year
where?	at the largest stadium in Great Britain
how?	by playing their very best
why?	because their rivalry was older than any of the current players
concession?	although the Bears always won

what kind?	veteran
which one?	with well developed skills
how many?	two
barebones sentence:	_____
when?	_____
where?	_____
how?	_____
why?	_____
concession?	_____
what kind?	_____
which one?	_____
how many?	_____

Sentence Writing Using Words Centered Around Specific Content:

Begin by providing a list of words that concern a specific topic. Ask students to generate sentences using the provided words (and ideas those words bring to mind). Students should be able to generate multiple sentences on any familiar given topic.

Below is a list of words concerning pirates (adapted from a list from enchantedlearning.com). First, have your students read over the words (or read them aloud to your students). Define any unfamiliar words (or omit them from the list), and ask students to conjure up pictures from the words. Then, give them focused sentence writing activities based on the words:

ahoy	coins	doubloon	hull	navigate	rob	swab
anchor	crew	earring	island	ocean	sail	sword
attack	crook	eye patch	keel	parrot	scar	treasure
aye-aye	crow's nest	first mate	knife	pegleg	scurvy	vessel
bandanna	cutlass	flag	landlubber	pirate	seas	violent
battle	dagger	fortune	loot	plank	ship	walk
boatswain	deck	gangplank	map	plunder	shore	(the plank)
buccaneer	deck hands	gold	maroon	quarters	silver	X (marks
cannon	desert	gun	mast	raid	skull and	the spot)
captain	island	hook	mates	rigging	bones	yo-ho-ho

- Write five sentences about pirates. Use at least two words from the list in each sentence.
- Write a compound sentence about a pirate ship. Use at least two words from the list.
- Use "keel" in a sentence of at least 10 words.
- Write three descriptive sentences about a pirate of your own creation. Use at least two of the words from the pirate list in your sentences.

Tandem Sentence Writing:
Provide a complete sentence, and ask students to write a sentence that would naturally follow it. You can provide a word that must be used in the follow-up sentence or leave the entire sentence up to the writer. A few examples follow:

- The athlete used a rowing machine each morning before work.

_____

- The police officer drew his gun as he stepped out of his car. (Use "immediately.")

_____

- I decided to get the chocolate avalanche dessert when we went out for my birthday. (Use "delicious" in a complex sentence of at least ten words.)

_____

- The United States dropped atom bombs on Nagasaki and Hiroshima to bring World War II to an end. (Use "however.")

_____

Analyzing Published Sentences:
Provide a sentence from a well known piece of writing (fiction or non-fiction), ask students to analyze it structurally, and, where appropriate, ask them to write an imitation of it. Here are a few examples:

- If you live to be a hundred, I want to live to be a hundred minus one day so I never have to live without you." (A.A. Milne, *Winnie-the-Pooh*)

Students can label the parts of speech. If the identity of certain words has not yet been studied, then the teacher can underline or highlight those words, indicating that students should skip identifying them. For example, there are four infinitives in the sentence above.

Students can also analyze the clause structure. The sentence above is a complex sentence with an independent clause surrounded by dependent clauses (D,ID).

An imitation sentence might look something like this:
When I went to see the movie, I hoped to stay to catch the credits with my friends even though afterwards I would have to rush to my house.

- "Destroying things is much easier than making them." (Suzanne Collins, *The Hunger Games*)

In this sentence there are two gerund phrases: <u>destroying things</u> and <u>making them</u>.

An imitation sentence might look something like this:
Crying babies are much more annoying than delayed flights.

- "If wishes were fishes, we'd all cast nets." (Frank Herbert, *Dune*)

This is a complex sentence (D,I). It also contains a predicate noun (fishes) and a direct object (nets).

An imitation sentence might look something like this:
Since the painting is a masterpiece, we will all make toasts!

- "This must be a simply enormous wardrobe!" (C.S. Lewis, *The Lion, The Witch, and the Wardrobe*).

<u>Wardrobe</u> is a predicate noun. <u>Enormous</u> is an adjective describing <u>wardrobe</u>, and <u>simply</u> is an adverb describing <u>enormous</u>.

An imitation sentence might look something like this:
That will be an extraordinarily good time!

COMMON SENTENCE TEMPLATES

clause: group of words with a subject and its verb

independent clause: clause that <u>can</u> stand by itself

dependent clause: clause that <u>cannot</u> stand by itself

Simple Sentence
1 independent clause

I

Many have a single subject and predicate.

Mac went to the store.

On Tuesday Will visited our grandmother at her cottage in the next town.

Others have compound subjects and/or predicates.

Wes and Ethan often play tennis on Saturdays.

Logan saw an excellent movie and then went to dinner with friends.

(For a group of words to be a clause, it must have its own subject and predicate. It cannot share either with another clause.)

Compound Sentence
2 independent clauses

I,I I;I
for, and, nor, but, or, yet, (so)

joined by comma and coordinating conjunction...

Jackson went to the store, but it was closed.

Tickets for the final game were scarce, yet Drew still got seats.

I love to jog through the park, and Isabelle often joins me.

I do not want to go to the movies, nor do I feel like playing baseball.

...or joined by a semi-colon.

A number of recent inventions have changed the way the world functions; cell phones and the internet are two of the most obvious.

The game got rained out; however, the coaches rescheduled it for the following Saturday.

(Words such as however are conjunctive adverbs rather than conjunctions; these adverbs often begin the second clause of a compound sentence that uses a semi-colon and are always followed by a comma.)

Complex Sentence
1 independent and 1 (or more) dependent clauses

D,I ID I⟨D

using subordinating conjunction...

While Rob was pulling out of his driveway, he accidentally bumped into another car. (D,I)

Even though the movie ran late, Charles still got in before curfew. (D,I)

Luke spent an extra $50 on his computer because it came with a printer. (ID)

Our mom banned drinks in the den after Jeb spilled soda on the good table. (ID)

...or using relative pronoun.

Taylor, who has played competitive sports since fourth grade, started at free safety this fall.

Jack loved any book that could hold his attention.

(The first of these adjective clause (or D-wedge) sentences uses the clause to define the subject. The second uses it to define the object.)

Figure 19

Concepts & Lessons

Students should build personal stacks of vocabulary cards representing the terms below. They should only have cards for terms the instructor has introduced. More advanced parts of a term's definition can be added once students have covered them. For example, a student may initially learn that compound sentences are joined by a comma and coordinating conjunction. Later, when she has learned that compound sentences can also be joined by a semi-colon, she (or her instructor) would add that fact to her concept card. Following this strategy, her cards are a stack of concepts she has actually covered. Sample cards are included with the discussion of each individual concept. (Concept cards are available for purchase from wvced.com.)

Figure 19 includes key information about the kinds of sentences. Organized in three columns -- simple, compound, and complex -- the chart provides visuals of D (dependent) and I (independent) clauses and the ways they can be combined to form sentences. It also provides most of the different sentence varieties with good, clear examples and elaborates on key issues. (A poster version of this chart is available for purchase from wvced.com.)

A Brief Overview

General Concepts for Teaching:

Term	Basic	Intermediate
declarative sentence	states an idea	
interrogative sentence	asks a question that requires an answer; ends in ?	
imperative sentence	commands; the subject is dropped and becomes understood "you"	
exclamatory sentence	spoken with great emotion or intensity; ends in !	
subject	who or what is doing the action	compound subject
predicate	contains verb plus its baggage	compound predicate
direct object		receives the action of the verb

Term	Basic	Intermediate
object of preposition		noun (or pronoun) that ends a prepositional phrase
clause	group of words with subject and its verb	
independent clause	clause that can stand by itself	
dependent clause		clause that cannot stand by itself
prepositional phrase	begins with preposition and ends with noun (or pronoun)	can act as adjective or adverb
simple sentence	1 independent clause	
compound sentence	2 independent clauses joined by comma and coordinating conjunction	2 independent clauses joined by semi-colon; optional use of conjunctive adverb
complex sentence	1 independent clause and 1 (or more) dependent clauses - D,I and ID	1 independent clause and 1 (or more) dependent clauses - I with adjective/relative clause

Advanced Concepts To Be Taught As Appropriate:

Concept	Advanced
indirect object	tells to whom or for whom the action is done; found between verb and direct object
predicate adjective	follows linking verb and describes subject
predicate noun	follows linking verb and renames subject
compound-complex sentence*	2 independent clauses and 1 (or more) dependent clauses
adverb clause	dependent clause that describes a verb
adjective clause	dependent clause that describes a noun (or pronoun)
noun clause	noun (or pronoun) placed after another noun (or pronoun) to rename or describe it
infinitive	to + pure form of verb; used as noun, adjective, or adverb (verbal)
gerund	verb ending in -ing used as noun (verbal)
participle	verb used as adjective (often ending in -ing or -ed) (verbal)

* Of the advanced concepts above, compound-complex is the most useful and important to address when students are ready for it.

A Word About Noun Function:

Nouns (and by association pronouns) can serve five different functions in sentences. As students learn about these functions, it is important to associate each new role with the previously learned ones. *Figure 20* below shows the different roles nouns can play. Below it is a sentence including all the roles (underlined and directly below each role and its definitions). Subsequent pages elaborate on each function:

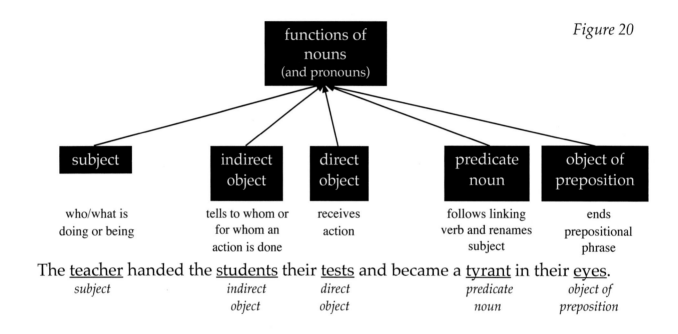

Figure 20

Four Kinds of Sentences

Overview:

By far the most common kind of sentence is the statement, called the **declarative sentence**. These sentences *state* or *declare* an idea. Most expository writing is comprised of declarative sentences:

> I had no milk for my cereal this morning.   The elevator stopped at the top floor.
>
> F.B.I. stands for the Federal Bureau of Investigation.
>
> Will plays defense for the school's football team while Jack plays offense.

Interrogative sentences are questions and end with a question mark:

> Why are you sleepy?   What were the causes of the Civil War?
>
> Is there a doctor in the house?   Which movie should we see this afternoon?

Imperative sentences are commands. Often, the subject is an understood <u>you</u>.

> Christopher, watch your mouth.   Eat your dinner.
>
> Please go to the post office before you head home.
>
> Consider this your final warning.

Exclamatory sentences show strong emotion and typically end with an exclamation mark.

> That's amazing!   The ship is sinking!
>
> I aced my test!   Jasmine's wallet is missing from her bedroom!

Focus primary attention on declarative sentences as they appear most frequently by far.

Common Core: The Common Core State Standards suggest that students

should be able to "produce and expand complete simple and compound declarative, interrogative, imperative, and exclamatory sentences in response to prompts" (grade 1).

declarative sentence

states an idea

examples: Melinda ate the muffin.
There is a bee caught in the fly trap.

declarative sentence

states an idea

I have read all the Harry Potter books.

We are allowed to watch only one hour of television each day.

On weekends my sister stays up later than I do.

Introduction:

- To be reviewed before teaching: capital letters, periods

- Define the term, writing it on the board. Include several examples.

- Hand students concept cards or have them create their own.

Application:

- Have students identify declarative sentences. (The instructor can do this by providing written examples or reading samples aloud or both.)

- Have students punctuate declarative sentences correctly and check that they begin with capital letters.

Subsequent Lessons (interrogative, imperative, and exclamatory sentences)

- Lessons should be similar in format and structure to the declarative sentence lesson. Do not commit too much time to these less important kinds of sentences, however. Introduce them, show students proper end punctuation, remind them that sentences begin with capital letters, and provide practice activities. Model concept cards are shown on this page.

- In the first and second grade, use the terminology *question*, *command*, and *exclamation*. As students enter third grade, begin to use the proper terminology interchangeably with the more common terms until students recognize and understand that *interrogative* means *question*, *imperative* means *command*, and *exclamatory* means *exclamation*.

interrogative sentence

asks a question that requires an answer; ends with a question mark

Who are you?

What is the capital of Nebraska?

How did the game go?

imperative sentence

commands; the subject is dropped and becomes an understood "you"

Clean up your room.

Please find a seat.

Consider yourself warned.

exclamatory sentence

spoken with great emotion or intensity; ends with an exclamation point

That really hurt!

Our team won the game!

This is the best field trip I've ever taken!

Suggested Exercises & Activities

Identification: Write a definition of each type of sentence:

imperative: _____

interrogative: _____

declarative: _____

exclamatory: _____

Sorting: Label each sentence as declarative (dec), imperative (imp), interrogative (int), or exclamatory (exc):

_____ This is a hot day!   _____ The doctor wore a lab coat.

_____ Eat your vegetables.   _____ That bug is enormous!

_____ Will you finish in time?   _____ Can you come out to play?

_____ The lamp needs a bulb.   _____ Run to the store for me.

Punctuation: Use the identity of the sentence to put end punctuation in each blank:

imperative: Do your homework or suffer the consequences_____

interrogative: Will you clean up the mess in the living room, please_____

declarative: The giraffe has trouble reaching water in the wild_____

exclamatory: That picture is beautiful_____

Sentence Generation: Ultimately, students must generate sentences containing every element they study. When they turn to sentence writing, you can engage them and develop their writing by providing parameters, including (a) minimum word count, (b) specific element required and/or located in particular position, and (c) specific content. That said, do not focus too much attention on sentence generation with the kinds of sentences:

- Write an interrogative sentence about your favorite food.   e.g., Can we have pizza?
- Write an exclamatory sentence about the weather.   e.g., Good gosh, it's stormy out!
- Write a declarative sentence about a chicken.   e.g., The chicken crossed the road.
- Write an imperative sentence about a chore.   e.g., Take out the trash, now.

Subjects & Predicates

Overview:

Every sentence has a subject. The subject is who or what is doing the action. Some methods define it as what the sentence is about, but this can be both misleading and confusing. Consider "The boy threw the ball." What makes <u>boy</u> the subject instead of <u>ball</u>? The boy is doing the throwing. <u>Ball</u> is the object or the thing being thrown. The subject, then, is doing the action. With linking verbs there is no action. Stick with subjects and their action verbs (predicates) first. Then, once students are comfortable with locating these important parts, they can turn to finding subjects and their linking verbs.

On the other hand, the predicate is what the subject is doing. It is always a verb and sometimes the only verb in the sentence. It would be nearly impossible to teach subjects without predicates or predicates without subjects. The two join together to form the core of every clause and of every sentence. Students can usually find predicates that are action verbs without too much difficulty. Consider these examples, where the <u>subject</u> is underlined and the *predicate* is italicized:

> The <u>Great Dane</u> *barked* ferociously at all passing cars.
>
> <u>Ursula</u> *biked* around the block in search of her friends.
>
> The strange young <u>woman</u> *looked* both ways three times before crossing the street.

Predicates that are linking verbs are a little more challenging to locate. If the predicate is linking (instead of action), it links the subject with the rest of the sentence. Students who have already practiced finding subjects and their action verbs will usually be able to transfer this knowledge of location over to subjects with linking verbs, provided they recognize the linking verbs themselves. Consider these examples, where the subject is underlined and the linking verb is italicized:

<u>John</u> *is* my brother.   <u>New Year's Eve</u> *will be* terrific.

The cranky <u>child</u> *was* in the seat behind me.

Though I rarely support rote memorization when it comes to writing, helping students become extremely comfortable with the most common linking verbs, both in isolation and in context, is often a good idea. At the very least, they should know the forms of the verb "to be" can serve as linking verb predicates. These include <u>am</u>, <u>is</u>, <u>are</u>, <u>was</u>, <u>were</u>, <u>be</u>, <u>being</u>, and <u>been</u>. <u>Predicate</u> is a somewhat abstract term to many students. Use it interchangeably with the term <u>main verb</u> so that students associate the two terms. Remember that every sentence has both a subject and a predicate; otherwise, it wouldn't be a sentence.

<u>Understood "you" as the subject</u>: One kind of sentence has an *understood* subject. In an imperative sentence, or command, the subject is an understood <u>you</u>. Consider these sentences:

Go to your room.   Eat your vegetables.

Run get some milk, please.   Redo this assignment for a better grade.

Stop yelling.   Pull over and come to a complete stop.

All of these sentences are imperatives, or commands, and all have the same subject -- a <u>you</u> that is not physically present in the sentence but is understood. With the exception of imperatives (commands), every sentence *requires* a subject that is physically present. This is a good understanding for students to have. Since subjects are the who or what of a sentence, they are always nouns or pronouns -- more good information to share.

Kinds & Categories:

Simple subject: The simple subject is the noun or pronoun doing the action. Most of the time in English, the subject precedes the main verb (or predicate).   S———P

Simple predicate: The simple predicate is the action of the subject. It is sometimes a single verb but can also be a main verb with its helping verbs. The simple subjects in the examples below are underlined while the simple predicates are italicized:

<u>John</u> *went* to the store.   Who is doing the "wenting?" John.

<u>Elijah</u> *doesn't like* me much.   Who is doing the "not liking?" Elijah.

The whiny <u>baby</u> *kept* us awake.   Who is doing the "kepting?" The baby.

The <u>table</u> *broke* into pieces.   What broke? The table.

This verb-questioning technique will make students chuckle or even look at you a little funny, but it will also help them learn to use the predicate to find the subject.

Compound subject: Sometimes, the subject is two or more nouns or pronouns that share the action. Below, several examples are at left, and a figure representing this compound subject structure is at right:

<u>Marcia</u> and <u>Shane</u> got married last summer.

The <u>trees</u> and <u>shrubbery</u> bent in the fierce wind.

<u>Dogs</u> and <u>cats</u> are not allowed in the theater.

The enormous gray <u>elephant</u> and the incredibly small <u>mouse</u> headed towards the
    nearby water.

$$S \underset{S}{\overset{}{>}} P$$

Compound predicate: Sometimes, the subject is doing two different things and therefore is the actor or doer for two different simple predicates or verbs. Examples are at left, and a picture of this compound predicate structure is at right:

The coach *hollered* and *screamed* at his team during practice.

My father *cooked* and *cleaned* in preparation for the party.

Jake *searched* everywhere and finally *found* his license underneath the seat cushion.

$$S \underset{P}{\overset{P}{<}}$$

Compound subject and predicate: Occasionally, there is both a compound subject *and* a compound predicate in the same sentence. Consider the examples below. Once again, the subjects are underlined while the predicates are italicized. A figure of this structure is to the right of the examples:

The <u>boy</u> and his <u>friend</u> *played* kickball and *jumped* in rain puddles on Saturday.

<u>Houses</u> and <u>stores</u> *were designed* and *built* in record time after the storm.

<u>You</u> and your <u>brother</u> *must clean* your rooms and *take out* the trash before dark.

S ⟍   ⟋ P

  ✕

S ⟋   ⟍ P

In the first sample sentence above, both the boy *and* his friend played *and* jumped. If the boy played and the friend jumped, the meaning would be quite different, and the sentence would have neither a compound subject nor a compound predicate.

Complete subject: The term complete subject refers to the simple subject and the words used to describe it. Usually, the split between complete subject and complete predicate occurs just before the main verb. Consider these examples, where the complete subject is underlined and the simple subject is in bold:

<u>The elderly **man**</u> sold his antique car for $100,000.

<u>**Roger**, my best friend,</u> had homework to finish and couldn't come out to play.

<u>The ugliest **dog** on the street</u> belongs to my neighbor, Sue.

Complete predicate: The complete predicate is the verb plus the baggage it carries. Consider the following sentences, where the complete predicate is italicized and the simple predicate is in bold:

Angela ***was** as tired as a dog.*

The guard ***drew** his pistol to defend the important official.*

The helicopter ***landed** on the roof of the building.*

Mrs. Jones *firmly **told** the class to sit down.*

While the terms *complete subject* and *complete predicate* are found in teaching materials about writing, do not spend too much time on them. The skill your students need in order to move forward is the ability to locate, and ultimately generate, simple subjects and their simple predicates. These words form the core of every sentence; therefore, they are necessary for most every step of good sentence writing instruction.

Notes: (Distinguishing between compound subjects/predicates and compound sentences)

Compound subjects and predicates are important to understand, particularly when students start discovering and creating compound *sentences*. Otherwise, there is likely to be confusion between the two. When a sentence has a compound subject, *both* subjects share the *same* verb. When a sentence has a compound predicate, *both* predicates (or main verbs) share the *same* subject. If both the subject and the predicate are compound, both subjects share both verbs.

compound subject:

> *The college student and his older sister stepped out of the rain.*

In this example the college student and his older sister are the subjects, and they are both stepping out of the rain. Hence, this is a single clause and a simple sentence, but it contains a compound *subject*.

compound predicate:

> *John ran out to his car in the hot summer heat and found his water bottle under the seat.*

In this example John is the only subject, and he is doing both the running and the finding. Hence, this is a single clause and a simple sentence, but it contains a compound *verb*.

compound sentence:

> *John ran out to his car in the hot summer heat, but his water bottle was nowhere to be found.*

John ran is the subject/predicate of the first clause while bottle was is the subject/predicate of the second. Since there are two separate subject/predicate pairs, the sentence contains two separate, independent clauses and is considered a compound sentence. More on this topic can be found in the compound sentence section of this text.

subject

who or what is doing the action

examples: John went to the store.
The door slammed in the wind.

subject

who or what is doing the action

John went to the store.

The door slammed in the wind.

advanced:
compound subject

John and Mary went to the store.

Introduction:

- To be reviewed before teaching: noun, pronoun, predicate (taught simultaneously)

- Define the term, writing it on the board. Include several examples.

- Hand students concept cards or have them create their own.

Application:

- Have students identify subjects from written sentences.

- Have students match complete subjects to complete predicates.

predicate

what the subject is doing
(contains a verb plus its baggage)

examples: John <u>went to the store</u>.
The door <u>slammed in the wind</u>.

---

predicate

what the subject is doing
(contains verb plus its baggage)

John <u>went to the store</u>.

The door <u>slammed in the wind</u>.

advanced:
compound predicate

John <u>went to the store and bought some eggs</u>.

Introduction:

- To be reviewed before teaching: verb, action verb, linking verb, helping verb, subject (taught simultaneously)

- Define the term, writing it on the board. Include several examples.

- Hand students concept cards or have them create their own.

Application:

- Have students identify predicates from written sentences.

- Have students match complete subjects to complete predicates.

Subsequent Lessons

- Basic Lessons: compound subjects & predicates

    imperatives and the understood "you"

    simple subjects versus complete subjects

    simple predicates versus complete predicates

- Note: A lesson helping students distinguish between compound subjects and verbs and compound sentences is discussed in the Overview information of this section and again, in more depth, in the Compound Sentence section later in this text.

Suggested Exercises & Activities

Identification: Identify subjects and/or predicates in sentences. A few examples follow:

- Underline the <u>simple subjects</u> in the sentences below:

    The young boy slipped on the ice.

    The cute puppy never barked at strangers.

- Underline the <u>complete subjects</u> in the sentences below:

    The bustling city's congested highways caused many accidents.

    My French exam was extremely difficult.

    The elderly man ran in a New York marathon.

- Underline the <u>subjects</u> in the sentences below. (Do not underline the *complete* subjects.) Be careful! The sentences contain compound subjects:

    Flight attendants and pilots board the plane before passengers.

    Long days and even longer nights left us exhausted.

    Mary and Sue loved to ride their bikes in the park after school.

    The students and their parents gathered in the gymnasium for convocation.

- Underline the <u>simple predicates</u> in the sentences below:

    The whiny infant disrupted the long flight.

    An angered lion attacked the safari group.

- Underline the <u>complete predicates</u> in the sentences below:

    The video game kept the boy occupied for hours.

    The unfair teacher gave a pop quiz first thing Monday morning.

    The helpful teacher went to purchase pencils at the store.

- Underline the <u>predicates</u> in the sentences below. (Do not underline the *complete* predicates.) Be careful! The sentences contain compound predicates:

    The phone rang but went unheard by its owner.

    The baby sitter gathered up the toys and stored them in the child's toy chest.

My dentist cleaned my teeth and checked them for cavities.

Sorting: Identify subjects and/or predicates from other elements in the lists below:

- Circle words or groups of words that could be subjects:

the baby polar bear	jogs quickly	under the old wooden bridge
in my mother's room	doesn't have a chance	we
us	the man in black	the used laptop

- Circle words or groups of words that could be predicates:

ran down the street	at the grand piano	the hilarious driver
three seats in a row	drinks a lot of water	dove into the ocean
under the blankets	cleans our house	an old top hat

Fill In The Blank: Fill in each blank with an appropriate subject or predicate:

- Fill in a single word subject:

_____ went to the closet to grab her coat.

_____ landed the plane safely on the runway.

_____ and _____ went to the movies together.

- Fill in complete subjects of more than two words:

_____ sat on his front porch and waved at passersby.

_____ stepped out for a one hour lunch break.

_____ shot a three-pointer to win the league game.

- Fill in a single word predicate:

The green Martian _____

My witty Uncle Ned _____

The angry crocodile _____

- Fill in complete predicates of at least five words:

The principal of our school _____

My angry sister _____

The purple fish _____

Matching: Match the subject with its predicate:

The shy boy   knocked things over with his spiked tail.

The unruly dragon   had trouble making new friends.

The evil gunman   drew his pistols and fired on the brave superhero.

Sentence Combining: Students can be asked to combine two related sentences:

- to create a compound subject

  Mark went to the store. Mary went with him.

  The truck ran into the car. The car ran into the truck.

- to create a compound predicate

  Andrew started his car. He pulled out of his driveway afterwards.

  The truck swerved on the ice. It ran into a tree.

  The doctor entered the room. He talked reassuringly to the patient.

Sentence Generation: Ultimately, students must generate sentences containing every element they study. When they turn to sentence writing, you can engage them and develop their writing by providing parameters, including (a) minimum word count, (b) specific element required and/or located in particular position, and (c) specific content:

- Write a sentence of at least ten words with a subject described by two adjectives.

  e.g., The *ancient maple tree* covered our yard with leaves this weekend.

- Write a sentence with a simple subject in the third position.

  e.g., The old *engine* roared to life after we turned it over a few times.

- Write a question with an abstract noun as the subject.

  e.g., Why is *peace* so hard to find?

- Write a sentence with "Harry Potter" as the subject.

  e.g., *Harry Potter* has two close friends, Ron and Hermione, who travel with him on many of his adventures.

- Write a sentence with "Teddy Roosevelt" as the subject.

  e.g., *Teddy Roosevelt* was an outstanding president, who also had a passion for hunting.

- Write a sentence of at least twelve words with "pool" as the subject..

    e.g., The *pool* was filled with leaves and beetles before we got out the net to clean it.

- Write a sentence of at least eleven words with a complete predicate that includes an adverb.

    e.g., I *stepped really quickly from the hot pavement into the cool water of the pool.*

- Write a sentence of at least twelve words with "ate" as the predicate.

    e.g., The piranha *ate* three rats, a small bird, and anything else we fed it.

- Write a sentence about President Reagan that uses the verb "spoke."

    e.g., *Ronald Reagan*, who was an actor before becoming president, *spoke* extremely well to the people of America.

- Write a sentence with the verb "played" that includes the word "basketball."

    e.g., We *played basketball* every Saturday afternoon once we had finished our lunch.

- Write a sentence with "Civil War" as the subject and "divided" as the predicate.

    e.g., The *Civil War divided* the nation, and it took many years for the wounds to heal.

- Include "ran," "biked," and "swam" as compound predicates in a sentence.

    e.g., The triathlon athletes *ran*, *biked*, and *swam* before finishing their Olympic race.

Direct Objects

Overview:

Nouns (and pronouns) serve five different functions in sentences. We have already covered subjects; direct objects receive the action in a sentence. They are located after an action verb and answer the questions who or what. Consider these examples, where the verb is underlined and the direct object is italicized:

John <u>ate</u> the *candy*. (ate what? the candy)

We <u>bought</u> *chicken*, *rice*, and *vegetables* for dinner.

(bought what? chicken, rice, and vegetables)

Sharon <u>found</u> her *mouth guard* on her bedside table. (found what? her mouth guard)

Bartholomew <u>met</u> his future *boss* yesterday over a nice lunch. (met whom? his boss)

All of these sentences follow a similar format:

Subject + Action Verb + Direct Object

This should come as no surprise. Remember that direct objects follow action verbs and answer the questions who or what.

direct object

receives the action of a verb
(noun or pronoun answering who or what)

examples: John hit the <u>ball</u>.
Mary and Susan ate <u>salad</u>.

---

direct object

receives the action of a verb
(noun or pronoun answering who or what)

John hit the <u>ball</u>.

Mary and Susan played <u>soccer</u>.

advanced: direct objects can also be noun phrases and clauses

Sue loves <u>working on her project</u>.

Introduction:

- To be reviewed before teaching: noun, pronoun, action verb, subject

- Define the term, writing it on the board. Include several examples.

- Hand students concept cards or have them create their own.

- Explain that nouns (and pronouns) have different functions in a sentence. All sentences must have subjects; direct objects are optional.

Application:

- Have students identify direct objects from written sentences.

- Have students match complete subjects and simple predicates to direct objects.

Suggested Exercises & Activities

Identification: Identify direct objects in sentences. A few examples follow:

- With support: Underline the subject, and then circle the action verb. Finally, underline the direct object twice:

    Ella whacked the ball with her bat.

    Christian ran the track each morning before practice.

    Under cover of darkness, the spy climbed the wall and entered the compound.

- With less support: Underline any direct object twice. Remember, many sentences do not have direct objects, and only sentences with action verbs can contain them.

    She is exhausted after her long flight. (linking verb - no direct object)

    My brother passed the difficult test. (action verb - direct object - test)

    My brother swam in our pond this morning. (action verb but no direct object)

    At the game Taylor intercepted a pass. (action verb - direct object - pass)

    The family ate chicken at the restaurant. (action verb - direct object - chicken)

Matching: Match each subject to an appropriate predicate and direct object:

A friendly truck driver	sampled	the gauges on her dashboard.
The plump chef	cheerfully honked	every dish he prepared.
The inexperienced pilot	carefully checked	his horn at the cheering children.

Fill In The Blank: Fill in each blank with an appropriate direct object or objects:

- Fill in the direct object:

    Andrew ate _____ for supper.

    Sue hit a _____ to win the softball game.

    In early December mom bought _____ for members of our family.

- Fill in the direct objects:

    I will buy _____, _____, and _____ at the store tomorrow morning.

The captain ordered the _____ and fired the first _____

_____.

Sentence Combining: Students can be asked to combine two related sentences:

- to create a direct object

  Mark got it. It was a new suitcase.

  The elderly woman really had a need. Her need was a new pair of shoes.

- to create a compound direct object

  Mark bought some eggs. Mark also bought some bacon.

  My sister, Irma, found her socks. She also found her shoes.

Sentence Generation: Ultimately, students must generate sentences containing every element they study. When they turn to sentence writing, you can engage them and develop their writing by providing parameters, including (a) minimum word count, (b) specific element required and/or located in particular position, and (c) specific content:

- Write a sentence of at least ten words with a direct object.

  e.g., The train operator stopped the *train* because of an accident up ahead on the track.

- Write a sentence with a direct object in the ninth position.

  e.g., My friend who lives in Alaska visits her *grandmother* here each summer.

- Write a sentence of at least ten words with a compound verb and two direct objects.

  e.g., Christian ate his chicken *sandwich* and drank a *rootbeer* before riding the roller coaster.

- Write a question with a pronoun as the direct object.

  e.g., Who bought *it* for him?

- Write a sentence with "British" as the direct object.

  e.g., The Americans finally defeated the *British* in the Revolutionary War.

- Use "Thomas Edison" as the subject and "light bulb" as the object in a sentence of at least thirteen words.

  e.g., *Thomas Edison* invented the *lightbulb*, which has revolutionized the way we live our lives.

Prepositional Phrases

Overview:

In order for a word to be a preposition, it must begin a phrase. Words such as <u>under</u>, and <u>through</u> are only prepositions when they begin phrases such as these:

<u>around</u> the corner   <u>through</u> the woods   <u>next to</u> the enormous ant

<u>under</u> the table   <u>beside</u> me   <u>by</u> Rick Riordan

Like all prepositional phrases, the ones above, all begin with <u>prepositions</u> and end with <u>nouns</u> (or the words that can stand for nouns, <u>pronouns</u>). Here's a template:

Preposition + (Articles/Adjectives) + Noun/Pronoun

Each of the nouns and pronouns in the examples above is the object of a preposition, yet another job (like subject and direct object) that a noun can have. No matter how long it is, no matter where in a sentence it exists, every prepositional phrase ends with one of these objects of a preposition. In the sentences below, each <u>preposition</u> is underlined and the *object of the preposition* is in italics:

Dana wore her hair <u>in</u> long, tight *braids* and tucked <u>under</u> a baseball *cap*.

The woman who stood guard <u>at</u> the castle *gate* scared the village families, who remained <u>off</u> the cobblestone *streets* whenever they could.

Each of the prepositional phrases in the sentences above begins with a preposition and ends with the noun or pronoun serving as the object of that preposition. Here's the first template with that slight modification:

Preposition + (Articles/Adjectives) + Object of Preposition

A list of prepositional phrases for reading and writing is on page 298.

Here's a general, easy-to-remember rule for punctuating *initial* prepositional phrases:

3 words or fewer, no comma: At the party we celebrated with our friends.

4 words or more, comma: In the antique oak desk, we found a stack of old letters.

Kinds & Categories:

Advanced: There are two different kinds of prepositional phrases: adjective and adverb.

| adjective | describes a noun (or pronoun) | The oak tree <u>in the woods</u> overshadows most others <u>in the area</u>. |
| adverb | describes a verb | I ran <u>in the woods</u>. |

Only students beyond a basic level of inquiry will find learning about the two kinds of prepositional phrases useful. However, it is important to realize that the terms <u>adjective</u> and <u>adverb</u> refer not just to words but also phrases and clauses. Words, phrases, and clauses serve to describe nouns/pronouns and therefore are *adjectival*. Likewise, words, phrases, and clauses serve to describe verbs and therefore are *adverbial*. Clauses serving these functions are described later in this text. However, sentence expanding almost always involves one of these forms, even when the terminology is not used:

core sentence:	The chef makes the best sandwich.
adjective:	The *elderly* chef makes me the best sandwich.
adjective phrase:	The chef *at the deli* makes me the best sandwich.
adjective clause: (also relative clause)	The chef, who has owned the corner deli for twenty years, makes me the best sandwich.
adverb:	The chef *usually* makes me the best sandwich.
adverb phrase:	*With skilled hands* the chef makes me the best sandwich.
adverb clause:	*Whenever I visit the corner deli*, the chef makes me the best sandwich.

Common Core: The Common Core State Standards suggest that students

should be able to "form and use prepositional phrases" (grade 4) and "explain the function of phrases in general and their function in specific sentences" (grade 7).

prepositional phrase

group of words that begins with a
preposition and ends with a noun
(or pronoun)

examples: at the lake
on the street
through the years

prepositional phrase

begins with a preposition and ends with a noun (or pronoun)

under the boardwalk   behind the old house

advanced: kinds of prepositional phrases
adverb phrase: describes a verb

We drove <u>around the corner</u>.

adjective phrase: describes a noun (or pronoun)

The store <u>around the corner</u> is closed.

Introduction:

- To be reviewed before teaching: noun, pronoun, preposition

- Define the term, writing it on the board. Include several examples.

- Hand students concept cards or have them create their own.

- Explain that prepositional phrases all begin with prepositions and end with nouns or pronouns.

Application:

- Have students identify prepositional phrases from written sentences.

- Have students write prepositional phrases using a chart or list of prepositions for reference.

object of preposition

noun (or pronoun) that ends a
prepositional phrase

examples: John went to the <u>store</u>.
The roof of the <u>car</u> was crushed
by the <u>branch</u> of the old oak <u>tree</u>.

object of preposition

noun (or pronoun) that ends a prepositional phrase

John went to the <u>store</u>.

The door of the <u>greenhouse</u> banged in the <u>wind</u>.

Come sit by <u>me</u>.

Introduction:

- To be reviewed before teaching: noun, pronoun, subject, direct object

- Define the term, writing it on the board. Include several examples.

- Hand students concept cards or have them create their own.

- Remind students that they have already covered subjects and direct objects. Object of a preposition is yet another role that a noun (or pronoun) can play.

Application:

- Have students identify prepositional phrases and objects of prepositions from written sentences.

- Have students write prepositional phrases in isolation.

Subsequent Lesson (adjective and adverb phrases)

- Advanced: Review adjectives, adverbs, and prepositional phrases with your students. Then, layer in this new information. There are two kinds of prepositional phrases: adjectival (acting as an adjective to describe a noun or pronoun) and adverbial (acting as an adverb to describe a verb).

In most instances prepositional phrases functioning as adjectives immediately follow the noun they describe. Consider these sentences, which contain prepositional phrases that serve as adjectives:

The game *of monopoly* takes hours.   The police officer *behind the car* took aim.

Mac, the boy *with the best three point average*, helped us win the game *against our rivals* last night.

The batteries were the wrong size *for my particular model*.

The attendant *at the gas station* helped the man *with the rental car* figure out where the oil gauge was.

The cyclops *on the island* smacked his chops hungrily.

Prepositional phrases serving as adverbs typically describe verbs. They can be in a variety of locations in the sentence. One helpful thing to know is that any introductory prepositional phrase is always adverbial:

I ran *with all my might*.   If we eat *at Wendy's*, the kids will eat free.

On a blanket under the stars, the couple talked *of their dreams for the future*. (This sentence has four prepositional phrases -- 2 at the beginning and 2 at the end -- all describing the verb <u>talked</u>.)

Once they understand this information, have students identify prepositional phrases in sentences and then mark them as either adjective or adverb. Have them draw an arrow from the phrase to the specific word it modifies.

188

Identification: Identify prepositional phrases in sentences. A few examples follow:

- With support: Remember, each prepositional phrase begins with a preposition and ends with a noun or pronoun. The number in parentheses at the end of each sentence indicates how many phrases you must find. Underline each prepositional phrase in the sentences below:

   In my mother's house, we always eat dinner at six o'clock. (2)

   We took the subway to Time's Square and saw many sights near the subway stop. (2)

   After the game we went out for pizza. (2)

   You should sit beside me at school this morning. (2)

- With less support: Put parentheses around each prepositional phrase.

   I forgot the name of the book that she borrowed from me.

   During the night a dead branch fell onto the roof and startled me.

   With no thought for others, the child screamed at the top of her lungs.

   We used the canister of spray paint to cover the gym wall in blue.

- In the context of a paragraph: Underline the prepositional phrases in this paragraph:
   On the fourth of July, people in the United States of America celebrate our independence from British rule. Many Americans have neighborhood cookouts on their streets. Typically, they purchase smaller fireworks from roadside stands and stores to light in their backyards. Large organizations also host professional fireworks shows, and people gather to see them. Some families hang American flags from their houses because of their pride in our country. The fourth of July is an enjoyable celebration that remembers a time of great pride in our country.

Sorting: Decide whether the underlined noun is the object of a preposition or a direct object:

Jake ate the pizza on his <u>couch</u>.   Martha drank <u>lemonade</u> because she was thirsty.

The frog bathed in the <u>sun</u>.   Andrew bought <u>eggs</u> and <u>bacon</u> at the store.

Matching: Match the sentence parts to create logical sentences.

prep. phrase	article/adjective	subject	verb	prep. phrase
In the schoolyard	the furry	woman	travelled	with a lot of machinery.
Under the bush	the unhappy	brother	supervised	with its paws.
Around the corner	the ancient	children	scratched	to France.
With my parents	a construction	rabbit	cried	with an iron fist.
On the farm	my older	company	cleared	for their mommies.

Positioning: Often, a specific prepositional phrase could exist in more than one location in a sentence. Activities helping students discover and practice with this concept will increase sentence variety:

- *prepositional phrases - relocate the phrase*

A friendly man sat quietly talking <u>beside me</u>.

<u>In the clock</u> a thousand gears worked together.

The troll lived <u>under the bridge</u> with his evil brother.

<u>On the long and winding road</u>, my friend and I grew closer because of our shared experiences.

The boy played cops and robbers <u>with his friends</u>.

- *prepositional phrases - place: draw an arrow at each point where the phrase could be placed.*

on the attic staircase:	I left the decorations in an old box.
with my hilarious aunts:	You are never sure when the fun will begin.
with purple hair:	The boy and the girl ran into their mother at the mall.
on the fast track:	Roger was headed towards a promotion.
in my brother's Toyota:	I learned how to drive standard.

Fill In The Blank: Fill in each blank with an appropriate object of a preposition:

- Choose a good object of a preposition for each blank:

  Chase slept in his _____ that night.

  I turned on the light in the _____ so I could find my way.

  Under the _____ I found my missing key.

- Fill in appropriate objects of prepositions for each sentence:

  Marcus found a tree for _____ at the edge of the _____

  _____.

  Eliza looked at her _____ beside the _____

  _____.

Sentence Generation: Ultimately, students must generate sentences containing

every element they study. When they turn to sentence writing, you can engage them and
develop their writing by providing parameters, including (a) minimum word count, (b)
specific element required and/or located in particular position, and (c) specific content:

- Write a sentence with an object of a preposition in the sixth position.

  e.g., The experienced pitcher at the *game* pitched a no-hitter until the fifth inning.

- Write a question with an object of a preposition. Use the noun "recital."

  e.g., Can you get to the *recital* if Elizabeth is out of town?

- Write a sentence of at least twelve words with an abstract noun as the object of a
  preposition. Use the verb "announced."

  e.g., In the heat of the *moment*, the candidate announced that he would run in the twelfth
  district for the *rights* of all people.

- Write a sentence of at least twelve words with "Percy Jackson" as the object of the
  preposition. Use the noun "Annabelle."

  e.g., Annabelle has a crush on *Percy Jackson* in the Lightning Thief Series.

Indirect Objects

Overview:

An indirect object is a noun (or pronoun) that tells to whom or for whom an action is done. In other words the indirect object *gets* the direct object. While direct objects can function without indirect objects, the inverse is not true. The indirect object always falls between an action verb and a direct object. Consider these examples, where the action verb is <u>underlined</u>, the *indirect object* is italicized, and the **direct object** is in bold:

Tony <u>showed</u> *Mark* a different **way** to the store.

Our history teacher <u>handed</u> *Marcie* the wrong **test**.

Granny <u>bought</u> my *sister* a new **jacket** for her birthday.

Here's a template for indirect objects:

Subject + Action Verb + Indirect Object + Direct Object

Indirect objects occur infrequently. In addition, understanding them won't do much to enhance student writing. A brief introduction and some quick identification drills come first. Then, providing some verbs that readily take indirect objects, have students generate sentences containing indirect objects.

indirect object

noun (or pronoun) tells to whom or for whom an action is done (always falls between the verb and a direct object)

examples: John hit <u>me</u> the ball.
We gave the <u>waitress</u> a hefty tip.
Abraham Lincoln gave his <u>country</u> the Gettysburg Address.

indirect object

tells to whom or for whom an action is done (always falls between the verb and a direct object; can be put into a prepositional phrase after the direct object as a test)

John hit <u>me</u> the ball.

Christine sent <u>Mary and Trey</u> the e-mail.

We bought <u>the neighborhood postal carrier</u> a gift certificate.

Introduction:

- To be reviewed before teaching: noun, pronoun, action verb, direct object, object of a preposition

- Define the term, writing it on the board. Include several examples.

- Hand students concept cards or have them create their own.

- Remind students that they have already covered subjects, direct objects, and objects of prepositions. Indirect object is yet another role that a noun (or pronoun) can play.

- Show students that indirect objects always fall between an action verb and a direct object.

- Show students that indirect objects can be placed into a prepositional phrase after the direct object as a test. Here is an example:

  I handed Mike the papers. can be turned into I handed the papers *to Mike*. In the first, *Mike* serves as an indirect object. In the second, *Mike* is the object of a preposition.

Since this second construction is plausible, the *Mike* in the first sentence is, indeed, the object of a preposition.

Application:

- Have students identify indirect objects from written sentences. For each indirect object, they should first locate the action verb and the direct object.

- Provide students with simple subjects and predicates and have them add indirect and direct objects to those barebones sentences. Be careful to use predicates that work well with indirect objects (e.g., buy, get, cook, keep, bring, make, pour, save, find).

- Have students match complete subjects and simple predicates to indirect and direct objects.

Suggested Exercises & Activities

Identification: Identify indirect objects in sentences. A few examples follow:

- With support: Remember, each indirect object falls between an action verb and a direct object. There <u>must</u> be a direct object to have an indirect object. First, find and underline the direct object. Then, put a circle around the indirect object:

    I handed Susie my passport for safekeeping.

    My teacher sent me an e-mail about the assignment.

    Just before dusk the King granted his son a favor.

- With less support: Circle the indirect object in each sentence. Some of the sentences may not have indirect objects:

    Jon gave Charisse a Valentine's Day Card.

    The Godfather made many people offers they couldn't refuse.

    Jake's parents offered their son an alternative to his punishment.

    Andrea bought several items from the store, including eggs, bacon, bread, and milk.

    We gave our grandparents a nice present for their anniversary.

Sorting: Nouns can play many roles. Decide whether each noun is a subject, a direct object, an indirect object, or the object of a preposition:

Abraham Lincoln gave <u>us</u> some fine speeches.

At the top of the <u>hill</u>, the troops gathered to view the valley.

The first man on the <u>moon</u>, Neil Armstrong said something that is still quoted today.

She jumped the <u>creek bed</u> in her rush to escape the villains.

The <u>key</u> was rusty and no longer fit into the lock.

Fill In The Blank: Fill in each blank with an appropriate indirect object or objects:

My parents bought _____ my first cell phone when I was fourteen.

Christy gave _____ the recipe that had been in her family for generations.

Sentence Generation: Ultimately, students must generate sentences containing every element they study. When they turn to sentence writing, you can engage them and develop their writing by providing parameters, including (a) minimum word count, (b) specific element required and/or located in particular position, and (c) specific content:

- Write a sentence of at least ten words with an indirect object. Use the verb "gave."

  e.g., My friends *gave me* a hard time when my mother drove me to school yesterday.

- Write a sentence of at least ten words with a compound indirect object. Use the verb "offered."

  e.g., The principal *offered Elizabeth and Chaivez* the *opportunity* to represent the school.

- Write a sentence with a verb in the future tense and an indirect object. Use the verb "earn."

  e.g., If I don't watch my sarcasm, it *will earn me* a trip to the principal's office.

- Write a sentence of at least nine words with you (your name) as the indirect object. Use the verb "gave."

  e.g., When the door slammed suddenly in the wind, it almost *gave* _____ a heart attack.

- Write a sentence with "Spain" as the indirect object. Use the verb "gave."

  e.g., The French *gave Spain* Louisiana as a result of the French & Indian War.

- Use "Henry Ford" as the subject, "car" as the direct object, and the "American people" as the indirect object in a sentence of at least fifteen words.

  e.g., Over a hundred years ago, *Henry Ford* gave *the American people* the *car*, and it has made a significant impact on transportation ever since.

- Use "the store owner" as the subject, "me" as the indirect object and "television" as the direct object in a sentence of at least ten words.

  e.g., The *store owner* sold *me* a new *television* for the living room today.

Predicate Nouns and Adjectives

Overview:

Understanding direct objects is an important pre-cursor to understanding predicate nouns. A direct object answers the question *who* or *what* in a sentence that contains an action verb. Consider this example, where the direct object is *snake*:

Mark killed the *snake*.

A predicate noun (also called predicate nominative) occurs in the same location and answers the same question -- *who* or *what*. However, the verb is a linking (or state of being) verb rather than one that expresses action. The predicate noun basically renames the subject noun. Consider these examples, where the <u>linking verb</u> is underlined and the *predicate noun* is italicized:

Mark <u>is</u> a *snake*. Susan <u>is</u> <u>becoming</u> a *team player*.

My sister <u>is</u> a *pig* when it comes to chocolate.

Hugo <u>was</u> a *lieutenant* in World War II.

A predicate adjective occurs in the same location -- directly after a linking verb -- but serves to describe rather than rename the subject noun or pronoun:

That wart <u>is</u> *ugly*. The girl <u>became</u> *embarrassed* when they laughed.

The shotgun <u>was</u> *unloaded*. The team <u>felt</u> *exhausted* after the championships.

Though the italicized words above are adjectives, they appear in an unusual location and are sometimes tricky for students to locate.

predicate noun and adjective

follows a linking verb and describes or renames the subject

examples:

Isabelle appears <u>excited</u>. (predicate adjective)

My headache is <u>worse</u>. (predicate adjective)

The Prime Minister was a <u>woman</u>. (predicate noun)

predicate noun & adjective

follows a linking verb and describes or renames the subject

Trey seems <u>exhausted</u>. (predicate adjective)

My cell phone is <u>broken</u>. (predicate adjective)

The pilot was a <u>woman</u>. (predicate noun)

The frog became a <u>prince</u>. (predicate noun)

Introduction:

- To be reviewed before teaching: noun, pronoun, adjective, linking verb, subject, direct object, object of a preposition, indirect object

- Define the term, writing it on the board. Include several examples.

- Hand students concept cards or have them create their own.

- Remind students that they have already covered subjects, direct objects, objects of prepositions, and indirect objects. Predicate noun is yet another role that a noun (or pronoun) can play.

- Remind students that they already know what adjectives are. Predicate adjectives are merely adjectives in a certain position -- after a linking verb.

Application:

- Have students identify predicate nouns and adjectives from written sentences. They should first locate the linking verbs in those sentences.

- Have students write sentences containing predicate nouns and adjectives.

Identification: Identify predicate nouns and predicate adjectives in sentences. A few examples follow:

- With support: Underline the subject, and then circle the linking verb. Finally, underline the predicate noun or adjective twice:

    Krista seemed exhausted by the morning's activities.

    By Friday the locker room smelled disgusting.

    She was an unwilling participant in our family games each Sunday.

    This recipe tastes delicious!

- With less support: Underline any predicate noun or adjective twice. Remember, many sentences do not have predicate nouns, and only sentences with linking verbs can contain them.

    She is exhausted after her long flight. (linking verb - predicate adjective)

    My brother passed the difficult test. (action verb - no predicate noun or adjective)

    My brother swam in our pond this morning. (action verb - no p.n. or p.a.)

    In the game Joseph was the real star. (linking verb - predicate noun)

    The governor was a lieutenant in the army for over five years. (linking verb - p.n.)

Sorting: Put one of the following in each blank to label the underlined sentence component: subject (S), direct object (DO), object of a preposition (OP), indirect object (IO), predicate adjective (PA), predicate noun (PN):

___ The <u>pianist</u> played beautifully, but the students didn't pay attention. (S)

___ My cousin, a *Star Wars* fan, was <u>Darth Vader</u> for Halloween. (PN)

___ You grab the <u>soda</u>, and I'll get the pizza. (DO)

___ Who spilled coffee on the *carpet*? (OP)

___ Everett dealt <u>Shade</u> a nice hand. (IO)

Matching: Match each subject + verb to an appropriate predicate noun or adjective

and its describers:

The foraging wolf was	loyal
My best friend is	extremely hungry
The blackberry pie smelled	delicious

The Olympic gold medalist is	an embarrassing relic.
Our nosey next door neighbor was	a thorn in my side.
The beat up old Ford is	a tremendous athlete.

Fill In The Blank: Fill in each blank with an appropriate predicate noun or

adjective:

- Fill in with predicate adjectives:

  The hot lunch smelled _____.

  Sue was truly _____, and so I asked her out.

  In the bitter cold, it feels _____ in the back bedroom.

- Fill in with predicate nouns:

  That boy remains a _____.

  It appears to be a _____ that you have a cell phone.

  He was appointed a _____ yesterday.

Sentence Combining: Students can be asked to combine two related sentences:

- to create a predicate noun

  Mark became something. That something was an A student.

  The boxer remained something. That something was a good fighter.

- to create a predicate adjective

  The dog appeared a certain way. That way is calm.

  The musician sounds a certain way. That way is awesome.

Sentence Generation:
Ultimately, students must generate sentences containing every element they study. When they turn to sentence writing, you can engage them and develop their writing by providing parameters, including (a) minimum word count, (b) specific element required and/or located in particular position, and (c) specific content:

- Write a sentence with a predicate noun.

  e.g., I am a new *man*!

- Write a sentence of at least ten words with a predicate adjective; include the word <u>lecture</u> in the sentence.

  e.g., I will remain *silent* during the *lecture*, but we should discuss it afterwards.

- Write a sentence with a predicate adjective in the seventh position about your favorite sweet.

  e.g., My family's fudge pie is quite *delicious*, and I eat it whenever I can.

- Write a sentence of at least ten words with two predicate adjectives.

  e.g., New York State is both *beautiful* and *cool* this time of year.

- Write a sentence about John Tyler with "the President" as the predicate noun.

  e.g., *John Tyler* was the first vice president who became *President* when the sitting president died.

- Use Jay Gatsby as the subject and the word "character" as the predicate noun in a sentence of at least thirteen words.

  e.g., *Jay Gatsby* is perhaps F. Scott Fitzgerald's most well known *character*.

Clause

Overview:

As I mentioned previously, the clause is the core concept in the Sentence Parts unit of study. Often, both teachers and students come to this study with a number of misconceptions. A clause is a group of words with a subject and its predicate (or mail verb). Nothing more and nothing less. Some can be sentences, and some can't. Some are two words long, and some are forty-two. Some contain prepositional phrases, and some do not. Consider these clauses, where the simple subject is underlined and the simple predicate (or main verb) is italicized:

my <u>brother</u> *is* on the baseball team   <u>Dr. Nelson</u> *cured* my headache

while <u>I</u> *was studying* for the final exam   though <u>Louann</u> *broke* her kneecap in a fall

All four of these examples are clauses. The top two could also be sentences. If you read them, you can tell they could stand by themselves. The bottom two, however, could not be sentences. They do not stand by themselves as complete thoughts. Nonetheless, each contains a subject and its predicate, and therefore each is a clause.

Clauses are the building blocks of all sentences. With the exception of coordinating conjunctions standing between independent clauses (the conjunctions in compound sentences), every single word in every single sentence exists within a clause. We are able to combine clauses in many different ways; this is how we achieve sentence variety and interest.

Kinds & Categories:

There are two different kinds of clauses: independent and dependent. They are covered in the next section of this text.

Common Core: The Common Core State Standards suggest that students should be able to "explain the function of clauses in general and their function in specific sentences" (grade 7).

---

clause

group of words with a subject and its predicate (verb)

examples: John went to the store
while the cat was sleeping
we love eating ice cream after dinner

clause

groups of words with a subject and its verb

John went to the store

if it starts raining

because we left early

Introduction:

- To be reviewed before teaching: subject, predicate
- Define the term, writing it on the board. Include several examples.
- Hand students concept cards or have them create their own.
- Explain that clauses are the building blocks of all sentences. The way we combine clauses gives us sentence variety and therefore reader interest.

Application:

- Have students sort clauses and phrases. Students should defend their answers by locating subjects and predicates in the groups of words they identify as clauses.

Suggested Exercises & Activities

Identification: Identify the clauses.

- Put a C next to each clause. Make sure each has a subject and predicate (verb):

    _____ the doctor found the man's problem

    _____ in my friend's house

    _____ when we found all of the missing toys

    _____ after I saw the latest movie in the series

    _____ during the long, boring game

Sorting: Sort the sentence parts.

- Mark each clause with a C and each phrase with a P. For each clause underline the subject once and the predicate (verb) twice:

    _____ on the roof of the old house   _____ until the team gathers

    _____ we should celebrate anyway   _____ before we sleep

    _____ Mark saw Andrew at the film   _____ in spite of the bitter cold

    _____ in the rain under cover of darkness

Matching: Match subjects and predicates to make appropriate clauses:

when the football game   got angry with the messy kids

the fifteen year old boy   went into overtime

the restaurant owner   played video games until 1 a.m.

after the dark clouds   got married in an outdoor wedding

the bride and groom   covered the sun entirely

the rap artist   rocked the house

Fill In The Blanks: Fill in the missing sentence part.

- missing predicate:

subject	predicate
the barnacle covered ship	_____
my older brother	_____
three runners in the race	_____

- missing subject:

subject	predicate
_____	ate three hotdogs at the game.
_____	shot a three pointer in overtime.
_____	should study more for tests.

Sentence Generation:

Sentence generation activities for this unit of study would serve to confuse rather than develop a student's sentence sense. Once students begin learning about the kinds of sentences, focus attention in this area.

Independent & Dependent Clauses

Overview:

There are two kinds of clauses: independent and dependent. Independent (or main) clauses *can* stand by themselves and serve as sentences. Dependent (or subordinate) clauses can*NOT* stand by themselves. They must lean on or *depend* on independent clauses in order to function. Most every word in every sentence is contained in a clause. (Coordinating conjunctions that join independent clauses in compound sentences are not included in the clause count, but they are the only exception.)

Use an **I** to identify and label an independent clause. Since the **I** has a base to it, it cannot be knocked over. Therefore, it represents independence -- or a clause that *can* stand by itself as its own sentence. Use a **D** to identify and label a dependent clause. Since the **D** has a rounded bottom, it can easily be knocked over. With its rounded bottom, it can*NOT* stand by itself.

Sentences are built using different patterns and combinations of I (independent) and D (dependent) clauses. Varying sentence structure is a key to writing at a more sophisticated level. A list of clauses for reading and writing is on page 299.

Model Eliciting Dialogue – What Makes A Clause Dependent?:

Teacher: [writes "after the game ended" on the board.] *Is this independent or dependent?*

Kennedy: It's dependent.

Teacher: Prove it to me.

Wes: It has a subject, "game," and a verb or predicate, "ended." That's why it's a clause.

Martha: *Yes, and it can't stand by itself. You need something before or after it to make the sentence complete.*

Teacher: *Excellent. Now, everybody put your thumbs over the word "after" on your paper. Read what is left. What just happened?*

Kennedy: *Wait, it's independent now!*

Teacher: *That's right. Good job. Try this one.* [writes "if we finish our homework" on the board, and students copy it] *This is a dependent clause. Now, cover the "if" with your thumbs. What just happened?*

Wes: *This one is independent now too.*

Teacher: [after using a few additional examples to cement the point.] *These thumb words are conjunctions. Without these conjunctions, the clauses become independent, and they cannot join with independent clauses to form sentences. These conjunctions, the ones that begin dependent clauses, are called subordinating conjunctions.*

Notes:

If students find independent clauses daunting, wait until the next lesson to introduce dependent clauses.

Independent clauses are sometimes called *main*, and dependent clauses are sometimes called *subordinate*. The terms are interchangeable, and M and S work equally well to help students visualize which clause is principal and which must rely on another for support.

Dependent clauses should not be studied until a student has reached at least third grade.

Do not underestimate the significance of clauses. Every sentence is made up of these building blocks. Students should be able to define and recognize both kinds of clauses and then create their own independently.

Common Core: The Common Core State Standards suggest that students should be able to explain "the function of phrases and clauses in general and their function in specific sentences" (grade 7). However, they will need to be able to understand and use them to build sentences before that.

independent clause

clause that can stand by itself

examples: John went to the store
I like ice cream
she found her shoe under the chair

independent clause

clause that _can_ stand by itself
(also called main clause)

John went to the store

pizza is my favorite food

the wind blew the shutter off the house

dependent clause

clause that cannot stand by itself

examples: while we were sleeping
if the time runs out
since Mary is really hungry

dependent clause

clause that _cannot_ stand by itself
(also called subordinate clause; begins with
subordinating conjunction or relative pronoun)

whenever I see your smiling face

since it started raining

although we raked all the leaves

Introduction:

- To be reviewed before teaching: subject, noun, predicate, verb, clause
- Ask students to help you define the words _independent_ and _dependent_. One good way to do this is by asking them to list things they can do independently and list separately

things they are dependent on others to do.

- Define independent clause, writing it on the board. Include several examples.
- Hand students concept cards or have them create their own.
- Explain that independent clauses can be sentences, but that they can also be combined with other clauses to form more sophisticated sentences.
- Explain that each sentence must contain at least one independent clause.
- Use an **I** like the one at right (serif font) to represent the independent clause. The **I** has a base and therefore cannot be toppled. It can stand by itself without support.

I

- Define dependent clause, writing it on the board. Include several examples.
- Hand students concept cards or have them create their own.
- Explain that dependent clauses do have subjects and predicates but cannot stand by themselves.
- Use a **D** like the one at right to represent the dependent clause. The **D** has a rounded bottom and therefore will fall over if not supported by an **I**. Dependent clauses (**D**'s) cannot stand by themselves as sentences. Adding dependent clauses (**D**'s) to independent clauses (**I**'s) creates sophisticated sentences.

D

- In other words, the **I** and the **D** are letter symbols for the concepts they identify.

Application:

- Have students sort independent and dependent clauses. Students should make sure that independent clauses stand by themselves and sound like complete thoughts. Dependent clauses, on the other hand, will sound as if there is something else to come. Remember, though, that both contain subjects and predicates. Once this portion of the lesson is mastered, move to the next element, which may in fact be in an entirely separate lesson.
- Dependent clauses begin with subordinating conjunctions. Over time with appropriate practice, students will learn to recognize these in the context of the sentences they read and write.

Suggested Exercises & Activities

Sorting: Sort the sentence parts.

- Mark each independent clause with an I and each dependent clause with a D:

    _____ since Will has already seen that movie

    _____ under the couch we found the missing money

    _____ apples make the best pies

    _____ because apples make the best pies

    _____ once you improve your grade in science

    _____ his freestyle time improved considerably

- Mark each independent clause (I) and each dependent clause (D). Also, mark any phrase (P).

    _____ the fan cooled the room considerably

    _____ while I slept on Saturday morning

    _____ I shut the closet door in my bedroom

    _____ in the back of the garage under those boxes

    _____ I told her not to slam the door

    _____ beside the oak tree in my back yard

Matching: Match the sentence parts.

- Match subjects and predicates to make appropriate independent clauses:

    the battery operated car   took me shopping at the new mall

    my best friend   ran out of juice after an hour of play

    I   filled my glass with fresh lemonade

- Match subjects and predicates to make appropriate dependent clauses:

    as soon as we   finish studying for our exams

    although lunch   gets a brand new cell phone

    even if my best friend   is just sandwiches and drinks

Sentence Generation:

Sentence generation activities for this unit of study would serve to confuse rather than develop a student's sentence sense. That said, either here or when students are introduced to complex sentences, it makes sense to ask students to generate dependent clauses in isolation. You will find more about this in the activities for complex sentences.

Simple Sentence

Overview:

A simple sentence is made up of one independent clause (**I**). As a clause, it has a subject and its predicate (verb). Take these examples:

> John went to the store.
>
> I found the key to the chest in the drawer of my desk.
>
> After the basketball game, we should go grab some dinner.

Sometimes, compound subjects, compound predicates, or both exist in a simple sentence. As long as there is only one subject-predicate *relationship,* it is a simple sentence. Consider these simple sentence examples:

> Andrea put her books in the car and then texted her friend.
>
> Mom and my brother went out to eat.
>
> The umpire and the coach yelled and screamed at each other throughout the game.

Students must thoroughly understand simple sentences before they can move to compound sentences.

Teachers often ask the difference between simple sentences and independent clauses. Independent clauses <u>can</u> be simple sentences. They can also be combined with other clauses to make more sophisticated sentences. Visually, the only difference is that an independent clause lacks a capital letter and end punctuation whereas a simple sentence does not.

It's important to understand that the term <u>simple</u> is about structure, not complexity. A simple sentence can be structurally interesting and sophisticated. At its core, however, it is made up of a single independent clause. Below are several sophisticated simple sentences:

Using the ancient, leather-bound book, the hunched over, elderly scholar explained early scientists' thoughts about the stars to her group of students.

Out of time with no energy remaining, the lone traveller considered his options and leapt from the cliff into the frothy sea.

John F. Kennedy, the thirty-fifth president of the United States, was assassinated in Dallas, Texas.

Common Core: The Common Core State Standards suggest that students should be able to "produce, expand, and rearrange complete simple and compound sentences" (grade 2).

simple sentence

1 independent clause

examples: John went to the store.
The door slammed in the wind.

simple sentence

1 independent clause

John went to the store.

We burned the toast.

I finished my homework before history class.

Introduction:

- To be reviewed before teaching: subject, predicate, independent clause

- Define the term, writing it on the board with an **I** like the one at right because the simple sentence is made up of 1 independent clause. Include several examples.

- Hand students concept cards or have them create their own. Include the **I** on the front of the cards.

I

- Explain that simple sentences are comprised of 1 independent clause. Also, draw attention to the fact that your examples, for the first time, begin with capitals and end with periods (or other end punctuation).

Application:

- Have students capitalize the first word and add appropriate end punctuation to independent clauses to turn them into sentences.

- Have students read simple sentences and identify their subjects and predicates.

- Have students read barebones simple sentences and expand them with adjectives, adverbs, and prepositional phrases.

- Have students locate subjects and predicates in simple sentences that have compound subjects and/or predicates.

Identification: Identify simple sentences. A few examples follow:

- Use an S to mark each simple sentence. Fragments should be marked with F. In the sentences underline the subject once and the predicate (verb) twice. All of these begin with capital letters and end with periods, but don't let that fool you!:

  _____ 1. From here to eternity.

  _____ 2. The fire fighter pointed the hose at the blazing second story windows.

  _____ 3. Pastries on the counter by the sink.

  _____ 4. Elizabeth parked her car near the main entrance to the mall.

  _____ 5. As soon as the bell rings to mark the end of the day.

- Use an S to mark each simple sentence. Fragments should be marked with F. In the sentences underline the subjects once and the predicates twice. Watch out for compound subjects and predicates. All of these begin with capital letters and end with periods, but don't let that fool you!:

  _____ 1. Lady Jessica and Duke Leto ruled House Atreides at the beginning of *Dune*.

  _____ 2. Although Huckleberry Finn is a moral and decent character.

  _____ 3. The pitcher fell from the shelf and shattered into a thousand pieces.

  _____ 4. We swam all day and gamed all night.

  _____ 5. Since mom asked us to carry the boxes to the basement.

Sorting: Unscramble the sentence parts to make logical sentences by numbering the blanks in the correct order. Then, write the finished product on the line below. Do not forget to capitalize the first word and use proper end punctuation (If students need more support, you may include end punctuation for the appropriate sentence part.):

1. _____ fearfully nibbled   _____ on grain in an open sack

   _____ a small gray mouse   _____ in the kitchen pantry

   Unscrambled sentence: _____

   _____

2. _____ my family and I   _____ at the local Target

   _____ an inexpensive trampoline   _____ luckily found

   Unscrambled sentence: _____

_____

Imitating: Imitate the given sentence or template.

- Read each simple sentence and notice the template it follows. Then, write a sentence of your own using the same format. Parts in parentheses are optional:

1. *(Article) noun*   *action verb*   *(article) common noun - direct object.*
   The   child   ate   steak.

   _____

2. *(Article) noun*   *verb*   *(article) noun*   *phrase.*
   The   boys   should quit   the game   at the playground.

   _____

3. *(Article) adjective(s)*   *noun*   *verb*   *(article) noun.*
   The   obnoxious   students   found   the teacher.

   _____

4. *Adjective plural noun*   *verb*   *prepositional phrase*
   Ugly   towers   stood   in the way.

   _____

5. *(Article) adjective*   *common noun*   *action verb*   *adverb*   *prepositional phrase.*
   (or Poss. Pro.)
   The   majestic   giraffe   chomped   quietly   on the hay.

   _____

6. *(Article) common*   *action*   *adverb*   *prepositional*   *prepositional*
   (or Pos. Pro.) noun   *verb*   *phrase*   *phrase.*
   The   building   swayed   eerily   from the impact   of the explosives.

   _____

- Read each simple sentence and identify its parts. Without benefit of a pre-written template, create a sentence that follows the same exact structure. Articles are optional:

216

1. The   dwarves   climbed   out of the caves.

    _____

2. An   antelope   leapt   the stream   near the overpass.

    _____

3. Scary   teenagers   roamed   on Halloween.

    _____

4. An   awesome   batter   swung   flawlessly   at the ball.

    _____

5. My   partner   lost   quickly   in the finals   of the tournament.

    _____

6. Next to the store,   the   high school   students   boldly   threw   rocks.

    _____

• Study each sentence template. Without benefit of a pre-written sample sentence, create a
  sentence that follows the same exact structure. Use articles as needed:

1. *(Article) noun   verb   prepositional phrase.*

    _____

2. *(Article) noun   verb   (article) noun phrase.*

    _____

3. *(Article) adjective(s)   noun   verb   (article) adjective   noun.*

    _____

4. *Adjective plural noun   verb   noun.*

    _____

5. *Article   common   action   adverb   prepositional   prepositional*
    (Pos. Pro.) noun   verb   phrase   phrase.

    _____

6. *Prepositional   prepositional   noun   verb   (article) noun   prepositional*
    phrase   phrase,   phrase.

    _____

Combining: Combine the sentences into one simple sentence. Omit words as necessary.

1. The dog barked.

   He did it ferociously.

   A burglar was there.

   The burglar was dressed in dark clothing.

   The burglar was tall.

   _____

2. The singer lost her voice.

   She was sad.

   She couldn't perform.

   The performance was for her fans in Houston.

   _____

3. The truck got a flat.

   It was on the interstate.

   The truck was a gas truck.

   The truck was an 18-wheeler.

   _____

4. The quarterback scored a touchdown.

   His touchdown was in front of thousands of fans.

   His touchdown was impressive.

   The quarterback was excited.

   _____

Tandem Writing: Tandem writing is more effective for sentences with more than one clause.

Sentence Generation: Ultimately, students must generate sentences containing every element they study. When they turn to sentence writing, you can engage them and develop their writing by providing parameters, including (a) minimum word count, (b) specific element required and/or located in particular position, and (c) specific content:

1. Write a simple sentence of at least 10 words.

    e.g., The jet took off fifteen minutes early and avoided thunderstorms from the east.

2. Write a simple sentence of at least 12 words with a compound predicate:

    e.g., Jamie studied for the challenging test and earned a 90 for his efforts.

3. Write a simple sentence on your favorite president.

    e.g., President Jimmy Carter was a peanut farmer before leading the nation.

4. Write a simple sentence on a movie you enjoy.

    e.g., *Shawshank Redemption* is based on a novella written by Stephen King.

5. Write a simple sentence with a compound subject about World War II.

    England and the U.S.A. remained allies through the conflicts of World War II.

6. Write a simple sentence of at least 10 words about birds.

    e.g., The ostrich is the largest and fastest land-moving bird in existence today.

Compound Sentences

Overview:

A compound sentence is made up of 2 independent clauses. Since independent clauses *can* stand by themselves, each side of a compound sentence could stand as its own sentence. Students can begin working with compound sentences as early as first grade, provided they are comfortable with simple sentences with their subjects and predicates (verbs). There are two ways to join independent clauses to make a compound sentence.

The most common is with a comma and a coordinating conjunction. Students often come to the table with misconceptions regarding commas and other punctuation. Begin with a clean slate regarding mid-sentence punctuation. This is the first sentence structure we have covered that requires mid-sentence punctuation. Use a comma immediately after the first independent clause, then a coordinating conjunction, and finally the second independent clause. A figure representing this is at right, and examples are below:

John went to the store, but it was closed.

I gathered vegetables from the garden, and my sister made a delicious cold soup.

$$I, \begin{matrix} \text{for} \\ \text{and} \\ \text{nor} \\ \text{but} \\ \text{or} \\ \text{yet} \\ \text{(so)} \end{matrix} I$$

There are only six useful coordinating conjunctions: for, and, nor, but, or, yet. Students find the mnemonic *fanboy* (each letter the first letter of one of these six words) useful in recalling these conjunctions. (See Notes for information about so as a coordinating conjunction.) Other conjunctions cannot serve the function of coordinating conjunctions. (Instructors sometimes incorrectly assume because is a coordinating conjunction; it actually serves as either a preposition or a subordinating conjunction, depending on the sentence.) These six conjunctions keep the clauses they join on equal footing; neither clause in a compound sentence takes priority or dominance over the other.

A more sophisticated method of joining compound sentences is the semi-colon (;). It replaces the comma and coordinating conjunction. It functions much like a period would; therefore, if you can't replace the semi-colon with a period in your sentence, you have probably used it incorrectly. Second graders are capable of handling basic compound sentences joined by semi-colons, but the examples they usually generate are overly simplistic. Sophisticated compound sentences of this type often include conjunctive adverbs immediately following the semi-colon. These transitional adverbs allow the clauses to flow together more smoothly. Since they are adverbs that begin an independent clause, they are followed by a comma. Here is an example:

I;I

Eliza finished her math assignment; nevertheless, she still had to do her Spanish.

Remember, the semi-colon splits the two independent clauses, and a comma follows the conjunctive adverb. Even many adults make the mistake of thinking words like <u>however</u>, when they separate independent clauses, are surrounded by commas:

We studied a lot for the test, however, it did not go well.

incorrect I,I -- run-on sentence

We studied a lot for the test; however, it did not go well.

correct -- I;I -- second I begins with conjunctive adverb <u>however</u>

The football game wore us out, therefore, we slept soundly that night.

incorrect -- I,I -- run-on sentence

The football game wore us out; therefore, we slept soundly that night.

correct -- I;I -- second I begins with conjunctive adverb <u>therefore</u>

Notes on Individual Coordinating Conjunctions:

- Of the six coordinating conjunctions, <u>and</u>, <u>or</u>, and <u>but</u> are most common. Consider these examples:

> The bowl broke, <u>and</u> shards flew everywhere.
>
> We could go to the movies, <u>or</u> you could go alone.
>
> I turned on the fan, <u>but</u> the room remained hot.

When students begin writing compound sentences in isolation, they often try to take one idea and stretch it across two clauses, particularly with the conjunction <u>and</u>. They will write sentences like these:

> I like ice cream, and I like cake.
>
> Drew went swimming, and then he went home.

Though these examples are structurally accurate, they are weak. The first should be written with merely a compound object:

> I like ice cream and cake.

The second should be written with merely a compound predicate:

> Drew went swimming and then went home.

When students use the conjunction <u>and</u> to join independent clauses in a compound sentence, encourage them to use two *different* subjects. They should bring two different ideas together rather than stretching one idea across two clauses. These compound sentences using <u>and</u> are stronger:

> The creaking door scared me, and I screamed.
>
> I am wearing purple to prom, and you need a flower to match.

Though not used as often, <u>yet</u> functions much like <u>but</u>:

> We ate a huge dinner, <u>yet</u> we still saved room for dessert.

Though <u>for</u> as a coordinating conjunction has become increasingly rare, students still encounter it in textbooks and older novels. Its meaning is similar to <u>because</u>, but <u>because</u> is a subordinating conjunction, which means its function is somewhat different:

> We enjoyed the gathering, <u>for</u> a number of our friends showed up.
> I gathered all of the dry cleaning together, <u>for</u> my brother was headed to the
> > cleaners that afternoon.

The final coordinating conjunction is <u>nor</u>. A compound sentence with <u>nor</u> as its coordinating conjunction requires two special things: a *negative* word (e.g., <u>never</u>, <u>not</u>) in the first clause and a verb-subject format (similar to how a question would be worded) in the second clause:

> I do not like broccoli, <u>nor</u> **do I like** mushrooms.
> We never liked the movie *Friday the 13th*, <u>nor</u> **did we** like its sequels.
> You should not buy a compact, <u>nor</u> **should you buy** a huge S.U.V.

- <u>So</u> as a conjunction can be both subordinating and coordinating. (It can also serve as an adverb of degree!) Since it is often overused and not a particularly strong word, I do not typically teach it when I teach the other six coordinating conjunctions (*fanboy*). If you do elect to teach it, you can change the mnemonic to fanboy<u>s</u> to include it.

You can add <u>and</u> before <u>so</u> in a sentence to see if it is being used as a coordinating conjunction. If <u>and</u> does not change the sentence's meaning, and the clauses still flow together naturally, then <u>so</u> is being used as a coordinating conjunction:

> Katherine has difficulty studying for long periods of time, (and) <u>so</u> she
> > struggles during exam time.

Additionally, since it is a coordinating conjunction, <u>so</u> cannot be repositioned at the beginning of the sentence. The restructuring below does not make sense:

<u>So</u> it is no surprise that she struggles during exam time, Katherine has difficulty studying for long periods of time.

The use of <u>so</u> as a subordinating conjunction is in the complex sentences section of this text. In brief, though, if when you follow the word <u>so</u> with the word <u>that</u> the sentence still works well, <u>so</u> is serving as a subordinating rather than a coordinating conjunction. Additionally, in most complex sentences using <u>so</u> as the subordinating conjunction, you should be able to switch the order of the clauses, moving the <u>so</u> to the beginning of the sentence, without altering meaning.

Common Core: The Common Core State Standards suggest that students should be able to do the following (Italics identify elements that later concepts will address.):

- Produce, expand, and rearrange complete simple and compound sentences. (2)
- Produce simple, compound, *and complex* sentences. (3)
- Use a comma before a coordinating conjunction in a compound sentence. (4)
- Explain the function of phrases and clauses in general and their function in specific sentences. (7)
- Choose among simple, compound, *complex, and compound-complex* sentences to signal differing relationships among ideas. (7)
- Use a semi-colon (and perhaps a conjunctive adverb) to link two or more closely related independent clauses. (9-10)

compound sentence

2 independent clauses joined by comma and coordinating conjunction

examples: John went to the store, but it was closed.
We went out to dinner, and Mary met us afterwards for dessert.

compound sentence

two independent clauses joined by a comma (,) and a coordinating conjunction: for, and, nor, but, or, yet

John went to the store, but it was closed.

Sue served the ball, and Marshall returned it easily.

Introduction:

- To be reviewed before teaching: subject, predicate, independent clause, coordinating conjunction.

- Define the term, writing it on the board. Include several examples. Tell students that there are only 6 useful coordinating conjunctions: <u>for</u>, <u>and</u>, <u>nor</u>, <u>but</u>, <u>or</u>, <u>yet</u>. Tell them about the mnemonic *fanboy*, which is useful for remembering them. (<u>So</u> can be added, changing the mnemonic to *fanboys*.)

- Draw the figure at right on the board. Explain that the **I**'s represent independent clauses, and that they are joined by a comma and one of the six words listed.

- Hand students concept cards or have them create their own. Include the figure on the front of the concept card as well.

I, for and nor but or yet (so) **I**

Application:

- Have students read compound sentences, identifying their independent clauses, commas, and coordinating conjunctions. Have them identify each clause's subject and predicate. Have them read each independent clause in isolation to make sure it can, indeed, stand by itself.

- Have students read compound sentences and place the commas appropriately.

- Have students join pre-written simple sentences with a comma and coordinating conjunction. For example...

John went to the store. It was closed.

answer: John went to the store, but it was closed.

It started raining. We ran inside.

answer: It started raining, and we ran inside.

We could all go to the movies. Mary could stay home.

answer: We could all go to the movies, or Mary could stay home.

(w/semi-colon)

compound sentence

2 independent clauses joined by
comma and coordinating conjunction
<u>or</u> a semi-colon (;)

examples: John went to the store,
but it was closed.
We went out to dinner, and Mary met us
afterwards for dessert.
I love chocolate; I eat it all the time.

---

compound sentence

two independent clauses joined by a comma (,) and a coordinating conjunction: for, and, nor, but, or, yet

John went to the store, but it was closed.

advanced:
two independent clauses joined by semi-colon (;)

Sarah saw three plays; *Cats* was her favorite.

I;I

Introduction:

- To be reviewed before teaching: subject, predicate, independent clause, compound sentence with comma and coordinating conjunction

- Note that student writers can now use semi-colons instead of commas/coordinating conjunctions to join independent clauses and form compound sentences. This is merely a new way of connecting independent clauses. Draw the figure above on the board. They will already know that the **I**'s represent independent clauses. Here are two additional examples:

  Ethan considered the problem; he found three different solutions.

  Mac is not a fan of his swim coach; they have a contentious relationship.

- Hand students replacement concept cards that include additional information regarding semi-colons, have them create their own, or have them add the additional information to the cards they already created. Include the figure (**I;I**) on the front of the concept card as well.

- Punctuation: Explain to students that semi-colons <u>replace</u> the comma and coordinating conjunction. Since a semi-colon separates two independent clauses (**I;I**), a period could also be used instead. Students should be warned against using semi-colons in other circumstances as people often use them incorrectly. Then, explain to students that the comma and coordinating conjunction can be replaced with a semi-colon to add sentence variety and sophistication to a piece of written text. Although you cannot hear a semi-colon when a sentence is read aloud, this variety is good to spice up written text on an occasional basis.

Application:

- Have students read compound sentences that use semi-colons, identifying their independent clauses and semi-colons. Have them identify each clause's subject and predicate. Have them read each independent clause in isolation and make sure it can, indeed, stand by itself.

- Have students read compound sentences and place the semi-colons appropriately.

- Have students join pre-written simple sentences with a semi-colon. For example...

> Jeb is tired. Logan is not.
>
> > answer: Jeb is tired; Logan is not.
>
> Martha should study the material carefully. She will earn an A.
>
> > answer: Martha should study the material carefully; she will earn an A.
>
> Eat your breakfast. We have to go!
>
> > answer: Eat your breakfast; we have to go!

228

Advanced: (with semi-colon, conjunctive adverb, and comma)

- To be reviewed before teaching: subject, predicate, independent clause, compound sentence, semi-colon usage

- Add the following example to your concept card (The term and definition remain the same as in the previous lesson.):

example: Mary loves ice cream;
however, she only eats it on special occasions.

- Explain to students that sometimes the transition between clauses in an I;I is awkward or abrupt. Often, a transition word (or phrase) can help the independent clauses work better together. This word (or phrase) is <u>not</u> a conjunction. It is an adverb, called a conjunctive adverb because it does help join two ideas together. Since it is only an adverb, the clauses still need a semi-colon to connect. This conjunctive adverb becomes the first word of the second independent clause.

- <u>Punctuation</u>: A conjunctive adverb may be inserted into a compound sentence immediately following the semi-colon. This adverb becomes the first word of the second independent clause and is preceded by the semi-colon and followed by a comma:

> We found all the missing pieces; <u>however</u>, we still couldn't put the puzzle together.
>
> I like mint chip ice cream best; <u>therefore</u>, I always order it at the local ice cream parlor.

Conjunctive adverbs such as <u>however</u> and <u>therefore</u> are *adverbs* that serve to connect groups of words together. It is important not to confuse them with conjunctions. Otherwise, you will punctuate the sentences that contain them incorrectly.

All introductory adverbs are followed by commas. Consider these examples:

<u>Usually</u>, we have pizza for lunch on Thursdays.

<u>Sometimes</u>, I get a headache if I stay up too late.

Just like <u>therefore</u> or <u>however</u>, these two adverbs begin independent clauses and therefore are followed by commas.

Application:

- Have students read compound sentences, identifying their independent clauses and semi-colons. Have them identify each clause's subject and predicate. Have them identify the conjunctive adverbs and notice the commas that follow them. Have them read each independent clause in isolation to make sure it can, indeed, stand by itself.

- Have students read compound sentences and place the semi-colons and commas appropriately.

- Have students join pre-written simple sentences with a semi-colon, conjunctive adverb, and comma. (Note: the conjunctive adverb becomes the first word of the second independent clause.)

Jeb is tired. Logan is not. (however)

answer: Jeb is tired; however, Logan is not.

The thief considered a number of entrances to the building. He hoisted himself through an open window. (finally)

answer: The thief considered a number of entrances to the building; finally, he hoisted himself through an open window.

Note that in the examples above I've provided the conjunctive adverb to be used. As students become accustomed to the format of these more challenging sentences, provide them with a list of conjunctive adverbs like the one on the following page (*Figure 21*) and allow them to choose an appropriate word. Specific instruction on individual words may prove beneficial in some situations. For example, many students are unclear on the meaning of words such as <u>consequently</u>, <u>subsequently</u>, and <u>hence</u>. Even <u>however</u> or <u>nevertheless</u> can prove difficult. Mini-lessons can be constructed on one or two conjunctive adverbs at a time, as needed. This will not only enhance sentence variety but also comprehension of textbooks and novels as well as standardized testing passages and questions.

Conjunctive Adverbs

conjunctive adverbs (optional for I;I compound sentences):

template for usage: use a semi-colon before and a comma after the conjunctive adverb

<u>additionally</u>	<u>actually</u>	<u>accordingly</u>
also	certainly	as a result
furthermore	indeed	consequently
likewise	in fact	hence
moreover		therefore
similarly	<u>afterwards</u>	thus
in addition	later	
	next	<u>alternatively</u>
<u>however</u>	subsequently	instead
nevertheless	then	
nonetheless		<u>for example</u>
notwithstanding	<u>at the same</u>	for instance
on the contrary	<u>time</u>	
on the other hand	meanwhile	<u>certainly</u>
still	simultaneously	clearly
		obviously

Figure 21

Activities for the three different compound sentence lessons are combined below. You should only use activities supporting concepts that have already been introduced to your students.

Identification: Label each group of words simple sentence (S), compound sentence (C), or fragment (F). Underline all subjects once and their predicates (verbs) twice. If the sentence is compound, put parentheses around each independent clause. Do NOT include coordinating conjunctions that connect clauses inside the parentheses.

_____ 1. My brother got home late, and our parents grounded him.

_____ 2. We got our paint ball equipment and headed to the park.

_____ 3. As soon as I get home from the mall.

_____ 4. I do not want to do my homework, for I had a long day at school.

_____ 5. The rug in the den is filthy, but the vacuum is broken.

_____ 6. I would like to watch the latest episode of that funny comedy.

_____ 7. Cindy and Will served me dinner last Wednesday, but I brought dessert.

_____ 8. Although I can't find my calculator anywhere.

_____ 9. I will bring in the trash; therefore, you have to do the dishes.

_____ 10. Mammals have fur; moreover, they produce live young.

Sorting: Unscramble the sentence parts to form logical sentences by numbering them in the blanks. Then, write the finished product on the line below. Do not forget to capitalize the first word and use proper end punctuation (If students need more support, you may include end punctuation for the appropriate sentence part.):

1. _____ the lacrosse player   _____ told him to sit out

   _____ , but the doctor   _____ sprained his foot

   _____ in last night's game   _____ for only one game

   Unscrambled sentence: _____

   _____

2. _____ the veteran judge   _____ in the city courthouse

    _____ told the lawyers to sit down   _____ ; then,

    _____ he   _____ sternly lectured everyone there.

    Unscrambled sentence: _____

    _____

Matching: Draw lines between the 1st independent clause and coordinating conjunction and the appropriate 2nd independent clause to form a sentence:

I prepared steaks for dinner, but	I entered the woods cautiously.
The grove of trees moaned in the wind, and	my friends had already eaten.
You are grounded until the end of time, yet	I will let you go to the dance tonight.

Combining: Combine the sentences into one compound sentence.

*   Combine the sentences into one compound sentence and write it on the blank below. Delete words as necessary. (Appropriate conjunctions can be provided, or students can generate their own.)

1. The football game started.

    It was the last game of the season.

    The fans screamed their heads off.

    Their screaming was done energetically.

    _____

2. The beach bum scared the tourists.

    She was dirty and grumpy.

    The tourists ran.

    They ended up back at their hotel.

    _____

3. The photographer captured the family.

   They were eating a delicious lunch.

   The lunch was on a picnic blanket.

   Rain started.

   The rain was hard and happened soon after.

   _____

- Combine the following simple sentences into compound sentences using the recommended conjunctive adverb:

   1. The exam is on Friday. You must study each and every night until then. (therefore)

      answer: The exam is on Friday; therefore, you must study each and every night until then.

   2. It is a Monday night. You should make reservations at the restaurant anyway. (nevertheless)

      answer: It is Monday night; nevertheless, you should make reservations at the restaurant anyway.

Imitating: Imitate the given sentence or template. A few samples of each are provided:

- Read each compound sentence and notice the template it follows. Then, write a sentence of your own using the same format. Parts in parentheses are not required:

1. *Subject + verb + direct object, coordinating conj. + subject + verb + direct object.*
   Mark considered the problem, but he could not find a good solution.

   _____

2. *Subject + verb + direct object + adverb, conj. + subject + verb + prep. phrase + prep. phrase.*
   We celebrated our anniversary early, for our children were with their grandparents for the night.

   _____

3. *Subject + verb + prep. phrase; conjunctive adverb, subject + predicate + prep. phrase.*
   Doctor Holder retired in March; however, his partner took over as the family's physician.

   _____

- Read each compound sentence and identify its parts. Without benefit of a pre-written template, create a sentence that follows the same exact structure. Articles are optional:

1. The elderly man swam dozens of laps, and the younger swimmers looked on in awe.

   _____

2. In my house we do not eat mushrooms, nor do we think much of lima beans.

   _____

3. The girls were up late last night; hence, their dad is letting them sleep in this morning.

   _____

- Study each sentence template. Without benefit of a pre-written sample sentence, create a sentence that follows the same exact structure. Articles can be inserted or omitted as needed:

1. *Prep. phrase + prep. phrase + subject + verb, conjunction + subject + verb + direct object.*

   _____

2. *Subject + linking verb + noun; conjunctive adverb, subject + action verb + direct object.*

   _____

3. *Prep. phrase + subject + predicate + direct object, conjunction + subject + prep. phrase + verb.*

   _____

Tandem Writing: Finish the sentences.

- Read the first half carefully, and notice the conjunction provided. Then, finish the compound sentence:

1. The trick-or-treaters rang the doorbell, but _____.

2. My best friend is coming over, and _____.

3. I do not like that movie, nor _____.

- Read the first half carefully. Then, provide a coordinating conjunction and finish the compound sentence:

1. The teacher caught a cold from a student in her class, _____.

2. The boys tracked mud across my new carpet, _____.

3. A local farmer brought corn to the market, _____.

- Read the first half carefully. Notice the semi-colon and conjunctive adverb and finish the compound sentence:

1. The teacher caught a cold from a student in her class; nevertheless, _____.

2. On the third day, the explorer discovered a huge ruby; consequently, _____.

Sentence Generation:

- Ultimately, students must generate sentences containing every element they study. When they turn to sentence writing, you can engage them and develop their writing by providing parameters, including (a) minimum word count, (b) specific element required and/or located in particular position, and (c) specific content:

1. Write a compound sentence of at least 10 words.

   e.g., We could go meet at the movies after work, or you could come by my house instead.

2. Write a compound sentence of at least 12 words that uses the word "nor."

   e.g., I do not like history class, *nor* do I think much of Spanish.

3. Write a compound sentence on a recent president. Use "subsequently."

   e.g., Barack Obama became a senator in 2005; *subsequently*, he became president.

4. Write a compound sentence using the phrase "on the other hand" as a conjunctive adverb:

   e.g., I am surprised by his anger; *on the other hand*, he has had a rough day today.

5. Write a compound sentence about Mark Twain:

   Mark Twain wrote a number of important novels; *Huckleberry Finn* is his most famous.

6. Write a compound sentence of at least 10 words about clouds.

   e.g., Dark clouds rolled over the playing field, and it began to thunder and lightning.

- Students can also be asked to create sentences using clause structure templates. Templates can be reused frequently. Create a sentence for each template provided below:

   1. I,fanboyI   3. I;I   5. I

   2. I;I - use <u>consequently</u>   4. I,fanboyI - use <u>for</u>

Complex Sentences

Overview:

A paragraph or essay that includes complex sentences sounds markedly more sophisticated than one that does not. Complex sentences use both independent and dependent clauses. In fact, by definition a complex sentence is 1 independent and 1 or more dependent clauses. This is the first instance where students will encounter and create sentences that contain dependent clauses. These should not be attempted until students have reached at least third grade because the way these clauses join is more sophisticated than the coordinating conjunction that joins two independent clauses in a compound sentence.

Take these two sentences:

Charlie watched a movie about astronomy, **and** his son wanted to be a N.A.S.A. astronaut.

Charlie watched a movie about astronomy **because** his son wanted to be a N.A.S.A. astronaut.

In the first, a compound sentence, there is no contextual relationship between the two ideas. He watched a movie about astronomy, and his son also wanted to be an astronaut. In the second, a complex sentence, the ideas are interrelated. He watched a movie about astronomy *because of* his son's interest in becoming an astronaut. Younger students and those with fledgling language skills are not yet ready to handle the relationship between ideas expressed in complex sentences.

Clauses can be ordered in different ways to create different kinds of complex sentences. Remember that every sentence must have at least 1 independent clause.

Kinds & Categories:

Subordinating Conjunctions		
time:	*place:*	*purpose:*
after	where	in order that
as	wherever	so that
as soon as		
before	*cause:*	*concession:*
just as	as	although
now that	because	even though
once	since	though
since		whereas
till	*comparison:*	while
until	as	
when	just as	*condition:*
whenever	than	as long as
while		even if
	manner:	if
	as	unless
	as if	whether
	as though	

Figure 22

There are three kinds of dependent clause:

1. **adverbial**: The adverbial clause typically describes (or modifies) the main verb in another clause, most often the independent one in the sentence. These dependent clauses typically appear in two positions -- before the clause they are describing (with a comma separating the clauses):

> ## Dependent Clause, Independent Clause.

> # D,I

> *While Jeff ate his pizza*, Evelyn poured some lemonade.
>
> *When Celeste is running*, nothing can stop her.

or after it (with no comma separating the clauses):

> ## Independent Clause Dependent Clause.

> # ID

> I finished printing my paper *once I got toner for the printer.*
>
> The movie was excellent *although I didn't care much for the ending.*

In this kind of complex sentence, which is the most common and useful one for students to learn to write, the dependent clause begins with a subordinating conjunction (*Figure 22*), which allows that clause to join with the independent clause. The subordinating conjunctions in the sentences above are underlined. If the dependent clause does not have its subordinating conjunction, the clause becomes independent, a useful fact for students to realize:

> *although* Marvin finished the race - dependent
>
> Marvin finished the race - independent
>
> *if* my friend is late - dependent
>
> my friend is late - independent

Without the subordinating conjunction, a **D,I** or an **ID** becomes an **I,I** -- a run-on. Consider this with the subordinating conjunction <u>although</u>:

> Although Marvin finished the race, he came in last. (**D,I** - complex sentence)
>
> Marvin finished the race, he came in last. (**I,I** - run-on)

In the second version, both clauses are independent, and therefore the comma must be replaced with a period, a semi-colon, or a comma and coordinating conjunction (fanboy) or the sentence will be a run-on.

Since adverbial dependent clauses begin with subordinating conjunctions, in **D,I** sentences the conjunction is actually the first word of the sentence. In other words in a complex sentence (unlike compound sentences where the conjunction always appears between the clauses), since the dependent clause can come first, the conjunction actually can be the first word in the sentence. Here are two more detailed templates of what we have been discussing:

Subordinating Conjunction + Subject + Predicate, Subject + Predicate.

or

Subject + Predicate + Subordinating Conjunction + Subject + Predicate.

Most students and even quite a few teachers think of only <u>for</u>, <u>and</u>, <u>nor</u>, <u>but</u>, <u>or</u>, and <u>yet</u> (coordinating conjunctions) when asked to recall conjunctions. Subordinating conjunctions are more sophisticated and a bit more confusing as well. Beginning a sentence with <u>although</u>, <u>since</u>, or <u>unless</u> will usually yield a **D,I** complex sentence without any conscious effort:

<u>Although</u> Marvin finished the race, he still came in last.

<u>Since</u> you keep arguing with me, I am going to stop listening to you.

<u>Unless</u> Mac finishes the lawn, he cannot go to the movies with us.

2. **adjectival or relative**: The adjectival clause has a fitting name in that it describes the noun or pronoun that immediately precedes it. Also called a relative clause because it relates back to that noun or pronoun, the adjective clause will never begin a sentence, but it can come after any noun or pronoun in another clause, even if it breaks that clause into two parts. Consider these examples, where the adjective clause is italicized and the relative pronoun, which is also the D-wedge's subject, is underlined:

The chair, *<u>which</u> is covered in expensive fabric*, now has coffee stains on it.

The cat, *<u>which</u> has orange fur and sharp claws*, is a little scary to watch.

My best friend, *<u>who</u> is moving to Florida*, will stay in touch.

In all three of the sentences above, the relative or adjectival dependent clause comes between the subject and predicate of the independent clause. In other words, it is *wedged* into the independent clause. I typically nickname these clauses D-wedges because they are dependent clauses that can be wedged anywhere after a noun or pronoun they describe. Use the figure at right to illustrate this with students. All of the above examples follow this template:

> **Main Subject, Relative Pronoun + Its Predicate, Main Predicate.**

Relative pronouns include <u>who</u>, <u>whom</u>, <u>whose</u>, <u>that</u>, <u>which</u>. Since adjective clauses can follow any noun or pronoun, their location isn't set in stone. Consider this sentence, where the D-wedges are in italics:

The man, *who wore a top hat*, and the woman, *who had on a hoop skirt*, twirled around the dance floor, *which sparkled with lights*.

This sentence is obviously a little overdone, but it clearly shows that these adjectival or relative clauses can exist after most any noun.

Briefly, there are two other varieties of D-wedge. Sometimes, the relative pronoun does not serve as the D-wedge's subject. Below, the D-wedge is in italics, and the subject of that clause is underlined:

The clock, *which <u>Ethan</u> had repaired last week*, is once again broken.

Martha, *whose <u>mom</u> grounded her for a month*, pouted in her room.

Here's what these look like:

Main Subject, Relative Pronoun + Its Subject + Its Predicate, Main Predicate.

As we have already seen, the Relative Pronoun + Its Subject + Its Predicate can follow *any* noun or pronoun in the sentence, though.

* * *

Sometimes, a relative clause begins with a relative adverb -- <u>when</u>, <u>where</u>, <u>why</u>:

I found my keys *where <u>I</u> left them*.

That is not the reason *why <u>you</u> are behaving that way*.

There will be a time *when <u>you</u> may make your own decision about this*.

I include these for teacher reference. They are tricky because all three relative adverbs can serve other roles as well. In order for them to serve as relative adverbs, they *must* directly follow the noun or pronoun that the D-wedge describes. Here's what these look like:

Main Subject, Relative Adverb + Its Subject + Its Predicate, Main Predicate.

<u>Punctuation</u>: Unfortunately, punctuating relative clauses is tricky. Non-essential (or non-restrictive) clauses always take commas because they can be removed from the sentence

without significantly altering meaning:

> The judge, who vacations in Florida, is known for his brilliant decisions.
>
> Our cat, which seems to have nine lives, fell from a tree but survived!

Essential (or restrictive) clauses are necessary to limit and clarify the meaning of the noun they follow. As a result, they do not take commas and cannot be removed from the sentence without making the noun (or pronoun) they describe unclear:

> The man who has no shoes is the one you should question.
>
> The present that I liked best is my new bicycle.

Without the relative clauses in the above examples, the meanings of the subject nouns become unclear.

As a general rule, always use <u>that</u> when it can replace <u>which</u> and not affect meaning. <u>That</u> marks an essential clause and never takes commas; <u>which</u> marks a non-essential clause and always takes commas. <u>Who</u> will depend on the situation:

> My best friend Brian, *who attended college with me*, is coming to visit.
>
> We should go to the doctor *who Laurie recommended*.

In the first of the above examples, because I've mentioned Brian's name, the D-wedge is non-essential (non-restrictive) and therefore takes commas and can be eliminated. Since the doctor in the second example is not specified, without the D-wedge there would be no way to know which doctor the sentence is discussing, so the <u>who</u> clause is essential and does not take a comma.

Remember that all D-wedges (relative or adjectival clauses) share one thing in common: they follow a noun or pronoun that they describe.

3. **noun**: Noun clauses should be taught sparingly and only to the most advanced students. They are structurally sophisticated, and they won't significantly improve a student's

writing. The entire noun clause takes the place of a noun in a sentence, which means it can serve as a subject, a direct object, the object of a preposition, or a predicate noun:

> *What I had for breakfast* has made me sick. (subject)
>
> We should all listen to *what he has to say*. (object of preposition)
>
> I don't know *what you are thinking*. (direct object)
>
> That table is not *where we should eat*. (predicate nominative)

Common Core: The Common Core State Standards suggest that students should

be able to do the following. (Italics identify elements that later concepts will address):

- Produce simple, compound, and complex sentences. (3)

- Use relative pronouns and relative adverbs. (4)

- Use punctuation (commas, parentheses, dashes) to set off nonrestrictive/parenthetical elements. (6)

- Explain the function of phrases and clauses in general and their function in specific sentences. (7)

- Choose among simple, compound, complex, *and compound-complex sentences* to signal differing relationships among ideas. (7)

- Place phrases and clauses within a sentence, recognizing and correcting misplaced and dangling modifiers. (7)

- Use various types of phrases (noun, verb, adjectival, adverbial, *participial*, prepositional, *absolute*) and clauses (independent, dependent; noun, relative, adverbial) to convey specific meanings and add variety and interest to writing or presentations. (9-10)

(with adverb clause)

complex sentence

1 independent clause and 1 (or more) dependent clauses

examples: The doctor saw twelve patients before she headed out for lunch.
While I considered all the alternatives, Logan was quick to make a decision.
If you take the larger suitcase, you'll have room for Emilio's toys.

---

complex sentence

1 independent clause and 1 (or more) dependent clause(s)

When Jack ran in the race, he came in last. (D,I)

We surprised Logan because we kept the party a secret. (ID)

subordinating conjunctions (used to start D clauses): after, although, as, because, before, even if, even though, if, once, since, so that, though, unless, until, when, while

D,I

ID

Introduction:

- To be reviewed before teaching: subject, predicate, independent clause, dependent clause, subordinating conjunction

- Ask students to write a sentence that begins with the word <u>although</u>. They will write complex sentences that follow the D,I pattern incidentally, and then you can use their sentences to explain the structure of a complex sentence. (Note: <u>Although</u> works well for this activity. Some of the other subordinating conjunctions can serve other functions in a sentence and shouldn't be used for this introductory activity. If students will struggle with understanding the meaning of <u>although</u>, try <u>since</u> instead.)

- Define the term, writing it on the board. Include several examples. Draw the **D,I** and **ID** images shown here on the board. Remind students that the **I** represents an independent clause and because of its base can stand alone. The **D** represents a dependent clause and can be knocked over. It needs an **I** to lean on. These visual representations are particularly effective.

- Explain that in this kind of complex sentence, the dependent clause always begins with a subordinating conjunction.

- Hand students concept cards or have them create their own. Include the figures on the front of the concept card as well.

- Remind students that these are the first sentences they have studied that contain dependent clauses.

- Explain that the dependent clause can begin or end the sentence (**D,I** or **ID**).

Application:

- Have students read complex sentences, identifying their independent and dependent clauses. Have them identify each clause's subject and predicate. Put parentheses around each clause, and use an I or a D to identify it.

- Explain that sentences beginning with dependent clauses separate the clauses with a comma while sentences ending with dependent clauses do not. For example...

  While I was watching television, the electricity went out. (comma between clauses)

  The electricity went out while I was watching television. (no comma)

Say this. If the dependent clause in a complex sentence comes first, it is followed by a comma:

> Since I am tired, I will take a nap.
>
> When I want your opinion, I will give it to you.
>
> Unless you hear back from me, you better go alone.

Say this. The complex sentence does not take a comma if the dependent clause is last:

> I will take a nap since I am tired.

> The river swept away our dock while we were out of town.
>
> The couple went shopping for a ring after the young man proposed to the young woman.

- Have students locate subordinating conjunctions and add commas where appropriate.
- Show students that oftentimes with this kind of complex sentence the clauses can be flipped, and the sentence still retains meaning:

> Since I am tired, I will take a nap. *could be* I will take a nap since I am tired.
>
> Until it stops raining, we should stay indoors. *could be*
>
> We should stay indoors until it stops raining.

Notes:

- Beginning a sentence with because: Teachers often tell students they may never begin a sentence with the word because. This is misleading and untrue. Instead, tell students not to begin sentences with because until they have learned how to do so correctly. We typically answer *why* questions verbally with fragments beginning with the conjunction because. While these dependent clause fragments serve us well in discussion, they are inappropriate for written expression. Consider responses to the question, "Why were you late?"

> appropriate *verbal* answer: "Because the bus wouldn't start." (fragment)
>
> appropriate written answer: "Because the bus wouldn't start, I was late."
> (D,I complex sentence)

- Because isn't a coordinating conjunction: Often, participants in workshops ask why because is subordinating (rather than coordinating). The answer is one of both structure and meaning. Realize that with compound sentences (I, fanboy I), the coordinating conjunction and the rest of the sentence cannot be moved to the beginning of the sentence:

compound with __and__ as conjunction: The first example below is an appropriate compound sentence. Each component stands on its own. In the second, however, the coordinating conjunction has moved to the beginning, and the result is no longer a sentence.

John went to the store, and it was open.

but not

And it was open, John went to the store.

complex with __because__ as conjunction: Both the first and second examples below are appropriate complex sentences. __Because it was open__ (the dependent clause) depends on __John went to the store__ (the independent clause).

John went to the store because it was open.

and also

Because it was open, John went to the store.

- __So used as a subordinating conjunction:__ When __so__ is used as a subordinating conjunction, you could add __that__ after it in the sentence without changing meaning:

We went to the movies so (that) we could see *Slumdog Millionaire*.

and also

So (that) we could see *Slumdog Millionaire*, we went to the movies.

When __so__ is used as a coordinating conjunction between independent clauses, such a switch is impossible. For additional information about __so__ used as a coordinating conjunction, see the section on compound sentences.

(with adjective or relative clause):

complex sentence

1 independent clause and 1 (or more) dependent clauses

examples: The doctor saw twelve patients before she headed out for lunch.
While I considered all the alternatives, Logan was quick to make a decision.
Susan, who is a doctor, works long hours each night.

complex sentence

1 independent clause and 1 (or more) dependent clause(s)

When Jack ran in the race, he came in last. (D,I)

We surprised Logan because we kept the party a secret. (ID)

advanced: adjective (or relative) clauses are wedged into a sentence immediately following a noun or pronoun they describe.

Susan, who is a doctor, works long hours each night.

The playground that was recently renovated is on the corner of 4th and Elm.

Introduction:

- To be reviewed before teaching: subject, predicate, independent clause, dependent clause, complex sentence

- Add the following example to your concept card, or make a new card just for this kind of complex sentence. (The term and definition remain the same as in the second lesson.):

example: The problem, which does not have an easy solution, will take all of our attention for the next few days.

- Also add the figure at right to the two already on the front of your card:
- Show your students some additional examples:

My grandmother, who lived through the depression, was always extremely careful with her money.

The table that my best friend bought me sits in our living room between two chairs.

- Teach students that these can be called **D**-wedge sentences because the relative clause is *wedged* immediately after the noun/pronoun it describes, often in the middle of an independent clause.

- Teach students that these D-wedge clauses begin with relative pronouns (<u>who</u>, <u>whom</u>, <u>whose</u>, <u>which</u>, <u>that</u>). They sometimes serve as the subject of the clause:

My grandfather, *who* was an exceptional gardener, had two homes .

In a follow-up session, explain that sometimes a relative pronoun introduces the clause, but another word serves as the subject:

The table that my best friend bought me sits in our living room between two chairs.

- Note: Teach these only when students are completely comfortable with **D,I** and **ID** sentences.

Application:

- Have students read complex sentences with adjective clauses, identifying their independent clauses with parentheses and their dependent clauses with brackets. Have them identify each clause's subject and predicate. Have them identify the relative pronoun that begins each adjective clause.

- Have students combine sentences using a D-wedge structure. For example...

The pie fell to the floor. The pie was hot out of the oven.
possible answer The pie, which was fresh out of the oven, fell to the floor.

- Have students add D-wedge clauses to existing barebones sentences. For example...

The officer chased the crook.

possible answer The officer, who was sweating in the heat, chased the crook.

Punctuation (to be introduced later to advanced students):

- There are two types of adjective clauses: essential (or restrictive) and non-essential (or non-restrictive). Essential adjective clauses can not be removed from the sentence without leaving the identity of the noun they describe unclear, and so they are *not* set off by commas:

  > In the crowd Nick saw a woman who looked like his sister.
  >
  > I handed your keys to the boy who claimed to be your son.

  Non-essential adjective clauses can be removed from the sentence without leaving the identity of the noun (or pronoun) they describe unclear, and therefore they *are* surrounded by commas:

  > James, who drank a lot of water before lunch, was unable to finish his meal.
  >
  > The outlaw shot the Hilsman County sheriff, who was unable to defend himself.

Subsequent Lesson (with more than one dependent clause):

Introduction:

- To be reviewed before teaching: subject, predicate, independent clause, dependent clause, complex sentence

- Remind students that the definition of a complex sentence is one independent clause and one (**or more**) dependent clauses. Introduce several examples:

> While I was driving on the highway, I found a good song on the radio so that I could keep myself awake.
>
> Because the house was quiet when Taylor arrived, he never expected the surprise party that we had planned for him.
>
> David became a police officer because he had always admired the uniform when he was a kid.

Application:

- Have students read complex sentences with multiple dependent clauses, identifying their independent and dependent clauses with parentheses. Have them identify each clause's subject and predicate. Have them identify the relative pronoun or subordinating conjunction that begins each dependent clause. Have students make sure that each sentence has at least one independent clause.

- Have students punctuate pre-written complex sentences correctly.

- Have students add dependent clauses to the ends of sentences that are in **D,I** format.

- Have students add dependent clauses to the beginnings of sentences that are in **ID** format.

- In subsequent lessons help students generate the following possible complex sentence templates and then examples that fit the templates:

Multiple adverbial clauses: Here are some of the most obvious multiple dependent clause sentence constructions:

D,D,I *Because I am a sound sleeper, unless there is a really loud noise,* nothing wakes me.

D,ID *While the plane was landing,* we experienced some turbulence *since the weather was bad.*

IDD My computer is broken *because I dropped it when I slipped on the ice.*

Multiple adjectival clauses: Here are some possibilities for multiple adjective clauses (or D-wedges). Remember that adjective clauses are inserted immediately following the nouns/pronouns they describe:

The man, *who wore baggy clothing,* and the woman, *who had on stiletto heels,* made quite a sight in our neighborhood, *which had a number of paths for walking.*

A pilot *who had no excuse to be flying while sick with the flu* conducted an emergency landing on the runway, *which was covered with ice.*

Mixing adjectival and adverbial clauses in a sentence together: Obviously, a sentence can also contain a mixture of adjectival and adverbial clauses as well:

John, *who was captain of the football team,* began with a pep talk *when he wanted to excite the other players.*

If you finish your homework, I will take you to the movie *that you have been wanting to see.*

Suggested Exercises & Activities Activities for the different complex sentence lessons are combined below. You should only use activities supporting concepts that have already been introduced to your students.

Identification: This activity should be cumulative. Thus, students should be asked to identify simple, compound, and complex sentences.

- Label each group of words simple sentence (S), compound sentence (CD), or complex (CX). Underline all subjects once and their predicates (verbs) twice. Put parentheses around the clauses. If a dependent clause occurs in the middle of an independent clause, use brackets to set it off. Do NOT include inside the parentheses coordinating conjunctions that connect clauses; all other words should be included. (Answers are included in parentheses here.)

_____ 1. My jeep is over fifteen years old, but it is still my favorite possession. (CD - I,fanboyI)

_____ 2. Four students from the basketball team are graduating this year, yet the team is still hopeful about next year's championships. (CD - I,fanboyI))

_____ 3. The closet, which was full of old socks and sports gear, smelled up the house. (CX - D-wedge)

_____ 4. Unless the printer operates properly, I will not be able to submit my paper. (CX - D,I)

_____ 5. She did not finish cleaning out the garage, nor did she mow the grass. (CD - I,fanboyI)

_____ 6. I should go swim some laps once I am finished with my homework. (CX - ID)

_____ 7. The dam held back millions of gallons of water that would have otherwise flooded the town. (CX - D-wedge)

_____ 8. The two sisters played outside on the street while their parents prepared dinner and talked. (CX - ID)

_____ 9. Because of the constant rain, we decided to take in a movie this afternoon. (S)

_____ 10. Would you like to walk the dog before dinner? (S)

Sorting: Unscramble the sentence parts to form logical sentences by numbering them in the blanks. Then, write the finished product on the line below. Do not forget to capitalize the first word and use proper end punctuation (If students need more support, you may include end punctuation for the appropriate sentence part.):

1. _____ until the aspirin bottle   _____ my mother

    _____ in the medicine cabinet   _____ was empty,

    _____ did not head to the store   _____ to buy a replacement

    Unscrambled sentence: _____

    _____

2. _____ the action movie   _____ was really poor

    _____ although the story line   _____ had an amazing cast

    Unscrambled sentence: _____

    _____

Matching: Match the sentence parts by drawing lines to form sentences:

1.   *dependent clause,*   *independent clause*

    Before I take the dog to the vet,   he did not realize how deep it was.

    When the explorer first discovered the cave,   we had to find a flashlight.

    Because the lights in the basement were out,   I am going to give him a bath.

2.   *independent clause*   *dependent clause*

    I enjoy a good football game   since it was pitch black inside.

    Alyssa has stopped studying for the night   if there is plenty of popcorn.

    The cave was a terrifying place   because she knows the material.

3. *subject,*   *relative clause,*   *predicate.*

    The energetic child,   which ate 100 pounds of grass,   had indigestion Tuesday.

    The enormous hippo,   who broke everything in sight,   texts frequently..

    My best friend,   who loves his cell phone,   was asked to leave the store.

254

Reordering:
Read the sentence. Then switch the clauses and rewrite the sentence. Keep the subordinating conjunction with its clause so that the meaning remains the same:

1. While I was watching the scary movie, I heard a creak on the stair landing.

   _____

2. Be sure to get some Tylenol if you get a headache.

   _____

3. Before the movie lets out, we need to get to the theater to pick up the kids.

   _____

4. I love to walk whenever it is raining outside.

   _____

5. Unless you hear more from me, consider the matter closed.

   _____

Combining:
Combine sentences to make one complex sentence.

- Combine each cluster of sentences into one complex sentence. (Correct conjunctions can be provided, or students can be asked to generate their own.) Add or remove words as needed:

1. We persevered.

   Our rivals played us.

   Our rivals seemed unbeatable.

   _____

2. You should clean your room.

   Your room is messy and filled with dirty clothes.

   _____

3. The lizard climbed onto the tree.

   The lizard did it for protection.

   The lizard was the same color as the bark of the tree.

   _____

- Combine the following simple sentences into complex sentences using the recommended subordinating conjunction:

    1. I broke my foot. I fell down the flight of icy stairs. (because)

        possible answers: Because I fell down the flight of icy stairs, I broke my foot.

                                        I broke my foot because I fell down the flight of icy stairs.

    2. I was swimming. The vicious shark approached me. (when)

        possible answers: I was swimming when the vicious shark approached me.

                                        The vicious shark approached me when I was swimming.

                                        When the vicious shark approached me, I was swimming.

                                        When I was swimming, the vicious shark approached me.

Imitating: Imitate the given sentence or template. A few samples of each are provided:

- Read each complex sentence and notice the template it follows. Then, write a sentence of your own using the same format. DO = direct object.

1. *Subordinating conj. + subject + verb + DO (noun), adjective + subject + verb + DO (pronoun)*
    As I was turning the corner, the beat up Chevy blindsided me.

    _____

2. *Subject + verb (w/adverb) + prep. phrase + sub. conjunction. + subject + verb + DO (noun)*
    The kids will not head to bed until I turn off the T.V.

    _____

3. *Subject, relative pronoun + verb + prep. phrase + adverb, verb + adjective + DO (noun).*
    The politician, who spoke to three audiences today, lost his voice.

    _____

- Read each complex sentence and identify its parts. Create a sentence that follows the same exact structure (no template provided). Articles can be inserted or omitted as needed.

1. Where you see a blue check mark, you need to find your own mistake.

    _____

2. I had a horrible headache because I had not eaten.

_____

3. We found the lamp, which had no shade, in my grandmother's closet.

_____

4. My swordfish was floating at the top of the tank when I went to feed him.

_____

- Study each sentence template. Create a sentence that follows the same exact structure (no sample sentence provided). Articles can be inserted or omitted as needed.

1. *Subordinating conj. + subject + verb + DO (noun), compound subject + verb + prep. phrase.*

_____

2. *Subject + linking verb + noun; conjunctive adverb, subject + action verb + DO (noun).*

_____

3. *Prep. phrase + subject + predicate + subordinating conj. + subject + prep. phrase + verb.*

_____

Tandem Writing: Read the first half of the sentence and finish it, making a complex sentence:

- Read the first half carefully, and notice the conjunction provided. Then, finish the complex sentence:

1. I am really sleepy whenever _____.

2. Once the bluebird landed on the feeder, _____.

3. I can't finish my homework unless_____.

4. When the tide comes in, _____.

- Read the first half carefully. Then, provide a subordinating conjunction and finish the complex sentence:

1. I got my new kite caught in the tree in our front yard _____.

2. The army captain gathered his team _____.

3. At dawn we will begin our trip _____.

Sentence Generation:

- Ultimately, students must generate sentences containing every element they study. When they turn to sentence writing, you can engage them and develop their writing by providing parameters, including (a) minimum word count, (b) specific element required and/or located in particular position, and (c) specific content:

1. Write a complex sentence of at least 10 words.

   e.g., As long as the tennis courts are open that early, I would love to play with you this Sunday morning.

2. Write a D-wedge complex sentence that uses the relative pronoun "that."

   e.g., The problems that we needed to solve last night really challenged me.

3. Write a complex sentence of at least twelve words in the ID format.

   e.g., The rhinos gathered near the fence whenever tourists visited the zoo.

4. Write a complex sentence beginning with "until." (These are particularly effective to develop complex sentence-writing ability, any subordinating conjunction can be used, and students can complete multiple sentences set up like this one in one sitting. Suggested content can be provided as needed.)

   e.g., Until the runways are clear of snow and ice, no planes will take off.

5. Write a complex sentence about a reality T.V. show:

   We watch *American Idol,* which is my favorite show, each week while we eat.

6. Write a complex sentence of at least 10 words about rivers.

   e.g., Most rivers flow from north to south until they reach a larger body of water, such as a pond, lake, or ocean.

- Students can also be asked to create sentences using clause structure templates. Templates can be reused frequently. Create a sentence for each template provided below:

  1. D,I

  2. ID - use <u>since</u>

  3. D,ID

  4. $\underset{D}{I}$

  5. D,D,I - use unless

  6. D,D,IDD

Compound-Complex Sentences

Overview:
The final sentence to discuss is the compound-complex sentence, which writers use incidentally more often than they might imagine. These sentences fit the definition of a compound sentence because they have 2 independent clauses joined by a comma and a coordinating conjunction or a semi-colon. They fit the definition of a complex sentence because they also have 1 (or more) dependent clauses. Adverbial dependent clauses can be inserted before or after either independent clause, and adjectival dependent clauses can be inserted after any noun or pronoun that they define. The possibilities are many. Students should be thoroughly familiar with both compound and complex sentences before studying, identifying, and creating compound-complex sentences intentionally.

Common Core:
The Common Core State Standards suggest that students should be able to do the following. (Italics identify elements that later concepts will address):

- Explain the function of phrases and clauses in general and their function in specific sentences. (7)

- Choose among simple, compound, complex, and compound-complex sentences to signal differing relationships among ideas. (7)

- Use various types of phrases (noun, verb, adjectival, adverbial, *participial*, prepositional, absolute) and clauses (independent, dependent; noun, relatively, adverbial) to convey specific meanings and add variety and interest to writing or presentations. (9-10)

compound-complex sentence

2 independent clauses and 1 (or more) dependent clauses

examples: When I gathered the toys from the playroom, I found the missing spoon, and my mom was quite relieved.
I asked for a Wii for Christmas, but, because my family was already going to New York City for winter vacation, we decided not to give presents this year.

compound-complex sentence

2 independent and 1 (or more) dependent clauses

John's parents bought him a used car for his sixteenth birthday, but he had to pay for his own insurance and gas because they wanted to teach him responsibility. (I, *but* ID)

If you find the time, you should study a few minutes each day, or you may find it difficult to master the material for the final test. (D,I, *or* I)

Introduction:

- To be reviewed before teaching: independent clause, dependent clause, compound sentence, complex sentence

- Define the term, writing it on the board. Include several examples.

- Hand students concept cards or have them create their own.

- Explain that students can create these easily by writing a compound sentence and then adding to the sentence a dependent clause in any position.

Application:

- Have students identify subjects and predicates in independent and dependent clauses.

- Have students locate subject/predicate pairs in compound-complex sentences.

- Have students generate compound sentences and add dependent clauses to them.

- Have students punctuate pre-written compound-complex sentences.

- Provide students with a different template for each subsequent lesson. Show them one model, and ask them to imitate it. Here are some models with single dependent clauses:

      core compound sentence: I, fanboy I

      basic possibilities: D,I, fanboy I

                         ID, fanboy I

                         I, fanboy, D,I

                         I, fanboy ID

- Another way to go about generating a compound-complex sentence is to start with a complex sentence. There are two basic templates, and an additional independent clause can be added anywhere:

	beginning A	*beginning B*
core complex sentence:	D,I	ID
basic possibilities:	D,I,fanboyI	ID,fanboyI
	I,fanboy,D,I	I,fanboyID

- Either approach will bring you to the same four basic alternatives. Additional variety can be created by (a) using a semi-colon instead of comma and conjunction or (b) using more than one dependent clause.

Suggested Exercises & Activities

Identification: This activity should be cumulative. Thus, students should be asked to identify simple, compound, complex, and compound-complex sentences.

- Label each group of words <u>simple</u>, <u>compound</u>, <u>complex</u>, or <u>compound-complex</u> in the blank above. Underline all subjects once and their predicates (verbs) twice. Put parentheses around the clauses. If a dependent clause occurs in the middle of an independent clause, use brackets to set it off. Do NOT include coordinating conjunctions that connect clauses inside the parentheses; all other words should be included. (Answers are included in parentheses here.)

_____

1. Before I can recharge my cell phone, I must find the charger. (complex - D,I)

_____

2. An icicle dangled from gutter of our garage; though it looked dangerous, it never fell before it melted. (compound-complex - I;D,ID)

_____

3. The front door must remain closed, but you may open the back door to catch the breeze. (compound - I,fanboyI))

_____

4. I could not find my keys anywhere because my daughter had put them in her pocket. (complex - ID)

_____

5. Though I love to procrastinate, I should not cram all of my studying into one night since I want to do well on my exams. (complex - D,ID)

_____

6. After we finally got a fire started at the campsite, a strong wind blew it out, and now we are freezing. (compound-complex - D,I,fanboyI

_____

7.   Barack Obama, who was elected President in November 2008, was a senator from Illinois. (complex - D-wedge)

_____

8.   My great uncle, who was a tobacco farmer, was over 100 when he died. (complex - ID with D-wedge as well)

_____

9.   The apples, which came from Mr. Esther's farm, are the most delicious that I have ever tasted. (complex - ID with D-wedge as well)

_____

10. The sports car that was in the driveway of my uncle's house has disappeared, and we are headed to the police department to report it stolen. (compound complex - ID,fanboyI)

_____

11. The first graders giggled uncontrollably whenever they had the chance, but their teacher kept them in line most of the time. (compound-complex - ID,fanboyI)

Sorting: Unscramble the sentence parts to form logical sentences by numbering them in the blanks. Then, write the finished product on the line below. For many of these, there will be more than one possible order. Do not forget to capitalize the first word and use proper end punctuation (If students need more support, you may include end punctuation for the appropriate sentence part.):

1.   _____   the Roman emperor   _____   while the people

     _____   under his control   _____   trembled in fear,

     _____   but luckily he   _____   ruled with an iron fist

     _____   was eventually overthrown.

Unscrambled sentence: _____

_____

2.   _____   , who was the third baseman,   _____   Zach

     _____   hit a home run   _____   with all his fans cheering,

     _____   in the third inning;   _____   unfortunately, that

     _____   to win the game   _____   was not enough

Unscrambled sentence: _____

Combining: Combine each cluster of sentences into one compound-complex sentence. (Correct conjunctions can be provided, or students can be asked to generate their own.) Add or omit words as needed.

1.   The coach sat with the team at halftime

     He gave the team a pep talk.

     Everyone had already given up.

     _____

2.   The employee at the fastfood restaurant took their order.

     He confused part of it.

     He corrected his mistake.

     Everybody ended up happy.

     _____

3.   The goalie on our field hockey team is excellent.

     She got injured in last week's game.

     She will be on the bench this week.

     We will most likely lose.

     _____

Imitating: Imitating sentences at this level is too complicated and not particularly fruitful. Instead, plan to have students create sentences using the clause templates in the Sentence Generation section.

Tandem Writing: Read the clauses provided and add the required clause to create a compound-complex sentence:

- Read the complex sentence, and add a coordinating conjunction and independent clause at the end to create a compound-complex sentence:

1. While my dad was repairing my old bicycle, I mowed the grass, _____ _____.

2. It starts pouring whenever we have a baseball game, _____ _____.

- Read the compound sentence, and add a dependent clause at the end to create a compound-complex sentence:

1. The S.C.U.B.A. diver carefully maneuvered between the enormous coral formations, for he didn't want to damage them _____.

2. My new T.V. is three-dimensional, but there isn't a lot of 3-D programming yet _____ _____.

- Read the compound sentence, put an X where you would like the dependent clause to appear, and write it in the blank provided, creating a compound-complex sentence:

1. My aunt and uncle catch lobster off the shores of Maine, and it is a real treat to eat at their table. _____.

2. I have not yet finished my homework, nor have I done my chores. _____ _____.

Sentence Generation:

- Ultimately, students must generate sentences containing every element they study. When they turn to sentence writing, you can engage them and develop their writing by providing parameters, including (a) minimum word count, (b) specific element required and/or located in particular position, and (c) specific content:

1. Write a compound-complex sentence that uses the word <u>unless</u>.

   e.g., Unless we get back in time, mom will be mad, but she will forgive us eventually.

2. Write a compound-complex sentence with at least two dependent clauses.

    e.g., When we heard the sirens, we went outside, and a firetruck was in front of our neighbors' house because there was a fire on their front porch.

3. Write a compound-complex sentence about the epic poem *Beowulf*.

    e.g., King Hrothgar angers Grendel, a horrible beast, who kills many in his otherwise happy kingdom, but Beowulf, a valiant warrior, comes to save the day!

4. Write a complex sentence about a novel.

    e.g., Kino discovers an enormous pearl in the opening chapters of *The Pearl*, and at first he and his wife believe that it will bring them great happiness though ultimately it brings them much pain and suffering.

- Students can also be asked to create sentences using clause structure templates. Templates can be reused frequently. Create a sentence for each template provided below:

    1. D,I;I
    2. ID,fanboyI

    3. D,I, fanboyD,I
    4. I,fanboy I / D

    5. ID;ID
    6. I,fanboyD,ID

Appositives

Overview:

An appositive is a noun (or pronoun) placed next to another noun (or pronoun) to rename or describe it. Some examples are italicized in sentences below:

> Homer Simpson, *a cartoon character*, has been on the air for over twenty years.
>
> <u>Star Wars</u>, *a famous science fiction film*, first came out in 1977.
>
> I finally saw our destination, *a rambling farmhouse on a hilltop.*
>
> *A fierce huntress,* Artemis is Apollo's twin sister.

Students are unlikely to use appositives incidentally in their writing without direct instruction. When properly introduced and internalized, however, these phrases add a level of sophistication and interest to sentences. Furthermore, students will encounter them in content area reading, so studying them will improve reading comprehension. Both science and social studies/history texts often use appositives because they allow text authors to define a person, place, thing, or concept. Take these examples:

> Winston Churchill, *the leader of Great Britain during World War II*, and F.D.R., *his American counterpart,* forged a strong friendship during the war.
>
> Homeostasis, *the property of a system that regulates its internal environment,* was first defined by Claude Bernard.

Appositives can occur in three locations in a sentence. As non-essential phrases, they are set off by commas:

> at the beginning: *An incredible soccer player,* Pelé broke many records and astounded fans across the globe.

between subject and predicate (verb): Mr. Hentschel, *our P.E. teacher,* also taught my mother.

at the end (notice that a noun/pronoun must immediately precede it): In the attic I finally found my grandmother's trunk, *a worn out leather box filled with photos.*

Appositives are typically set off by commas as is the case with the examples above. Single-word appositives do not need commas, however:

My friend *Mark* makes me laugh.

She sent the present to my sister *Sharon.*

Students (and teachers) sometimes confuse appositives with relative clauses (D-wedges), particularly when they occur between subject and predicate. Look at these two examples carefully:

Hilary Clinton, *a senator from New York,* became Secretary of State.

Hilary Clinton, *who was a senator from New York,* became Secretary of State.

Both sentences impart the same information to the reader. The italicized portion in the first sentence marks an appositive; in the second, the italicized portion is a relative clause (D-wedge). The appositive is a phrase with no subject or predicate; the relative clause, however, has both a subject (<u>who</u>) and a predicate (<u>was</u>).

Like any noun or pronoun, appositives can be described (or modified) by adjectives, adjective phrases, and adjective or relative clauses. Below, the appositives are underlined and the words, phrases, and clauses that modify them are in italics:

The President, *a kind* <u>man</u> *with an incredible intelligence,* won by a landslide.

My sister, *a* <u>woman</u> *who has a wicked sense of humor,* keeps us all laughing when we visit her.

appositive

noun (or pronoun) placed next to
another noun (or pronoun) to
rename or describe it
(often includes modifiers)

examples: My brother, <u>a good kid</u>, helps
our neighbor with her groceries.
<u>A bustling metropolis</u>, New York City is
home to over eight million people.

appositive

noun (or pronoun) placed next to another noun (or pronoun) to rename or describe it (often includes modifiers)

George Washington, <u>the first President of the United States</u>, is considered one of our country's greatest leaders.

Mark Twain, <u>author of *The Adventures of Huckleberry Finn*</u>, often wrote about life in the South.

<u>A happy and cheerful girl</u>, Gwelda enjoyed most everything about life.

Introduction:

- To be reviewed before teaching: noun, pronoun

- Define the term, writing it on the board. Include several examples.

- Hand students concept cards or have them create their own.

- Explain that students can create these by writing a sentence and then choosing a noun to rename. Start with examples that split the subject and predicate:

  The dog barked ferociously. (Rename "dog.")

  The dog, a German Shepherd, barked ferociously.

Application:

- Have students identify appositives in sentences.

- Have students correctly punctuate sentences containing appositives.

- Have students expand sentences using appositives.

Suggested Exercises & Activities

Identification: Underline the appositives in the sentences below. (You can also give students sentences containing appositives and ask them to insert necessary commas.):

1. An adventure no matter how you describe it, our trip to Disney World was fabulous!

2. Gregor Mendel, the discoverer of modern genetics, crossed pea plants to prove his hypotheses.

3. This weekend, I have got to mow the backyard, an overgrown jungle according to my dad.

4. When we visit my grandmother, I look forward to her lemonade, the best I have ever tasted.

Sorting: Unscramble the sentence parts to form logical sentences by numbering them in the blanks. Then, write the finished product on the line below. Do not forget to capitalize the first word and use proper end punctuation. (If students need more support, you may include end punctuation for the appropriate sentence part.):

1. _____ often enough   _____ Mac Milam

    _____ is also a family friend   _____ though we

    _____ do not see him   _____ my doctor

    Unscrambled sentence: _____

    _____

2. _____ would rather spend my money   _____ My phone

    _____ someplace else   _____ needs replacing,

    _____ , a relic from the dinosaur age   _____ but I

    _____ according to my daughter,

    Unscrambled sentence: _____

    _____

Combining: Combine each cluster of sentences into one sentence using an appositive. (Correct conjunctions can be provided, or students can be asked to generate their own.) Add and omit words as necessary:

1. The teacher took one look at the students.

    He was a veteran of twenty years.

    He knew something was wrong.

    _____

2. Our mail carrier was late today.

    He is a good man.

    His mail truck broke down last week.

    _____

3. The class went on a field trip.

    The trip was a nightmare.

    I doubt our teacher will ever take us anywhere again.

    _____

Expanding: Read the sentences and write an appositive to replace the X in each. (As they are ready, give students expansions in all three positions.):

1. Our dog, X, needs a bath.

    _____

2. X, the noise rattled me and made me jumpy for the rest of the day.

    _____

3. The performer completed his dance, X.

    _____

Sentence Generation:

- Ultimately, students must generate sentences containing every element they study. When they turn to sentence writing, you can engage them and develop their writing by providing parameters, including (a) minimum word count, (b) specific element required and/or located in particular position, and (c) specific content:

1 Write a sentence with an appositive between the subject and predicate.

e.g., My room, a complete mess, is never going to pass my mom's inspection.

2 Write a sentence of at least 10 words that opens with an appositive.

e.g., A beautiful antique from Italy, the lamp fell and broke into a million pieces.

3 Write a sentence about a foreign language that contains an appositive.

e.g., Mandarin Chinese, the language with the most speakers, has over 800 million native speakers today.

4 Write a sentence containing an appositive about dinosaurs.

e.g., Tyrannosaurus Rex, a fearsome dinosaur, became extinct about 65 million years ago.

5. Write a sentence about someone you admire with an introductory appositive.

e.g., A positive role model for young people, Michael Jordan also has some amazing records as a basketball player.

Verbals

Overview:

A verbal is a verb used as a different part of speech. Students will use them incidentally, and the instructor should be familiar with them so as to avoid confusion.

Though advanced students will benefit from some instruction with verbals, limit this to a brief introduction, a few quick identifying exercises, and then some sentence-writing activities. Most students will use infinitives and gerunds in their speech and writing without too much thought. Some work with participles, and particularly participial phrases, may prove fruitful, however. They appear commonly in published writing, including novels and textbooks, and yet students do not often use them automatically in their own writing.

Rather than separate verbals out into individual teaching lessons, I have included the necessary information, sample concept cards, and numerous examples to improve teacher understanding and allow for student instruction where appropriate. Sample exercises, with an emphasis on participial phrases, are at the end of the Overview.

Gerunds:

A gerund is an -ing verb used as a noun. Luckily, they *always* end in -ing, and they *always* serve in a role a noun would usually take. This makes them easier to identify than some other elements of grammar. They fortunately almost never require any special punctuation, a fact that makes them relatively easy to use in writing. One way to see if an -ing verb is a gerund is to replace it with a noun and decide if the sentence still works. Consider the following example:

Skiing took all my energy.

<u>Skiing</u> is the gerund. Now, replace <u>skiing</u> with <u>the math test</u>:

>   <u>The math test</u> took all my energy.

The complete subject, <u>the math test</u>, can serve as an appropriate replacement for <u>skiing</u>. Here are some additional examples of gerunds in sentences:

>   Those kids love <u>screaming</u>.
>
>   He trained in <u>flying</u> with an excellent instructor.
>
>   <u>Walking</u> is excellent exercise.
>
>   I plan to be finished with the <u>planting</u> next Tuesday.
>
>   He is still in the <u>running</u>.

Gerunds sometimes exist with other words to form a *gerund phrase*. In these examples the *gerund* is underlined, and the *gerund phrase* is in italics:

>   I love *<u>washing</u> the car.*
>
>   The game requires *<u>rolling the die</u>.*
>
>   *<u>Wearing</u> shoes* is smart.
>
>   *<u>Policing</u> your kids* takes time.
>
>   *<u>Stubbing</u> your toe* is no fun.
>
>   *<u>Singing</u> that song* makes me laugh.
>
>   *<u>Lifting</u> weights* is exhausting but builds muscles.
>
>   My grandmother enjoys *<u>baking</u> on the weekend.*
>
>   I love *<u>watching</u> television on weeknights.*
>
>   A difficulty with fluency can involve *<u>pausing</u> between words.*

With the exception of indirect objects, gerunds can serve any function a noun (or pronoun) typically serves:

>   <u>Eating</u> and <u>pooping</u> is all baby chicks seem to do. (subject)
>
>   I do not like your <u>texting</u> during class. (direct object)
>
>   I find great pleasure in <u>marking</u> the days till summer vacation. (object of prep.)
>
>   My dad's pet peeve is <u>whining</u>. (predicate noun)

Remember, though, that gerunds are *verbs* serving as nouns. As a result adverbs, adverb phrases, and adverb clauses (rather than their adjective counterparts) describe gerunds. Consider this example, which is useful for teacher understanding but probably not student instruction:

<u>Sleeping late when you make all that racket in the morning</u> is nearly impossible.

<u>Sleeping</u> is the gerund, serving as subject of the sentence. <u>Late</u> is an adverb describing <u>sleeping</u>. (Remember, the gerund is a *verb* functioning as a noun.) <u>When you make all that racket in the morning</u> is an *adverb clause* describing <u>sleeping</u>. The entire underlined portion, then, serves as the complete subject. Here's another example:

I love <u>watching television when I get home from school</u>.

<u>Watching</u> is the direct object of the main verb <u>love</u>. <u>Television</u> is the direct object of <u>watching</u>. (Remember, gerunds are *verbs* acting as nouns.) <u>When I get home from school</u> is an adverb clause telling when the <u>watching</u> occurs.

Participles:

A participle is a verb used as an adjective. Thus, they describe nouns or pronouns. *Present* participles always end in -<u>ing</u>:

the *wailing* siren   a *crushing* blow   a *boiling* pot

Past participles usually end in -<u>ed</u>:

my *busted* lip   the *sealed* vault   some *salted* fish

Since the past tense is sometimes formed irregularly, past participles sometimes form using irregular endings, including -<u>en</u>, -<u>d</u>, -<u>t</u>, and -<u>n</u>:

that *broken* window   the *dealt* hand   a *grown* boy

the *spoken* word   my *paid* bill   the *thrown* pot

Here are some examples of participles in sentences:

My <u>annoying</u> neighbor yells at us all the time.

I would like to present the <u>graduating</u> class of 2000!

The <u>stoked</u> team went out for dinner after their <u>amazing</u> win.

Like their gerund counterparts, participles can exist in *participial phrases*. Even advanced students may not use them naturally in their writing, and some work with generating participial phrases and expanding sentences using participial phrases may enhance student writing significantly. Look at these examples, where the <u>participle</u> is underlined and the *participial phrase* is in italics:

> *<u>Running</u> on empty*, the old car pulled into the gas station just in time.
>
> *<u>Slithering</u> across the grass*, the enormous snake approached the unaware picnickers.
>
> The card, *<u>chosen</u> with care from the local card shop*, really expressed the humor of my dad's fiftieth birthday.
>
> Into the sewer grate fell my keys, *<u>lost</u> forevermore*.

Like gerunds, participial phrases are described by adverbs, adverb phrases, and adverb clauses:

> <u>Climbing vigorously until he reached the top</u>, the mountaineer celebrated his ascent.

<u>Climbing</u> is the participle, describing <u>mountaineer</u>. <u>Vigorously</u> is an adverb telling *how* the <u>climbing</u> happened, and <u>until he reached the top</u> is an adverb clause telling *when* the <u>climbing</u> happened.

Participial phrases, which are non-essential elements, are usually isolated by commas and can be removed without losing the sentence's central meaning.

Most educators have heard of a dangling participle. While I would not devote too much time to their study, advanced students need to understand what one is and how to avoid them. Standardized testing such as the S.A.T. and A.C.T. includes questions regarding dangling participles as well. Consider this sentence:

> The runner was exhilarated by his fans, crossing the finish line.
>
> The crook outwitted the police officer, dressed as a clown.

In the first sentence, the fans crossed the finish line. In the second, who is dressed as a clown? The police officer? As a general rule of thumb, the participle needs to be closest to the noun or pronoun it describes (rather than another noun or pronoun in the sentence).

Infinitives:

An infinitive is the pure form of the verb. It is formed by joining <u>to</u> + the verb with no tense and can function as a noun, adverb, or adjective. Students taking foreign languages are usually familiar with them. <u>To run</u>, <u>to jump</u>, <u>to be</u>, and <u>to sleep</u> are all infinitives. They *never* serve as the main predicate of a sentence because that verb must have a tense. When students are identifying subjects and predicates, this is valuable information to have. Sometimes, it is a good idea to mention these "<u>to</u> + verb" structures to a younger student, just so that she will avoid choosing one as a sentence's predicate.

That said, students write infinitives naturally, even from a relatively young age. Some brief work identifying them is fine, but practice using them will do little to enhance student writing. Here are some examples:

> <u>To sleep</u> is what I want most in life.
>
> The score <u>to beat</u> is 35!
>
> The work that I want you <u>to finish</u> is in your binder.
>
> Prom was certainly a time <u>to remember</u>.
>
> Because the time <u>to withdraw</u> has passed, you will have to stay in this class.

Infinitives sometimes exist with other words to form an *infinitive phrase*. In these examples the *<u>infinitive</u>* is underlined and the *infinitive phrase* is in italics:

The place *to find good clothing at a low price* is T.J.Maxx.

We looked *to see if we could find a place to park near the theater.*

We're off *to see the wizard.* (*The Wizard of Oz*)

Our family likes *to eat at Chili's on Friday nights.*

I made an appointment *to have my hair cut.*

I want *to walk to the park today.*

The knight continued *to fight for his honor and for his maiden.*

Every time to + a verb exists in English, it will serve as an infinitive. Be careful, though, as the word to also serves as a common preposition. In the examples below, to is the preposition that begins a prepositional phrase rather than an infinitive:

Martha was taking her to the store.

The fight to the top is long and difficult.

I tripped over my son's toys and fell to the floor. I sent him to his room.

The road to the mall is under construction.

Infinitives can serve as nouns, adverbs, and adjectives. Consider these examples:

The captain looked to find brave soldiers for the mission.

(adverb describing looked)

I have posted the rules to follow by the door. (adjective describing rules)

He learned to speak with dignity. (noun serving as direct object of learned)

While the roles infinitives can serve is useful teacher information, it won't do too much to improve student writing.

Like gerunds and participles, infinitive phrases often have adverbial describers:

The problem to solve when we get there is where we should eat.

To solve is the infinitive and serves as an adjective describing problem. When we get

<u>there</u> is an adverb clause telling *when* the solving will occur.

Here are concept cards for the three verbals, from left to right in order of instruction.

gerund

verb used as a noun, always ending in -<u>ing</u> (verbal)

<u>Running</u> is good exercise.
Stop <u>burping</u>.

gerund phrase:

<u>Painting a house</u> is hard work.

<u>Drinking lemonade</u> on a hot day quenches one's thirst.

participle

verb used as an adjective (verbal)

<u>broken</u> knee   <u>talking</u> books
<u>barking</u> dog

participial phrase:

The chairs, <u>weathered by years of storms</u>, sat on the porch.

<u>Excited by the victory</u>, the soccer team went out for pizza.

infinitive

to + the pure form of the verb; used as a noun, adjective, or adverb (verbal)

to run   to sleep   to consider

infinitive phrase:

I would like <u>to run through the park tomorrow morning</u>.

<u>To eat dessert before dinner</u> is a true delight!

Common Core: The Common Core State Standards suggest that students should be able to do the following:

- Use punctuation (commas, parentheses, dashes) to set off nonrestrictive/parenthetical elements. (6)

- Place phrases and clauses within a sentence, recognizing and correcting misplaced and dangling modifiers. (7)

- Explain the function of verbals in general and their function in particular sentences. (7)

- Use various types of phrases (noun, verb, adjectival, adverbial, participial, prepositional, absolute) and clauses (independent, dependent; noun, relatively, adverbial) to convey specific meanings and add variety and interest to writing or presentations. (9-10)

Suggested Exercises & Activities

Identification: Students should be asked to locate elements in sentences.

- Underline the gerund, participle, or infinitive in each sentence. Then, in the blank, write G (gerund), P (participle) or I (infinitive) to identify the element you underlined.

  _____ 1. I enjoy snacking when I get home from school.

  _____ 2. I would like to see if I can find my own errors.

  _____ 3. His nose will not stop running.

  _____ 4. A sleeping baby is better than a crying one.

- Underline the gerund, participle, or infinitive in each sentence. Then, put parentheses around its phrase. Finally, in the blank, write G (gerund), P (participle) or I (infinitive) to identify the element you identified.

  _____ 1. My clock, glowing persistently throughout the night, served as a reminder that I could not sleep.

  _____ 2. I would like to find a solution to your problem.

  _____ 3. Drinking coffee in the morning is a requirement for me.

Sorting: Unscramble the sentence parts to form logical sentences by numbering them in the blanks. Then, write the finished product on the line below. (If students need more support, you may include end punctuation for the appropriate sentence part).

1. _____ sleeping late this Saturday   _____ found it difficult

   _____ the teenager   _____ to make it to the restaurant

   _____ to meet his grandmother

   Unscrambled sentence: _____

   _____

2. _____ scoring the winning goal   _____ was what Mac dreamed of

   _____ when he   _____ in a championship game

   _____ thought about the team   _____ at his prep school

   Unscrambled sentence: _____

2. _____ the teenager   _____ and careened into a ditch

   _____ lost control of the wheel   _____ driving through the neighborhood

   _____ at about 80 miles an hour   _____ but was luckily unharmed

   Unscrambled sentence: _____

   _____

Combining With Participles: Combine each cluster of sentences into one

sentence. Delete words as required. Your sentence should include a participial phrase.

1. The young man entered the expressway

   He was texting while he was driving.

   He barely missed having an accident.

   _____

2. The flight attendant told witty jokes.

   The jokes were made during her announcements.

   The flight was more enjoyable for the passengers because of her jokes.

   _____

3. The thief had stolen money and I-Pods from students' lockers.

   He was busted by the local police department.

   All the stolen articles were returned to their owners.

   _____

Replacing Nouns With Gerunds: Write a gerund or gerund phrase in

the blank provided to replace the underlined noun (and its describers).

1. I love <u>that bicycle</u>.   _____

2. <u>My uncle</u> makes me laugh.   _____

3. The chance of <u>a hole in one</u> is about 1 in a million.   _____

Expanding Sentences With Participles: Write a participle or

participial phrase in the blank provided to replace the X in the sentence.

1. The X pilot landed the plane safely despite heavy turbulence.

   _____

2. The singer, X, finished the song and then stormed off stage.

   _____

3. Elizabeth put an arm around her friend, X.

   _____

Sentence Generation:

*   Ultimately, students must generate sentences containing every element they study. When they turn to sentence writing, you can engage them and develop their writing by providing parameters, including (a) minimum word count, (b) specific element required and/or located in particular position, and (c) specific content:

1   Write a complex sentence that uses at least one infinitive.

   e.g., Unless I find a place *to exercise* in this hotel, I will go crazy!.

2   Write a compound sentence that contains at least one participial phrase.

   e.g., The boy, *swinging hard at the pitcher's throw*, missed the ball completely; nevertheless, he raised his bat to try again.

3. Write a simple sentence with a gerund in it.

   e.g., I am kept awake by his loud *snoring* every night.

4. Write a sentence about Thurgood Marshall that uses an infinitive.

   e.g., Before Thurgood Marshall became the first black supreme court justice, he defended some cases in front of the Supreme Court as a lawyer, and he was tough *to beat*.

5. Write a sentence about Leonardo DaVinci that contains a participial phrase.

   e.g., *Interested in the way the world works*, DaVinci, one of the most famous artists that ever lived, created a number of inventions as well.

Appendix 1:
Word, Phrase, and Clause Lists

On the pages that follow are reproducible word, phrase, clause, and sentence lists that instructors can use to generate writing activities and worksheets. Students can use them to expand the vocabulary they use when they write, to vary their sentence structure, and as topics for sentence writing. The lists are described below in the order in which they appear.

Nouns (284): This list, grouped by person, place, thing, and idea is a small selection of nouns, the part of speech with the most word members.

Verbs (5 pages - 285-289): Too often, students use linking verbs, particularly forms of the verb "to be," as the main verbs of their sentences. Strong action verbs lead to improved sentences. Included are transparent regular verbs (more accessible verbs that conjugate regularly), more advanced regular verbs (more challenging verbs that conjugate regularly), irregular verbs (verbs that have irregular conjugations), and phrasal verbs (verbs comprised of a verb and additional word(s), most of which are prepositions in other contexts).

Conjunctions (bottom of Linking & Helping Verbs page - 288): This list includes coordinating and subordinating conjunctions useful in helping students expand their sentence writing to compound and complex sentences with interesting and varied transition words. A list of the more rare correlative conjunctions is also included.

Adjectives (2 pages - 290-1): Students often limit their adjective use to simplistic words, such as big/little or tall/short. There are many adjectives in English. While some are beyond a given student's vocabulary, many are just difficult for him to retrieve from memory. These lists are an invaluable resource to address this retrieval issue.

Pronouns (292): This page includes a comprehensive list of all pronouns as well as smaller lists, broken into categories. For some English speakers, pronoun usage comes naturally. For others, lists like these may prove beneficial for reference.

Adverbs (2 pages - 293-4): The main adverb list is broken into two categories: those with the suffix -ly and those without. These lists can be used to add flavor to dry or simplistic writing.

Prepositions (295): This page includes a comprehensive list of prepositions as well as two break-out lists, one with concrete prepositions that would apply to "anything a plane can do to a cloud" and another that contains common but more abstract prepositions.

Conjunctions, Relative Pronouns, Prepositions, & Conjunctive Adverbs for Sentence Construction (296): Middle and high school students will benefit from a copy of this for their ready reference. They should refer to it when generating different kinds of sentences, particularly when they begin to overuse particular conjunctions. *(This chart is available in gloss, cover-grade tag as a binder insert from wvced.com. Significant discounts for bulk orders are available; for younger students, a simpler version is also available.)*

Transition Words for Reading, Writing, & Note-Taking (297): The words in the left column signify a change in direction, the words in the middle signal a continuing thought, and those in the right column signal a conclusion or summation statement. Below are temporal words. This list is useful for students working on transitioning between sentences. *(This chart is available in gloss, cover-grade tag as a binder insert from wvced.com. Significant discounts for bulk orders are available; for younger students, a simpler version is also available.)*

Prepositional Phrases (298): This list is in two parts. One includes phrases with concrete prepositions, and the other includes those that are more abstract. Sometimes, a single preposition is not enough to stimulate a sentence from a student. These lists can help.

Clauses (299): On the left are dependent clauses, and on the right are their independent counterparts. These can be used for tandem writing, where the teacher provides one half, and the student generates the other half to complete the sentence, for subject/verb identification, for clause matching exercises, and more.

Barebones Sentences (300-4): There are four lists, including basic subject-verb, basic subject-verb-object, advanced subject-verb, and advanced subject-verb-object sentences. The basic sentences are concrete while the advanced ones are more abstract, particularly in terms of verbs. These sentences can be used for adding adjectives and adverbs as well as their phrase and clause counterparts. They are also excellent for the interrogative expander questions.

Common Punctuation (305): This reference chart provides straightforward guidelines for punctuation usage with simple, easy-to-understand examples. Use it for teaching and reference. *(This chart is available in gloss, cover-grade tag as a binder insert from wvced.com. Significant discounts for bulk orders are available.)*

NOUNS GROUPED BY CATEGORY

person	place	thing	thing (continued)	idea
actor	airport	alligator	fur	adventure
advisor	apartment	animal	glove	anger
artist	attic	apple	grill	beauty
astronaut	backyard	arm	icicle	belief
aunt	bakery	ball	jar	bravery
baby	beach	balloon	jellyfish	chaos
baker	bedroom	banana	juice	confidence
boyfriend	bridge	bat	kite	courage
brother	cabin	bathtub	lamp	death
chef	camp	beast	lipstick	democracy
diver	castle	bed	lobster	despair
doctor	cathedral	belt	mask	education
driver	cemetery	blanket	needle	envy
explorer	church	book	nickel	evil
father	circus	boot	pail	faith
friend	city	brick	pancake	fear
girlfriend	coast	bucket	picture	freedom
golfer	condominium	bugle	pillow	friendship
grandparent	cottage	cactus	pizza	happiness
husband	country	cake	pumpkin	hatred
janitor	den	camera	puppy	honesty
lawyer	desert	canoe	quilt	imagination
magician	dungeon	cap	radio	intelligence
mother	farm	car	rifle	jealousy
neighbor	forest	chain	rock	justice
nephew	fortress	chair	roof	laughter
pediatrician	garden	chest	sack	liberty
pilot	gym	crate	seat	loyalty
professor	hospital	crib	ship	luck
queen	house	desk	snow	memory
sister	island	dock	soda	peace
soldier	kitchen	dollar	spider	poverty
supervisor	lake	eagle	tent	power
surgeon	library	ear	throne	skill
swimmer	office	eel	van	sorrow
teacher	palace	faucet	volcano	speed
technician	park	feast	wax	strength
tutor	porch	fish	weapon	success
uncle	store	flag	whale	sympathy
visitor	street	floor	window	talent
wife	synagogue	frame	word	wisdom
writer	zoo	fruit	yam	worry

TRANSPARENT REGULAR VERBS

add	complete	guide	melt	sail	taste
answer	copy	hammer	mend	save	tease
applaud	correct	harm	mess up	scrape	thank
argue	cough	hate	mix	scratch	tickle
ask	count	haunt	multiply	scream	tie
attach	cover	heat	murder	scrub	tip
attack	crack	help	nod	search	touch
arrive	crash	hook	obey	serve	tow
bake	crawl	hop	open	share	trace
bat	crush	hover	own	shave	trade
bathe	cry	hug	pack	shiver	train
battle	dance	hum	paddle	shock	trap
beg	deliver	hunt	paint	shop	tremble
behave	describe	hurry	park	shrug	trick
blink	destroy	inject	paste	sip	trip
blush	disagree	injure	phone	ski	trot
boast	dislike	instruct	pick	skip	trust
boil	divide	interrupt	pinch	slap	try
bomb	drag	introduce	plant	slip	tug
borrow	dress	invent	play	smash	tumble
breathe	drown	invite	point	smell	turn
bruise	enjoy	itch	poke	smile	twist
bump	enter	jam	pour	smoke	type
burn	escape	jog	press	sneeze	unlock
bury	explain	join	pretend	sniff	unpack
call	explode	joke	promise	snore	use
camp	fail	juggle	pull	snow	visit
carry	fit	jump	pump	spell	wait
carve	fix	kick	punch	spill	walk
chase	flip	kill	punish	spoil	wander
cheat	flow	kiss	push	spot	want
check	fool	kneel	reach	spray	warn
cheer	force	knock	refuse	squash	wash
chew	fold	laugh	relax	squeak	waste
choke	frighten	launch	remember	squeal	watch
chop	fry	learn	repair	stare	wave
clap	grab	lie	repeat	start	whine
clean	glue	like	report	stay	whip
close	greet	load	rescue	step	wink
coach	grin	lock	rinse	stir	wipe
comb	grip	look	rob	switch	wrap
compare	groan	love	rot	talk	wrestle
compete	guard	march	rub	tame	yawn
complain	guess	marry	rush	tap	yell

MORE CHALLENGING REGULAR VERBS

accept	clear	empty	increase	offer	regret	steer
admire	clip	encourage	influence	order	reign	stitch
admit	coil	end	inform	overflow	reject	stop
advise	collect	entertain	intend	owe	rejoice	store
afford	command	examine	interest	part	release	strap
agree	concentrate	excite	interfere	pass	rely	strengthen
alert	concern	excuse	irritate	pat	remain	stretch
allow	confess	exercise	jail	pause	remind	strip
amuse	confuse	expand	judge	peck	remove	stuff
analyze	connect	expect	knit	pedal	replace	subtract
announce	consider	extend	knot	peel	reply	succeed
annoy	contain	fade	label	peep	reproduce	suffer
apologize	continue	fasten	land	perform	request	suggest
appear	cross	fear	last	permit	retire	suit
appreciate	cure	fetch	level	pine	return	supply
approve	curl	file	license	place	rhyme	support
arrange	curve	fill	lighten	plan	risk	suppose
arrest	cycle	film	list	please	rock	surprise
attempt	damage	fire	listen	plug	roll	surround
attend	dare	flap	live	polish	ruin	suspend
attract	decay	flash	man	pop	rule	tempt
avoid	deceive	flood	manage	possess	sack	terrify
ban	decide	follow	match	post	satisfy	test
beam	decorate	form	mate	practise	scatter	thaw
belong	delay	found	measure	precede	scold	time
blind	delight	frame	meddle	prefer	scorch	tire
blot	depend	gather	memorize	prepare	scribble	tour
bolt	desert	gaze	milk	present	seal	transport
book	deserve	glow	mine	preserve	separate	travel
bore	detect	grate	miss	prevent	settle	treat
bounce	develop	grease	moan	print	shade	unite
bow	disappear	guarantee	mourn	produce	shelter	vanish
box	disapprove	hand	move	program	sigh	wail
brake	disarm	handle	muddle	protect	sign	warm
brake	discover	hang	mug	provide	signal	water
branch	double	happen	nail	puncture	slow	weigh
brush	doubt	head	name	question	snatch	welcome
bubble	drain	heal	need	race	soothe	whirl
buzz	dream	heap	nest	rain	sound	whisper
calculate	drum	hope	note	raise	spare	whistle
care	dry	identify	notice	realize	spark	wish
cause	dust	ignore	object	receive	sparkle	wobble
challenge	earn	imagine	observe	recognize	sprout	wonder
change	educate	impress	obtain	record	squeeze	work
charge	embarrass	improve	occur	reduce	stain	worry
claim	employ	include	offend	reflect	stamp	wreck

IRREGULAR VERBS

base form / past simple / past participle

regular verbs form like <u>ask</u>:
ask / asked / asked

irregular verbs form the past simple, past participle, or both without the regular -ed

awake / awoke / awoken
beat / beat / beaten
become / became / become
begin / began / begun
bend / bent / bent
bet / bet / bet
bid / bid / bid
bite / bit / bitten
blow / blew / blown
break / broke / broken
bring / brought / brought
build / built / built
burn / burned (burnt) /
    burned (burnt)
buy / bought / bought
catch / caught / caught
choose / chose / chosen
come / came / come
cost / cost / cost
cut / cut / cut
dig / dug / dug
do / did / done
draw / drew / drawn
dream / dreamed (dreamt) /
    dreamed (dreamt)
drive / drove / driven
drink / drank / drunk
eat / ate / eaten
fall / fell / fallen
feel / felt / felt
fight / fought / fought
find / found / found

fly / flew / flown
forget / forgot / forgotten
forgive / forgave / forgiven
freeze / froze / frozen
get / got / gotten
give / gave / given
go / went / gone
grow / grew / grown
hang / hung / hung
have / had / had
hear / heard / heard
hide / hid / hidden
hit / hit / hit
hold / held / held
hurt / hurt / hurt
keep / kept / kept
know / knew / known
lay / laid / laid
lead / led / led
learn / learned / learned
leave / left / left
lend / lent / lent
let / let / let
lie / lay / lain
lose / lost / lost
make / made / made
mean / meant / meant
meet / met / met
pay / paid / paid
put / put / put
read / read / read
ride / rode / ridden

ring / rang / rung
rise / rose / risen
run / ran / run
say / said / said
see / saw / seen
sell / sold / sold
send / sent / sent
show / showed / showed
    (shown)
shut / shut / shut
sing / sang / sung
sit / sat / sat
sleep / slept / slept
speak / spoke / spoken
spend / spent / spent
stand / stood / stood
swim / swam / swum
take / took / taken
teach / taught / taught
tear / tore / torn
tell / told / told
think / thought / thought
throw / threw / thrown
understand / understood /
    understood
wake / woke / woken
wear / wore / worn
win / won / won
write / wrote / written

LINKING & HELPING VERBS

Common Linking Verbs

"to be"	others
am	become
is	grow
are	look
was	prove
were	remain
be	seem
being	smell
been	sound
	taste
	turn
	stay
	get

The 23 Helping Verbs

am	does
is	did
are	will
was	would
were	shall
be	should
being	can
been	could
have	may
has	might
had	must
do	

COMMON CONJUNCTIONS

Coordinating Conjunctions

for	but
and	or
nor	yet
	(so)

Correlative Conjunctions

both...and
either...or
neither...nor
not only...but also
whether...or
not...but

Subordinating Conjunctions

after	even though	so that
although	if	though
as	if only	till
as if	in case	unless
as long as	in order that	until
as much as	just as	when
as soon as	lest	whenever
as though	now that	where
because	once	whereas
before	only if	wherever
by the time	provided that	whether
even if	since	while

Phrasal Verbs

ask (someone) out
ask around
back (something) up
back (someone) up
blow up
blow (something) up
break down
break (something) down
break in
break (something) in
break up
break out
bring (someone) down
bring (someone) up
bring (something) up
call (someone) back
call on (someone)
calm down
check out
cheer (someone) up
clean (something) up
come across (something)
come apart
come down with (something)
come from (somewhere)
count on (someone)
cross (something) out
cut (something) off
cut (someone) off
cut (something) out
do (something) over
dress up
drop back
drop in
drop (someone/something) off
drop out
eat out
fall apart
fall down
fall out
figure (something) out
fill (someone) in

find out
get along
get away
get back
get (something) back
get back into (something)
get together
get up
give (someone/something) away
give in
give up
go ahead
go back
go out
go over
grow apart
grow back
grow up
grow out of (something)
grow into (something)
hand (something) down
hand (something) in
hand (something) out
hand (something) over
hang on
hang up
hold (someone) back
hold on
keep on doing (something)
let (someone) down
let (someone) in
look after (someone/something)
look for (someone/something)
look forward to (something)
look into (something)
look out for (someone/something)
look (something) up
look up to (someone)
make (something) up

pass away
pass out
pass (something) out
pay (someone) back
point (something) out
put (something) off
put up with (someone/something)
put (something) on
run into (someone)
run over (someone)
run away
run out
set (someone/something) up
show off
sleep over
sort (something) out
stick to (something)
switch (something) off
switch (something) on
take (something) apart
take (something) back
take off
take (something) off
take (someone/something) out
tear (something) up
think back
think (something) over
throw (something) away
throw up
try (something) on
try (something) out
turn (something) down
turn (something) off
warm (something) up
warm up
wear off
work out
work (something) out

ADJECTIVES GROUPED BY CATEGORY

determiner **quantity**	*observation* **bad feelings**	*observation* **good feelings**	*observation* **condition**	*observation* **weather**	*sense observations* **taste/touch**	raspy screeching silent
abundant			alive	arid		soft
all	angry	agreeable	awkward	bad	bitter	shrill
empty	anxious	appreciative	better	bitter	bland	squeaking
few	apathetic	ecstatic	careful	balmy	delicious	silent
full	awful	brave	charismatic	calm	fruity	thundering
heavy	bewildered	calm	clever	cold	fresh	voiceless
light	crushed	delightful	clumsy	cloudy	greasy	whispering
many	defeated	eager	dead	clear	juicy	
most	defensive	earnest	dependent	damp	hot	**feel/touch**
no	depressed	empathetic	easy	dark	icy	
numerous	devastated	energetic	famous	drizzly	melted	boiling
some	dreadful	engaged	gifted	frosty	nutritious	bumpy
sparse	embarrassed	enthusiastic	helpful	good	rotten	chilly
substantial	fierce	faithful	important	hot	salty	cold
	grumpy	friendly	independent	humid	scrumptious	cool
	helpless	gentle	inexpensive	hazy	spicy	damp
	irritated	gregarious	mushy	icy	sticky	dry
	itchy	happy	odd	mild	strong	dusty
	jealous	jolly	powerful	misty	sweet	fluffy
	lazy	kind	proud	muggy	tangy	freezing
	livid	lively	rich	rainy	tart	fuzzy
	melancholy	nice	shy	raw	tasteless	hard
	morbid	obedient	tender	stormy	uneven	hot
	mysterious	proud	uninterested	snowy	weak	icy
	nasty	relieved	vast	steamy	wet	rough
	nervous	sympathetic	wrong	showery	yummy	silky
	over-	silly		scorching		smooth
	whelmed	thankful		sunny	**sound**	soft
	obnoxious	victorious		tempestuous		textured
	panicky	witty		warm	blaring	warm
	pessimistic	zealous		wet	booming	wet
	repulsive			windy	clicking	
	sad				cooing	
	scary				deafening	
	thoughtless				faint	
	unhappy				hissing	
	uptight				loud	
	worried				melodic	
					noisy	
					piercing	
					purring	
					quiet	

ADJECTIVES GROUPED BY CATEGORY (CONTINUED)

smell	size	shape	color	origin (proper)	material
acrid	big	broad	beige		brick
antiseptic	chubby	circular	black	Aboriginal	cashmere
bitter	colossal	crooked	blue	Aleutian	cardboard
burning	enormous	curved	brown	African	concrete
clean	fat	deep	colorful	American	copper
delicious	gargantuan	flat	colorless	Asian	cotton
fragrant	gigantic	high	crimson	Australian	gem-
fresh	great	hollow	dark green	Canadian	encrusted
medicinal	huge	low	drab	Catholic	enamel
musty	immense	narrow	gray	Chinese	fiberglass
pungent	large	oblong	green	Christian	gold
putrid	little	oval	light blue	Creek	leather
rancid	mammoth	rectangular	lime	Democratic	paper
rich	massive	round	mauve	Egyptian	plastic
rotten	miniature	shallow	orange	English	polyester
salty	miniscule	skinny	pink	European	nylon
smoky	petite	square	purple	French	rayon
sour	puny	steep	red	Indian	satin
spicy	scrawny	straight	rust	Italian	silk
stale	short	wide	tan	Japanese	stainless-
stinky	small		teal	Jewish	steel
strong	tall		turquoise	Latino	steel
sweet	tiny		white	Lilliputian	stucco
			yellow	Martian	wooden
				Marxist	wool
			noun + color	Mexican	woolen

possessive	age/speed			Muslim	
my	ancient		blood-red	Navaho	
your	brief		chocolate-	Nigerian	
his	early		brown	Puritan	
her	fast		crimson-red	Sioux	
its	late		dove-white	South	
our	long		eggplant-	American	
their	modern		purple	Spanish	
	old		emerald-	Republican	
	old-fashioned		green		
	quick		forest-green		
	rapid		lime-green		
	short		midnght-blue		
	slow		ruby-red		
	speedy		sky-blue		
	swift		lily-white		
	young				

PRONOUNS GROUPED BY CATEGORY

Personal Pronouns

used as subject	used as object	used as possessive
I	me	mine
you	you	yours
he	him	his
she	her	hers
it	it	its
we	us	ours
you	you	yours
they	them	theirs

* *Possessive <u>adjectives</u> (e.g., our, their) are listed with adjectives on the preceding page.*

Demonstrative Pronouns

this	these
that	those

Interrogative Pronouns

what	whom
who	whose
which	

Reflexive Pronouns

myself
yourself
himself
herself
itself
ourselves
yourselves
themselves

Relative Pronouns

that
which
who
whom
whose
whichever
whoever
whomever

Indefinite Pronouns

anybody	nobody	many
anyone	no one	several
anything	nothing	all
each	one	any
either	somebody	most
everybody	someone	none
everyone	something	some
everything	both	
neither	few	

Cumulative List of Pronouns

all	nothing
another	one
any	one another
anybody	other
anyone	others
anything	ours
both	ourselves
each	several
each other	she
either	some
everybody	somebody
everyone	someone
everything	something
few	that
he	theirs
her	them
hers	themselves
herself	these
him	they
himself	this
his	those
I	us
it	we
its	what
itself	whatever
many	which
me	whichever
mine	who
more	whoever
most	whom
much	whomever
myself	whose
neither	you
no one	yours
nobody	yourself
none	yourselves

Common Adverbs

accidentally	exactly	merrily	selfishly	weakly
angrily	faithfully	monthly	seriously	wearily
annually	fatally	mortally	shakily	wildly
anxiously	fiercely	mysteriously	sharply	yearly
awkwardly	finally	nearly	shrilly	
badly	fondly	neatly	shyly	adverbs that do
blindly	foolishly	nervously	silently	not end in -ly
boastfully	forcefully	noisily	sleepily	
boldly	fortunately	obediently	slowly	afterwards
bravely	frantically	obnoxiously	smoothly	almost
briefly	gently	only	softly	always
brightly	gladly	painfully	solemnly	even
busily	gracefully	perfectly	speedily	far
calmly	greedily	pleasantly	stealthily	fast
carefully	happily	politely	sternly	first
carelessly	harshly	poorly	strikingly	last
cautiously	hastily	powerfully	successfully	less
cheerfully	honestly	promptly	suddenly	more
clearly	hourly	punctually	suspiciously	never
correctly	hugely	quickly	swiftly	next
courageously	humorously	quietly	tenderly	not
crossly	hungrily	rapidly	tensely	often
cruelly	innocently	rarely	terrifically	seldom
daily	inquisitively	really	thoroughly	sometimes
defiantly	irritably	recklessly	thoughtfully	soon
deliberately	joyously	regularly	tightly	still
doubtfully	justly	reluctantly	truthfully	tomorrow
easily	kindly	repeatedly	unexpectedly	too
elegantly	lazily	rightfully	unfortunately	very
enormously	lightly	roughly	victoriously	well
enthusiastically	loosely	rudely	violently	yesterday
equally	loudly	sadly	vivaciously	
eventually	madly	safely	warmly	

COMMON ADVERBS GROUPED BY CATEGORY

that tell how		that tell where	that tell when (or how often)	
	loftily			today
	loudly			tomorrow
accidentally	loyally	abroad		usually
arrogantly	mechanically	anywhere	after	weekly
awkwardly	merrily	away	afterwards	when
badly	mysteriously	downstairs	already	yearly
beautifully	naturally	downward	always	yesterday
blindly	neatly	everywhere	annually	
boldly	nervously	far	before	
bravely	noisily	here	commonly	
briskly	obediently	home	continually	
brutally	oddly	in	daily	
busily	openly	inside	eventually	
calmly	painfully	off	finally	
carefully	patiently	near	first	
cheerfully	poorly	nearby	hourly	
competitively	properly	nowhere	immediately	
correctly	quickly	on	instantly	
coolly	quietly	out	just	
curiously	rapidly	outside	last	
deeply	really	over	later	
eagerly	recklessly	somewhere	less	
easily	rudely	there	monthly	
effortlessly	ruthlessly	under	more	
extremely	savagely	underground	mostly	
fairly	safely	up	never	
fatally	sloppily	upward	next	
ferociously	stylishly	upstairs	now	
foolishly	suspiciously		often	
fully	swiftly		periodically	
generally	terribly		promptly	
gracefully	thoroughly		punctually	
greedily	triumphantly		rarely	
grimly	truthfully		recently	
honestly	unfortunately		repeatedly	
intensely	urgently		second	
irritably	vaguely		seldom	
jealously	valiantly		sometimes	
justly	warmly		soon	
knowingly	well		still	
lazily	wrongly		then	
lightly	zealously		third	

COMMON PREPOSITIONS

Concrete Prepositions

above	by	out of
across	close to	outside
ahead of	down	outside of
alongside	far from	over
among	from	past
amongst	in	through
around	in front of	throughout
at	inside	to
atop	into	toward
behind	near	towards
below	near to	under
beneath	next to	underneath
beside	on	up
between	on top of	upon
beyond	onto	within

More Advanced Prepositions

aboard	in addition to
about	in case of
according to	in place of
after	in spite of
against	instead of
along	of
aside from	off
because of	on account of
before	on behalf of
besides	out
despite	prior to
due to	subsequent to
during	with
except (for)	with regard to
for	without

Exhaustive List of Common Prepositions

aboard	aside from	except	of	subsequent to
about	astride	except for	off	thanks to
above	at	far from	on	that of
according to	atop	following	on account of	through
across	barring	for	on behalf of	throughout
after	because of	from	on top of	till
against	before	in accordance with	onto	to
ahead of	behind	in addition to	opposite	toward
along	below	in case of	out	towards
alongside	beneath	in front of	out from	under
amid	beside	in lieu of	out of	underneath
amidst	besides	in place of	outside	unlike
among	between	in spite of	outside of	until
amongst	beyond	including	over	up
around	but	inside	owing to	upon
as	by	instead of	past	with
as far as	by means of	into	plus	with regard to
as well as	close to	like	prior to	with regards to
as of	concerning	near	regarding	with respect to
as per	despite	near to	regardless of	within
as regards	down	next to	round	without
as well as	due to	notwithstanding	save	
aside	during		since	

Conjunctions

coordinating (for compound sentences): I, fanboy I

    for   and   nor   but   or   yet

subordinating (for complex sentences to begin adverb clauses - grouped by purpose):   D,I   ID

time:
after
as
as soon as
before
just as
now that
once
since
till
until
when
whenever
while

place:
where
wherever

cause:
as
because
since

comparison:
as
just as
than

manner:
as
as if
as though

purpose:
in order that
so that

concession:
although
even though
though
whereas
while

condition:
as long as
even if
if
unless
whether

Relative Pronouns

(for complex sentences to begin adjective clauses):

  who   which   that   whom   whose

Conjunctive Adverbs

(optional for I;I compound sentences* - grouped by meaning):

<u>additionally</u>
also
furthermore
likewise
moreover
similarly
in addition

<u>however</u>
nevertheless
nonetheless
notwithstanding
on the contrary
on the other hand
still

<u>actually</u>
certainly
indeed
in fact

<u>afterwards</u>
later
next
subsequently
then

<u>at the same time</u>
meanwhile
simultaneously

<u>accordingly</u>
as a result
consequently
hence
therefore
thus

<u>alternatively</u>
instead

<u>for example</u>
for instance

<u>certainly</u>
clearly
obviously

Use a semi-colon before and a comma after the conjunctive adverb.

Prepositions

concrete prepositions
(to begin prepositional phrases)

above	near to
across	next to
around	on
at	on top of
behind	onto
below	out of
beneath	outside
beside	outside of
between	over
beyond	past
by	through
close to	throughout
down	to
far from	toward
from	towards
in	under
in front of	underneath
inside	up
into	upon
near	within

advanced prepositions
(to begin prepositional phrases):

aboard	except (for)
about	for
according to	in addition to
after	in case of
against	in place of
ahead of	in spite of
alongside	instead of
among	of
amongst	off
along	on account of
aside from	on behalf of
atop	out
because of	prior to
before	subsequent to
besides	with
despite	with regard to
due to	without
during	

This page is ideal for middle and high school students' notebooks.

Direction Change & Contrast: A change in ideas to follow.

alternatively
although
as opposed to
at the same time
but
conversely
despite (the fact that)
different from
even so
even though
for all that
however
in contrast
in spite of (the fact that)
instead
nevertheless
nonetheless
notwithstanding
on the contrary
on the other hand
or
otherwise
rather
still
though
unlike
whereas
while
yet

Addition: Similar ideas, additional support, or evidence to follow.

additionally
again
also
and
another
as an example
as well
because
besides (that)
equally important
following this further
for example
for instance
for one thing
further
furthermore
in addition
in light of the...it is easy to see
in particular
in the same vein
in the same way
just as
likewise
more (than that)
moreover
namely
next
other
pursuing this further
similarly
specifically
then
to illustrate

Conclusion, Summary & Emphasis: Conclusion, summary, or emphasis to follow.

accordingly*
after all
all in all
as a result*
because*
certainly
clearly, then*
consequently*
finally
for the reason (that)*
generally
hence*
in a word
in any event
in brief
in conclusion
in fact
in final analysis
in final consideration
in general
in short
in sum
in summary
in the end
indeed
last
lastly
naturally
of course
on account of*
on the whole
since*
so*
therefore*
thus*
to be sure
to conclude
to sum up
to summarize
truly

(* indicates cause and effect)

Sequence & Time:

after	during	now
afterwards	earlier	presently
always	eventually	recently
as long as	finally	shortly
as soon as	first... second...	simultaneously
at first	third	sometimes
at last	following	soon
at length	immediately	so far
before	in the first place	subsequently
before long	in the meantime	then
currently	later	this time
	meanwhile	when
	never	whenever
	next	while

Note: The bent arrow signifies a change in direction while the two straight arrows represent words that continue in the same direction. The arrow on the right crosses a line to indicate an end point.

PHRASES FOR EXPANSION USING CONCRETE PREPOSITIONS

above the tree line in the park
across the newly paved street
ahead of everybody else in line
alongside the abandoned freight train
among the members of my family
amongst the socks in Shane's top drawer
around the one mile track
at the corner of Elm Street and Alta
    Avenue
atop the smallest hill on the golf course
behind the front closet door
below the surface of the ocean
beneath a heap of dirty clothes
beside my best friend on the park bench
between two pages of the old text
beyond the horizon
by Anthony Horowitz
close to the point of no return
down the stairs and through the second
    door
far from a normal day
from my best friend in the world
in the leather-bound antique box
in front of several of her classmates

inside the cookie tin
into the old Chevy
near our home town
near to my new boss
next to his fifth floor office
on the weathered table at the beach
on top of everything else
onto Main Street
out of sheer will power
outside the family-owned grocery store
outside of the army fort
over insurmountable odds
past the locked wooden gate
through brambles and thorny branches to
    the creek bed
throughout the past three weeks
to my great shock and dismay
toward the end of the long day
towards Augusta Street
under the seat in front of me
underneath all of the old wool blankets
up the rickety ladder
upon my bedside table
within seconds of her arrival

PHRASES FOR EXPANSION USING ABSTRACT PREPOSITIONS

aboard the newly fitted jumbo jet
about your own problems
according to the front desk receptionist
after a really long afternoon
against my better judgment
along the way
aside from Susan
because of the quality of the work
before the judge in his chambers
besides Eli and Brett
despite my piercing headache
due to careful studying
during the fourth inning of the Reds game
except for her shiny new shoes
for minimum wage

in addition to a host of problems
in case of fire
in place of that old bathroom sink
in spite of her reservations
instead of a huge midday meal
of many different colors
off the shelf beside the painting
on account of a late start to the game
on behalf of all of the veterans here today
out the window in the bathroom
prior to his career as a newscaster
subsequent to the doctor's appointment
with potatoes and gravy
with regard to your earlier comments
without a prescription from the doctor

CLAUSES FOR EXPANSION

dependent clauses for expansion (with optional corresponding independent clauses at right)

independent clauses for expansion (with optional corresponding dependent clauses at left)

after she served us dinner	we thanked her for the excellent meal
although the plane landed safely	we were shaken by the bumpy ride
as the wind whistled through the grove of trees	I was reminded of several Halloween stories
as if night would never come	I paced the floor watching the clock
as long as Charles still plans to go to prom	we must help him find a date
as soon as first period begins	everybody must be in a classroom
as though we did not have a care in the world	we danced and sang in the rain
because Mary stopped the discussion right away	no real harm was done to our friendship
before the rain began falling	we quickly darted into the store
even if he sleeps until noon	he will still be exhausted from his difficult journey
even though our favorite restaurant is usually closed on Mondays	I will make a quick call to check tonight
if she puts her mind to it	she can accomplish next to impossible things
if only I can find the time	I will clean out all the closets this Saturday
in order that you ace the next test	you must prepare the material carefully
just as I turned onto Edgehill Road	the bicyclist raced into the intersection
now that he has gotten his license	he is able to drive himself to school
once she has dealt the cards	Sarah is headed to the kitchen for a soda
since my cell phone died	I cannot text my friends
so that I am not starving by dinner	I will eat a banana on the way home from school
though Sue squinted in the bright sunlight	she did not put on her sunglasses
till I consider all of my options	I cannot tell you my final decision
unless Jackson makes a hole in one	he cannot overtake the lead golfer
until Nicolas, the team's safety, broke his leg	he had started every game
when the doctor checked Beth for measles	he discovered a rash on both her forearms
whenever Phil saves money for a new car	he intends to choose a used Toyota
where the bridge crosses Elderberry Creek	I buried the gold coins under a tree
whereas you love avocados	I prefer broccoli
wherever Drew can get the best deal	he will spend his birthday money
whether the President serves a second term or not	he has accomplished a great deal
while Lance warms up	you should get the bats out of the car

Basic Subject-Verb Barebones Sentences for Expansion

I laughed.
You should eat.
He burped.
She sneezed.
We slept.
They wrote.
The soldiers attacked.
The chef baked.
The player batted.
The dog begs.
The children never behaved.
The planes bombed.
The actors bowed.
The truck braked.
The bee buzzed.
Grandpa called.
The hikers camped.
The bull charged.
The audience clapped.
The housekeeper cleaned.
My dad coached.
My sister coughed.
The boats crashed.
The lizard crawled.
The infant cried.
The girl cheats.
The cow chewed.
The general commanded.
The students copied.
The athlete cycled.
The ballerina danced.
The sink drained.
Our family dressed.
The faucet dripped.
The rat drowned.
The movie ended.
The man will exercise.
The tunnel exploded.
The dog fetched.

The basement floods.
The munchkin grinned.
The students groaned.
The security officers guarded.
The police officer guessed.
The worker hammered.
The outlaw hanged.
The cut healed.
The farmer hunts.
The warrior attacks.
The woman jogs.
The clown will juggle.
The boy jumped.
The girl knitted.
Her classmates learned.
His ship landed.
A rocket launched.
Martha will lie.
The band marched.
Three carts moved.
Cardinals nested.
Spot obeyed.
We packed.
The crew paddled.
Sophie painted.
The truck parked.
Ned phoned.
The children played.
The musician practiced.
The minister preached.
The boy pedaled.
The cars raced.
It rained.
The cat never returned.
Those vegetables rotted.
The opposing team rushed.
The tourists will shiver.
My cousin will shrug.
They skied.

The minivan stopped.
My team stretched.
The children screamed.
The toddler scribbled.
Our team scrubbed.
The squad searched.
The travellers settled.
My uncle shaves.
Edna slipped.
The motorcycle slowed.
Valinda smiled.
My grandpa and grandma will smoke.
It snowed.
My guinea pig squeaked.
The rat squealed.
The boy stared.
The cook stirred.
Meg talks.
The delivery boy tapped.
Her vase tipped.
His hands trembled.
The brat tripped.
Black Beauty trotted.
The receptionist typed.
The sides united.
Our family unpacked.
My cousins visited.
Five customers waited.
My friends will walk.
Fans will watch.
My family will wave.
The puppy will whine.
The girl will whirl.
My brother whistles.
Our mother worries.
The class yawned.
My classmate yelled.

ADVANCED SUBJECT-VERB BAREBONES SENTENCES FOR EXPANSION

Mark agreed.

Sue will answer.

Juan apologized.

Krista appeared.

Mom and dad applauded.

My brother argues.

Grandma arrives.

The bully boasts.

My aunt breathed.

The two teams competed.

The boy should concentrate.

The child should confess.

The flight was delayed.

The old folks were delighted.

It depends.

The plan developed.

The siblings disagreed.

The magician disappeared.

Mom and dad disapprove.

The young girl dreamed.

We were embarrassed.

The villain escaped.

The memory will fade.

The teenager failed.

Her thoughts flowed.

A plan formed.

My niece was frightened.

My nephew was found.

The tiger followed.

A crowd gathered.

The fire glowed.

Her voice grated.

The day improved.

The temperature increased.

My sister interfered.

My brother interrupted.

The thief was escaping.

A comedian jokes.

A warrior kneeled.

One soldier lasted.

Richard listens.

Jason will live.

Charles looked.

The couple will marry.

The ice melted.

The bullet missed.

The spirit moans.

The hall monitor noticed.

The lawyer objected.

Marsha observed.

Luke offered.

The couple parted.

The car passed.

The lecturer paused.

The cork popped.

The family prayed.

The boys will promise.

The machine gun pumped.

The orchestra performed.

Rachel pointed.

Meryl pretended.

James refused.

The Queen reigned.

The girls rejoiced.

The couple relaxed.

One cupcake remains.

I remember.

Our friends replied.

Grandmother retired.

The entire city rocked.

The schooner sailed.

The rose petals scattered.

The winner succeeded.

Her garden suffered.

The meat thawed.

The visitors toured.

The swimmer trained.

The twins tried.

His rabbit vanished.

The mourners wailed.

BASIC SUBJECT-VERB-OBJECT SENTENCES FOR EXPANSION

The child added the numbers.
I admitted the mistake.
The teen could afford the car.
We amused ourselves.
I announced the victory.
My friend attached a pic.
She bleached her hair.
He boiled the water.
She bruised her shin.
He buried his pets.
The author carried the books.
Dad will carve the turkey.
I changed my shirt.
The cook chopped the onions.
He claimed his prize.
I cleared the room.
They completed the test.
That confuses me.
He crossed the yard.
The doctor cured the patient.
The cop chased the man.
Sue combs her hair.
The teacher corrected the tests.
I deceived the bully.
The bomber destroyed the base.
The villain disarmed the guards.
We divided our belongings.
The teacher educated the students.
Fasten the luggage.
The waitress filled our glasses.
Spielberg filmed the movie.
His boss fired him.
Logan folded the paper in half.
Grandma Ella framed those prints.
Don't frighten the baby.
Jake fixed the latch.
The poodle followed her.
The child glued the pieces.
I grabbed your coat.
The child gripped the saddle.

Elliott will hand in the paper.
Josh will handle that.
He wouldn't harm a flea.
Don't hate me.
The ghost haunted the mansion.
We will head out.
The fire heated the room.
The tutor helped Aaron.
My mother hovered over my brother.
Grandma will hug me.
The hero hurried.
Mark improved his chances.
Suzanne included everybody.
The soldiers informed his brother.
Jeb joined the club.
The movers loaded the truck.
His big brother lightened his load.
Her great aunt liked chocolate.
We will man our posts.
His mom matched his socks.
The girl and her uncle measured the
   ingredients.
We must memorize the state capitals.
The farmer milked the cow.
Astra needed some cash.
The doctor noted the time.
The parrot obeyed his owner.
Mike offered a hand.
She ordered him.
My cousin owes me.
Her grandma pecked her cheek.
Doctor Pruitt permitted food.
Linda raised her hand.
Andy reached the end.
Alex received Shane's gift.
The artist recorded three songs.
Abe released the birds.
My sister remembers everything.
Mom reminds me.
We should remove our shoes.

BASIC SUBJECT-VERB-OBJECT SENTENCES FOR EXPANSION (CONT.)

The rain ruined the game.

The snack satisfied Amy.

The monster scared the boys.

Susie scraped her knee.

The branch scratched his face.

The movie shocked my family.

The teacher skipped the chapter.

My aunt sipped her tea.

The child will spell her name.

The housekeeper stripped the beds.

The gardener stuffed the bags.

Her partner served the ball.

The lifeguard shaded his eyes.

The kids smashed the pumpkins.

He stamps his feet.

Gretchen stepped to the left.

Dad supplied the snacks.

Our grandparents surprised us.

The principal suspended the student.

The pro tamed the lion.

We tasted all the cakes.

The hosts thanked everybody.

My sister tickles me.

The referee times games.

My grandmother tires easily.

The truck towed my car.

The pickpocket tricked the tourists.

My daughter tugged on my shirt.

My son will unlock the door.

I wanted that ring.

Tom warmed his feet.

Nancy washed her hands.

We wandered the beach.

Morris wastes his lunch.

Garth wiped the table.

Ann wraps our presents.

ADVANCED SUBJECT-VERB-OBJECT SENTENCES FOR EXPANSION

The owner accepted the offer.

We admired the monument.

The secretary advised the president.

The teacher alerted the principal.

I allowed the question.

A scientist analyzes the results.

My granddaughter appreciated the gift.

The flower attracted a bee.

We avoid conflict.

He attempted the problem.

Three schools banned the book.

We challenged her authority.

You concern me.

Cover that!

We will collect donations.

Liz contained her anger.

The midwife delivered the baby.

The witness described the crime.

I detect some anger.

She dislikes him.

Double the recipe.

The captain drummed up support.

The sisters earned a good living.

The auto industry employs workers.

I enjoy your company.

She examined the splinter.

I can't face her.

The queen fancies him.

John flashed a smile.

Officer Jones forced the door.

Her fiancee gazed into her eyes.

We cannot guarantee your loan.

The mountaineer guides the group.

He still had hope.

The actress will impress you.

A nurse injects the medicine.

The admiral instructed her men.

The bear intended no harm.

He invented a cure.

Her attorney knotted his tie.

My neighbor meddles in my business.

The family mourned their loss.

She will obtain all the quarters.

Dinner occurred after the movie.

The mirror reflected her face.

The leader signaled his troops.

Mom soothed Collette.

The lawyer suggested a solution.

Ice cream tempts dieters.

The heat tests her patience.

COMMON PUNCTUATION

Comma

1. after a dependent clause that begins a sentence (D,I)

   Before we finish the game, we must score.

2. before a coordinating conjunction to separate two independent clauses (I, fanboy I)

   We arrived late, and the bus was gone.

3. to separate a nonessential phrase or clause from the rest of the sentence (e.g., appositive, adjective clause)

   Mr. Jones, a good speaker, ran for mayor.

   Eliza, who has two cars, frequently walks.

4. to separate an initial adverb or initial adverb phrase of more than 3 words

   Usually, we eat dinner before a movie.

   In the ancient warehouse, I found a chest.

5. to separate words and word groups in a series of three or more

   We bought eggs, bacon, yogurt, and butter.

6. to separate two adjectives when the word *and* can be inserted between them

   The wise, friendly woman helped many.

7. after day in a date

   I was born on May 27, 1968.

8. between city and state

   We celebrated in Louisville, Kentucky.

9. after city and state/country

   We will stop in Greenville, South Carolina,

   on our way. London, England, is awesome.

10. before the quotation mark when quoting

    She said, "Let them eat cake."

11. after the greeting of a personal letter

    Dear Mary,

12. after the closing of a letter

    Yours truly,

Question Mark

- at the end of a question

  What time is it?

Exclamation Point

- at the end of a word, phrase, or sentence to express strong emotion

  I have had enough of this!

Period

- at the end of a sentence

  The play lasted over three hours.

- after an abbreviation or initial

  Mr. W. G. Jones joined the N.A.A.C.P.

Semi-Colon

- to join two independent clauses I;I

  You should run for mayor; I would vote for you.

Colon

- to introduce a list, an explanation, or a quote after a complete sentence

  You should get the following supplies: a pencil, pens, paper, and a binder.

  Sally had one true vice: she loved chocolate more than life itself.

  In Berlin Ronald Reagan made the following statement famous: "Tear down this wall."

- after the greeting of a business letter

  To whom it may concern:

Apostrophe

- in a contraction to show where letters have been omitted

  shouldn't   haven't   don't

- to show possession in a singular word before the s

  Mike's car   shirt's collar   woman's book

- to show possession in a plural word after the s

  states' capitals   markers' tops

Appendix 2:
Instructional Content & Sequences of Skills

Anybody who has investigated as many as two teaching guides or workbooks on written expression is aware that there is no definitive sequence for concepts of instruction. It is a challenge to place concepts in a sequence and to determine at what grade level students should encounter and understand those concepts for the first time. As such, the sequences on the pages that follow are meant as guidelines. Adhering too rigidly to them ignores the individual student's or group's needs as well as outside influences, such as state and federal guidelines and school or program curriculum. Be aware that the grade level designations are designed for students who are not experiencing significant struggles with writing. Pacing and thoroughness of introduction and instruction should be adjusted to suit the needs of individual students, groups, and classes as necessary.

Since writing is skills-based, concepts must be repeated and developed over time. Most concepts are introduced more than once during a student's school career. With each successive introduction, the student becomes more comfortable with the concept and applies it to his expanding vocabulary and writing ability. Additionally, as a new layer to a concept (for example, that a noun can name an idea in addition to a person, place, or thing) is added, the previous layers should be reviewed and further cemented. Writing, like any skills-based subject, should be taught in a spiral, with the instructor and students covering a new concept and then spiralling back to incorporate it with previously learned material.

Remember to maintain focus. A writing lesson where students spend the entire time underlining or identifying has missed the mark. Students must write -- lists of words, phrases, clauses, and lots and lots of sentences over multiple years to internalize the important structures you are teaching. While a solid sense of the terminology used in understanding, manipulating, replicating, and generating various sentence structures is useful, do not let it limit the student writer. Identification is a small piece of the big picture: generating written language remains the key means to an end in the writing process.

Pages 308-9 provide the instructor with appropriate grade levels for introducing the various concepts. Clearly, once a concept is introduced in a grade, it should be covered again in subsequent grades. Pages 310-2 provide a logical sequence of skills per grade level to help individual instructors, classroom teachers, and even schools and districts develop curricula as needed.

PARTS OF SPEECH INSTRUCTIONAL CONTENT BY GRADE LEVEL (1-6): INITIAL CONCEPT INTRODUCTION

Parts of Speech: Use	1-2	3-4	5-6
noun	person, place, thing singular/plural - regular frequently used singular/ plural - irregular (2) common/proper collective (2) possessive (2)	idea singular/plural - irregular	predicate noun

verb	action
	past - regular
	frequently used past -
	  irregular
	common irregular
	  (introduction - 2)
	linking (rote memory of "to
	  be" only)
		linking (to be)
		linking (other - 4)
		past/present/future verbs
		helping (4)
		progressive tense for use
		not identification (4)
			transitive/intransitive

pronoun	personal reflexive possessive indefinite	demonstrative interrogative relative (4)	proper case (6) intensive (6)
adjective	standard (attributive) articles	comparative/superlative order (4)	predicate adjective
adverb	standard (describes verb)		standard (describes adverb/adjective - 6)
preposition	concrete (introduction - 2)	concrete abstract (4)	
conjunction	frequently occurring	coordinating subordinating	correlative
Parts of Speech: Discuss Function		*core standards:* nouns, pronouns, verbs, adjectives, adverbs	*core standards:* conjunctions, prepositions, interjections

PARTS OF SPEECH INSTRUCTIONAL CONTENT BY GRADE LEVEL (1-6): INITIAL CONCEPT INTRODUCTION

Sentence Parts	1-2	3-4	5-6
declarative	as statement	as declarative (statement)	
interrogative	as question	as interrogative (question)	
exclamatory	as exclamation	as exclamatory (exclamation)	
imperative	as command	as imperative (command)	
functions of nouns	simple subject compound subject	complete subject	object of preposition direct object predicate noun (indirect object as needed)
predicate	simple predicate compound predicate	complete predicate	
prepositional phrase		prepositional phrase (4)	
simple sentence	simple sentence (capitalization + end punctuation)	simple sentence (1 independent clause)	
clauses		independent + dependent	
compound sentence	basic: 2 complete sentences (and, but, or only)	2 independent clauses joined by comma + coordinating conjunction	2 independent clauses joined by semi-colon
complex (D,I + ID)	finish ID sentences with subordinating conjunction already supplied	1 independent and 1 (or more) dependent clauses (D,I + ID only)	1 independent and 1 (or more) dependent clauses (more than one D - 6)
complex (relative clause)			complex with 1 relative/ adjective clause (6)

A SUGGESTED SEQUENCE BY GRADE LEVEL

GRADES 1 & 2

concrete nouns (person, place, thing)
action verbs (regular)
simple subjects
simple predicates
simple sentences
concrete nouns (common, proper; singular, plural - regular)
statements
questions
exclamations
commands
compound subjects
compound predicates
standard adjectives
nouns (irregular singular and plural - 2nd grade only)
personal pronouns (subject and object)
action verbs (irregular - frequently used - 2nd grade only)
action verbs (past tense)
article adjectives
standard adverbs (describe verbs)
nouns (collective - 2nd grade only)
concrete prepositions (2nd grade only)
common coordinating conjunctions (and, but, or)
compound sentences (taught as 2 sentences joined by comma and and, but, or only)
linking verb (taught by rote memory: am, is, are, was, were, be, being, been)
nouns (possessive - 2nd grade only)
pronouns (reflexive)
pronouns (indefinite)

GRADES 3 & 4

concrete nouns (person, place, thing; common, proper; singular, plural - regular and irregular)
action verbs (regular)
simple subjects and predicates
simple sentences
complete subjects and predicates
compound subjects and predicates
kinds of sentences (taught as declarative, interrogative, exclamatory, imperative)
verb tenses (past, present, future); helping verbs
adjectives (standard, article)
pronouns (subject and object)
adverbs (describe verbs)
prepositions (concrete)
prepositions (abstract - 4th grade only)
prepositional phrases (4th grade only)
clauses and phrases
independent and dependent clauses
simple sentences (as independent clauses)
conjunctions (coordinating)
compound sentences (taught as I,fanboyI)
nouns (idea)
linking verbs (verb "to be")
linking verbs (other than "to be" - 4th grade only)
comparative/superlative adjectives
adjective order (4th grade only)
pronouns (reflexive, indefinite, demonstrative, interrogative)
pronouns (relative - 4th grade only)
verb tenses (progressive); helping verbs
conjunctions (subordinating)
complex sentences (with adverb clauses - D,I and ID only)

From the Common Core: "Throughout 3rd grade, students should develop the ability to explain the function of nouns, pronouns, verbs, adjectives, and adverbs."

A Suggested Sequence By Grade Level

Grades 5 & 6

nouns
verbs (action, linking, helping)
simple and complete subjects
simple and complete predicates
simple sentences
compound subjects and predicates
clauses and phrases
clauses (independent and dependent)
simple sentences (1 independent clause)
verb tenses (action - standard)
direct objects (transitive/intransitive verbs)
verb tenses (linking - standard)
predicate nouns and adjectives (6th grade only)
adjectives (standard, article)
pronouns (subject, object)
adverbs (describe verbs)
prepositions, prepositional phrases, objects of a preposition
conjunctions (coordinating)
compound sentences (I,fanboyI)
conjunctions (subordinating)
complex sentences (with adverb clauses)
compound sentences (I;I with conjunctive adverb)
conjunctions (correlative)
verb tenses (action - perfect, progressive)
verb tenses (linking - perfect, progressive)
adjectives (comparative, superlative, order)
appositives
pronouns (demonstrative, interrogative, reflexive, indefinite)
pronouns (correct number, person, case - 6th grade only)
intensive pronouns (6th grade only)
pronouns (relative)
complex sentences (with adjective/relative clauses - D-wedge)
adverbs (describe adjectives, adverbs - 6th grade only)

From the Common Core: "Throughout 5th grade, students should develop the ability to explain the function of conjunctions, prepositions, and interjections."

Grades 7 & 8

nouns
verbs (action, linking, helping)
simple and complete subjects and predicates
compound subjects and predicates
clauses and phrases
clauses (independent and dependent)
simple sentences (1 independent clause)
verb tenses (action - standard)
direct objects (transitive/intransitive verbs)
verb tenses (linking - standard)
predicate nouns and adjectives
adjectives (standard, article)
pronouns (subject, object)
adverbs
prepositions, prepositional phrases, objects of a preposition
conjunctions (coordinating)
compound sentences (I,fanboyI)
conjunctions (subordinating)
complex sentences (with adverb clauses)
compound sentences (I;I with conjunctive adverb)
appositives
adjectives (comparative, superlative, order)
pronouns (demonstrative, interrogative, reflexive, indefinite, intensive; correct number, person, case)
conjunctions (correlative)
pronouns (relative) and adverbs (relative)
complex sentences (with adjective/relative clauses - D-wedge)
compound-complex sentences
verb tenses (perfect, progressive)
indirect objects
active and passive voice (8th grade only)
use (not identify) verbs in the indicative, imperative, interrogative, conditional, and subjunctive moods (8th grade only)

From the Common Core: "Throughout 7th grade, students should develop the ability to explain the function of phrases and clauses and their specific function in sentences. Also, they should develop the ability to choose among different clause configurations and sentence types to convey different relationships between ideas."

CONCEPTS TO BE COVERED WITH HIGH SCHOOL STUDENTS

GRADES 9-12

The Common Core states that "throughout 7th grade, students should develop the ability to explain the function of phrases and clauses and their specific function in sentences. Also, they should develop the ability to choose among different clause configurations and sentence types to convey different relationships between ideas." Thus, students must be able to apply but also explain the application of these elements.

The Common Core also states that students in the 9th and 10th grades should have the ability to "use various types of phrases (noun, verb, adjectival, adverbial, participial, prepositional, absolute) and clauses (independent, dependent; noun, relative, adverbial) to convey specific meanings and add variety and interest to writing or presentations." Though this piece of text does not indicate that students must know how to explain their knowledge, they are building on the base they established in middle school. As they add structures to their knowledge, they should understand how those structures interplay with previously learned concepts, and also, ultimately, they should be able to create examples of those structures in isolation and in application in paragraphs and longer pieces of writing.

As they *enter* high school, students should have a thorough understanding of and be able to recognize and create examples of the following:

- parts of speech: noun, pronoun, adjective, verb, adverb, preposition, conjunction.
- sentence parts and structures: subject and predicate, phrase and clause, object of preposition and adjective and adverb phrase, direct and indirect object, predicate adjective and noun, independent and dependent clause, adverb and adjective/relative clause, simple, compound, complex, and compound-complex sentence.

Struggling writers entering high school may have difficulty with some or even most of the concepts above. Instructors will need to assess competency and then provide instruction, combined with intensive sentence-writing activities to develop those skills as quickly and yet thoroughly as possible.

During high school students should develop their knowledge of and ability to recognize and create examples of the following:

- a thorough and flexible understanding of the ways in which clauses combine to create different kinds of sentences
- the ability to combine clauses to create all different kinds of sentences, both in isolation and in application
- a thorough understanding of punctuation necessary to cluster words, phrases, clauses, and ideas together properly, including comma, semi-colon, colon (and, perhaps, dash)
- an understanding of appositives (and, perhaps, absolutes)
- an understanding of noun clauses
- an understanding of verbals, including gerunds and gerund phrases, participles and participial phrases, and infinitives and infinitive phrases

Appendix III: References

Anderson, Jeff. *Mechanically Inclined: Building Grammar, Usage, and Style into Writer's Workshop.* Portland, ME: Stenhouse Publishers, 2005.

Berninger, Virginia and Beverly J. Wolf. *Teaching Students with Dyslexia and Dysgraphia*: Lessons from Teaching and Science. Baltimore, MD: Brookes Publishing Co., 2009.

Brimo, Danielle, Kenn Apel, and Treeva Fountain. "Examining the contributions of syntactic awareness and syntactic knowledge to reading comprehension." *Journal of Research in Reading.* Oxford, UK: John Wiley & Sons, Ltd, April 2015.

Coker, David. "Writing Instruction for Young Children: Methods Targeting the Multiple Demands That Writers Face." *Best Practices in Writing Instruction.* New York, NY: The Guilford Press, 2007.

Dahl, Karin L. & Nancy Farnan. *Children's Writing: Perspectives from Research. Literacy Study Series.* : Newark, DE: International Reading Association, 1998.

Eberhardt, Nancy Chapel & Monica Gordon-Pershey, eds. *Perspectives on Language and Literacy - Theme Issue: Syntax: Its Role in Literacy Learning.* Baltimore, MD: The International Dyslexia Association, Summer 2013.

Ecalle, J., H. Bouchafa, A. Potocki, and A. Magnan. "Comprehension of written sentences as a core component of children's reading comprehension." *Journal of Research in Reading,* Vol. 36. 117–131. 2013.

Fearn, Leif. "Measuring Mechanical Control in Writing Samples." July 1982.

Fearn, Leif & Nancy Farnan. "When Is a Verb? Using Functional Grammar to Teach Writing." *Journal of Basic Writing,* Vol. 26, No. 1, 2007.

Fearn, Leif & Nancy Farnan. "The Influence of Professional Development on Young Writers' Writing Performance." *Action in Teacher Education,* Vol. 29, No. 2. 17-28. 2007.

Fearn, Leif & Nancy Farnan. *Interactions: Teaching Writing and the Language Arts.* Boston, MA: Houghton Mifflin Company, 2001.

Graham, Steve. "Want to Improve Children's Writing? Don't Neglect Their Handwriting." *American Educator.* Winter 2009-2010.

Graham, Steve, Charles A. MacArthur, and Jill Fitzgerald, Eds. *Best Practices in Writing Instruction.* New York, NY: The Guilford Press, 2007.

Graham, Steve & Dolores Perin. *Writing Next: Effective Strategies to Improve Writing of Adolescents in Middle and High Schools.* www.all4ed.org.

Graham, Steve & Dolores Perin. "A Meta-Analysis of Writing Instruction for Adolescent Students." *Journal of Educational Psychology,* Vol. 99, No. 3. 445-476. 2007.

Graham, Steve & Karen R. Harris. *Writing Better: Effective Strategies for Teaching Students With Learning Difficulties.* Baltimore, MD: Paul H. Brookes Publishing Co., 2005.

Jones, S., Debra Myhill, & Trevor Bailey. "Grammar for writing? An investigation of the effects of contextualized grammar teaching on students' writing." University of Exeter, UK. 14 September 2012.

Konnikova, Maria. "What's Lost as Handwriting Fades." *New York Times.* New York, NY. 2 June 2014.

MacArthur, Charles A., Steve Graham, & Jill Fitzgerald. *Handbook of Writing Research.* New York, NY: The Guilford Press, 2006.

Mather, Nancy, Barbara J. Wendling, and Rhia Roberts. *Writing Assessment and Instruction for Students with Learning Disabilities*. San Francisco, CA: Jossey-Bass, 2009.

Myhill, Debra and Annabel Watson. "The role of grammar in the writing curriculum: A review of the literature." *Child Language Teaching and Therapy*. Vol. 30(I), 41-62. Sage Publications, 2014.

National Council of Teachers of English. *Writing Now: A Policy Research Brief*. 2008.

National Governors Association Center for Best Practices, Council of Chief State School Officers. *Common Core State Standards*. Washington, DC: National Governors Association Center for Best Practices, Council of Chief State School Officers, 2010.

National Writing Project & Carl Nagin. *Because Writing Matters: Improving Student Writing in Our Schools*. San Francisco, CA: Jossey-Bass, 2006.

Kolln, Martha and Robert Funk. *Understanding English Grammar*, 7th Ed. New York, NY: Pearson Education, 2006.

Pick, Anthony C. *Discourse and Function: A Framework of Sentence Structure*. 2009.

Risher, Douglass, Nancy Frey, Leif Fearn, Nancy Farnan, & Frank Peterson. "Increasing Writing Achievement in an Urban Middle School." *Middle School Journal*, Vol. 36, No. 2. 21-26. Westerville, OH: National Middle School Association, Nov. 2004.

Schlagel, Bob. "Best Practices in Spelling and Handwriting." *Best Practices in Writing Instruction*. Eds. Charles A. MacArthur, Steve Graham, and Jill Fitzgerald. New York, NY: The Guilford Press, 2007.

Schleppegrell, Mary J. and Ann L. Go. "Analyzing the Writing of English Learners: A Functional Approach." *Language Arts*, Vol. 84, No. 6. 529-538. Urbana, IL: National Council of Teachers of English, July 2007.

Schleppegrell, Mary J. "Grammar as Resource: Writing a Description." *Research in the Teaching of English*, Vol. 32, No. 2. 182-211. May 1998.

Schleppegrell, Mary J. "Subordination and Linguistic Complexity." *Discourse Processes*, Vol. 15, No. 1. 117-31. Jan-Mar 1992.

Scott, Cheryl M. "A Case for the Sentence in Reading Comprehension." *Language, Speech, and Hearing Services in Schools*, Vol. 40. 184-91. April 2009.

Smith, Michael W., Julie Cheville, and George Hillocks, Jr. "'I Guess I'd Better Watch My English': Grammars and the Teaching of the English Language." *Handbook of Writing Research*. Eds. Charles A. MacArthur, Steve Graham, and Jill Fitzgerald. The Guildford Press: New York, NY, 2006.

Strong, William. *Sentence Combining: A Composing Book*. New York, NY: Random House, 1973.

Strong, William. *Sentence Combining and Paragraph Building*. New York, NY: Random House, Inc., 1981.

Torrance, Mark and David Galbraith. "The Processing Demands of Writing." *Handbook of Writing Research*. Eds. Charles A. MacArthur, Steve Graham, and Jill Fitzgerald. The Guildford Press: New York, NY, 2006.

Troia, Gary A. "Writing Instruction for Students with Learning Disabilities." *Handbook of Writing Research*. Eds. Charles A. MacArthur, Steve Graham, and Jill Fitzgerald. New York, NY: The Guilford Press, 2006.

Weaver, Constance. *Grammar to Enrich and Enhance Writing*. Portsmouth, NH: Heinemann, 2008.

Willows, D.M., & E.B. Ryan. "The development of grammatical sensitivity and its relation to early reading achievement." *Reading Research Quarterly*, Vol. 21. 253-266. 1986.

Appendix IV: Suggested Supplementary Teaching Materials

Tools that Accompany the *Writing Matters* Approach
by William Van Cleave - Available at wvced.com

Binder Inserts. (several different styles for students at different grade levels, emphasizing quick and easy access to word lists and rules for sentence and essay construction)

Grammar Dice. (grammar/sentence generating dice activities)

GrammarBuilder Concept Cards. (concept cards including parts of speech and sentence parts for student and instructor use)

Sentence Sense. (workbook series for student practice in sentence skill development)

Sentence Stretches I & II. (sentence expansion card games)

Sentence Templates and Writing Expansion posters.

Words at Work I & II. (grammar/sentence construction card games)

Writing Skills Concept Charts. (with co-author Heather Redenbach) (8.5x11 visuals for parts of speech and sentence parts)

Writing Skills Sorters. (grammar/sentence sorting activity packs)

Tools that Complement the *Writing Matters* Approach
by Other Authors - Published by wvced.com

King, Diana. *Learning Cursive - Elementary Level* (left- & right-handed versions). (new cursive workbooks for instructing elementary students)

Other Useful Writing Tools at wvced.com

Killgallon, Don. *Sentence Composing* series. (7 sentence composing workbooks including sentence combining, parsing, and imitating)

King, Diana. *Cursive Writing Skills* (left- and right-handed versions). (remedial workbooks for older students who struggle with handwriting)

King, Diana. *Keyboarding Skills*. (revolutionary method of instructing students in keyboarding)

King, Diana. *Learning Cursive - Elementary Level* (left- & right-handed versions). (new cursive workbooks for instructing elementary students)

King, Diana. *Writing Skills*, Books A, One, Two, and Three. (workbooks involving grammar and sentence and paragraph development)

King, Diana. Posters. (1 covering Phrases and 1 covering Clauses).

Padgett, Patricia. *Writing Adventures Books 1 & 2*. (workbooks involving sentence and paragraph writing)

Pencil Grips. (assorted pencil grips to improve or correct pencil grasp)

Tactile Surfaces for Writing. (Brain Freeze, Gelboard, and Smart Sand)

Terry, Bonnie. *The Sentence Zone*. (sentence construction game)

Useful Student Books from Outside Sources

Schuster, Edgar. *Sentence Mastery*, Levels A, B, and C. phoenixlearningresources.com. (workbooks - sentence combining skills)

Praise for This Manual...

When I saw this in action, I immediately wanted it for my class. I went to school the following Monday and began teaching it. Within a few lessons, my students were already becoming stronger writers.

Mary Baldwin, Sixth Grade Department Chair
The Briarwood School

* * *

While there is a plethora of research concerning writing, practical applications are sparse. Van Cleave has provided teachers with a transparent structure for guiding students through the maze of parts of speech and their role in writing, both in the creative process and in response to text. Writing Matters focuses on using parts of speech as a vehicle to expression of thought rather than a subject taught in isolation.

The models for instruction allow the reader to feel that she is actually involved in the exchanges between Van Cleave and his students. The lesson structure is explicit and easy to follow. Use of manipulatives to create sentence parts leads to the creation of sophisticated sentences within the context of a paragraph idea. The teacher is provided with a lesson structure and an appendix of words in usage. Throughout the book, reference is made to Common Core Standards.

This is the book teachers have been asking for.

Sandy Thompson C.A.L.T., Q.I. Licensed Dyslexia Therapist

* * *

Van Cleave has given teachers a tool for group and one-on-one writing instruction that increases student writing ability linked to the Common Core State Standards and raises writing expectations for students. After using this book, teachers and students should be able to see an increase in writing levels which will transcend into post-high school.

Rhonda E. Hlavaty, M.Ed.
Adjunct Professor, Oklahoma State University-OKC
Teacher, SeeWorth Charter Academy